D0292243

Russian Literature and Ideology

NICHOLAS RZHEVSKY

Russian Literature
and Ideology:

Herzen, Dostoevsky,
Leontiev, Tolstoy, Fadeyev

UNIVERSITY OF ILLINOIS PRESS

Urbana Chicago London

Library of Congress Cataloging in Publication Data

Rzhevsky, Nicholas, 1943-
Russian literature and ideology.

Includes bibliographical references and index.
1. Russian fiction—19th century—History and
criticism. 2. Authors, Russian—20th century—
Political and social views. 3. Ideology in litera-
ture. 4. Russian literature—History and criticism
—Theory, etc. I. Title.
PG3098.3.R93   891.73'3'09   82-1977
ISBN O-252-00964-9   AACR2

TO TANIA

Contents

Transliteration Note

With the exception of some names, I use Transliteration System I as defined by J. Thomas Shaw in *The Transliteration of Modern Russian for English-Language Publications* (Madison, Wis., 1967).

"Буян задумчивый и важный,
Хирург, юрист, физиолог,
Идеолог и филолог,
Короче вам — студент присяжный."

А. С. Пушкин, "Послание Дельвигу," 1828.

Preface

The present book began with my Princeton dissertation, "Herzen in Russian Literature." My intention at the time of the earlier work was to use Alexander Herzen's central position in Russian culture as a means of exploring literary ideas and procedures. As I added to my reading, however, I became increasingly convinced that this perspective did only partial justice to the texts under consideration. I began to rethink and rewrite my observations and subsequently published some of my new conclusions in academic journals. At the same time I felt the need to develop a consistent critical approach which would help clarify the cultural patterns and historical reality of Russian fiction without neglecting the individual literary achievements of different writers. The methodological problem came down to finding a set of critical premises that were valid in their own right but that were also of particular and immediate relevance in defining Russian literature.

The idea of using ideology as a critical tool came out of these impulses and hopes. I was struck initially by the emotional and ethical weight of the term. Not unlike most students of literature in the sixties, I came in frequent contact with textual analyses based on the premises of new criticism and formalism. In many instances the narrow technical concerns of such critical languages as they were used in academic research seemed to be inadequate before the intellectual-emotional exuberance and intensity of the fiction I was studying or before its tragic sociopolitical history in the twentieth century. Ideology, on the other hand, even in its pejorative political meaning, was seldom used to indicate anything but deep and total commitment, a condition I thought to be especially characteristic of Russian texts. The issue of commitment and involvement in turn led me to face questions of objectivity and bias which had particular relevance within the history of Russian literary scholarship. Last of all, ideology seemed to offer a means for using what was once called world view or *Zeitgeist* to validate an interpretation, but in a less vague sense than some common variants of Hegelian-inspired critical procedure and closer to the actual textual and experiential reality of writers.

Initially I found evidence for such uses of ideology in the fiction of Herzen, Fyodor Dostoevsky, Leo Tolstoy, Constantine Leontiev, and Alexander Fadeyev. In proceeding wih my explorations, however, I found it unsatisfactory to interpret these highly idiosyncratic creative sensibilities using only one ideological measure; there were general patterns of Russian ideology in which all five authors participated, but I could not argue for a uniform response in their literary texts. A recognition of the unique literary identity of each writer led to key adjustments in my approach. I ultimately imagined an open-ended analytical procedure which would move back and forth between hypothesis, cultural evidence, and the writer's individual fiction. After this methodological adjustment the structure of the study rapidly evolved into its present shape: in the first chapter I offer an initial hypothesis and suggest modes of literary analysis that incorporate some well-known definitions of ideology; in the second, I argue for the specific historical validity of such definitions in the Russian instance; in chapters three to six—the core of the book—I interpret the creative world of four nineteenth-century writers and reappraise my proposed ideological postulates in light of these particular writers; finally, in the last two chapters I review the hypothesis of specifically Russian literary ideologies and muster evidence from the most recent period of Soviet literature. The study thus depends throughout on meanings of ideology that are used both for a method of literary analysis and for a definition of the substance of Russian fiction.

Two additional emphases of the work should be noted. First, my basic premises, stressing as they did the ideological identities of the writers, allowed an adjustment in critical perspective in light of different problems raised by each of the subjects. Herzen's fiction, it thus seemed to me, could be best understood in terms of the

responses he wanted to inspire in his readers. I used this critical point
of view—particularly fashionable in the 1970s—to clarify my understanding of the core processes of 1830s-40s literature in which
Herzen took part. Dostoevsky raised issues of intellectual-emotional
biography; Tolstoy's *War and Peace* the problem of influence study;
Constantine Leontiev the questions of literary typology, that of
romanticism in his instance; and Fadeyev that of literary evaluation.
Each of these critical perspectives responded to my first sense of
ideology and provided it with evidence of a specific nature. Second,
as I reviewed the scholarly apparatuses pertaining to the authors, I
became increasingly convinced that a full understanding of their
individual ideological responses required extensive work in the religious component of Russian literature. In turn this conclusion led me
to intensify my readings in Russian history, and to make the
attempt—using the tools of contemporary literary studies—to
determine the effects of a religious culture on different works of
fiction.

In many respects I find this labor to be incomplete. In emphasizing
the basic values and ideas underlying Russian texts and literary
patterns, I condensed and compacted issues of critical theory and
problems of Slavic literary scholarship that need much more detailed
investigation. The first part of the study is deliberately concise
because I did not want to get bogged down in the metacriticism which
seems so often to preclude interpretations of specific texts and
authors. My intention was to delineate the primary critical values and
preconceptions with which I approach Russian literature but not to
make my methodological preferences the central concern. The other
sections, however, are less easily justified and require the reader's
indulgence. I took numerous risk as at various moments and sometimes assumed a deliberately polemical stance in the hope of prodding a reexamination of long-standing value judgments, attitudes,
and prejudices. In several instances much more would be required to
finish the critical job of defining a writer's ideology and its role in
fiction, and there were, of course, aspects of literary tradition that lie
outside the purview of my hypothesis. I did not, it should be noted at
the outset, intend to find some one key to all of Russian literature,
and indeed could not hope to do so in a work that neglects Alexander
Pushkin, Ivan Turgenev, Nikolai Gogol, and Nikolai Leskov. Suggestive as the opening citation from Pushkin might be of native ideologi-

cal apperception, I would be the first to admit that his complex talent, as well as the talent of other Russian authors, requires more analysis and research than available here. I have no special principles to offer in support of the writers I do include, except to note that the study of ideology inspires some wariness of *all* principles of literary selection extended beyond the critic's honest tastes and open interests.

Neither the tasks undertaken in this work nor the means to their successful completion could have been arrived at alone. I owe a large intellectual debt to two scholars in particular: Father Georges Florovsky, who left a widely felt legacy of brilliant scholarship based on his love of Russian culture and who prodded my awareness of the breadth of knowledge required to understand it, and Joseph Frank, who set standards of critical theory and practice that I could always look to for guidance in difficult moments of undergraduate studies, graduate research, and the first years of teaching. The dialogue—at times two-sided, at times solitary—that I carried on with these two men always inspired the best of my insight and research. Valuable assistance in commenting on earlier versions of the manuscript was given by Victor Terras, William Mills Todd III, George Hendrick, Vasilii Kuleshov, David Ransel, Frank Gladney, Stephen Hill, Susan Zorn, and John McCormick. My colleagues at the Universty of Illinois provided intellectual support and friendship that made the critical job easier than it would have been if it had been faced alone. Particular acknowledgment and thanks are due the Fulbright-Hays faculty programs, which enabled me to write and conduct research abroad in 1968–69 and 1977–78. The Rutgers Research Council, the International Research and Exchanges Board, and the Research Board of the University of Illinois provided supplementary grants which were of considerable help in finishing the project. Finally, the book owes a strong debt to the faith and high editorial standards of Richard L. Wentworth, director of the University of Illinois Press; his colleagues, Ann Prisland Thorpe, Elizabeth G. Dulany, and Ann Lowry Weir performed heroic labors in bringing the manuscript to its present printed form.

The extraordinary support of my wife, Tatiana Goncharenko-Rzhevsky, is recorded in the dedication.

Nicholas Rzhevsky
Urbana, 1982

PART I

CHAPTER 1

Critical Method:
Mirrors and Identities

THE COMPLEX and sometimes confused etymological history of ideology—beginning with Destutt de Tracy's condillacian notion of empirically based thought and extending to the twentieth-century meaning of mass sociopolitical syndromes—suggests that one must be extremely careful in delineating unmuddled critical functions for the term.[1] Of the many nuances provided by literary scholarship, two in particular offer promising methods of critical procedure. The first is the definition of ideology as the literary audience's unquestioned attitudes and prevalent beliefs, and this definition is profitably evoked to focus, refine, or reject preconceptions which condition readings of texts; the second expresses basic values and ideas held by writers and helps determine the central denotations of their works. Both uses of the word can be seen as steps along a critical journey to discover the cultural identity of some one creative vision in fiction.

Most of the following interpretations of Russian literature will originate in critical procedures suggested by these two definitions. Such methodological preferences allow a committed yet temperate investment in ideology's sociopolitical nuances and contribute to the controlled appraisal of volatile issues central to literary meaning. Frederic Jameson, inspired by similar considerations, argues that ideology raises "healthy problems which make the critical process a perilous adventure, a process requiring a kind of uncomfortable and acute self-consciousness at all times, rather than a neutral exhibition of technical skills."[2] Ideology is thus a reminder, for both writers and critics, of emotional involvements and totalities of experience frequently neglected or constricted in literary analysis; and an ideological concern, with its aura of commitment, action, and ethical vitality, is a convenient way of putting to question literary criticism's withdrawal from substantive human issues to the dehumanized analysis of a technocratic age.[3] But the attractions of sociopolitical adventure should not stand in the way of accepting another major challenge of the term, which is to establish full contact with experiential issues of literature without subordinating the critical task to extraliterary views or using texts for one's own political preferences.

Ideology viewed in this way, as a tool of scholarship put to work in the endeavor of defining specifically literary identity, depends on a broad history ranging from Hegelian aesthetics to twentieth-century hermeneutics.[4] Kindred methodological and textual explorations provide both models of literary discovery to be followed and cautionary examples of frustrations and blind alleys to be avoided. One such qualified use is suggested by the pejorative evocation of ideology as a subjective and empirically invalid world view. This primary nuance, known to Napoleon and brought into world prominence by Marx and his followers, is most often found in political disputes and propaganda. It has acquired a secondary, more complex field of activity, however, in the widespread endeavor of social scientists and men of letters to understand the subjective factor in knowledge and to face squarely the attitudes and preconceptions which hinder impartial judgment.[5] Among the best-known expressions of such analysis— spurred by Hegel's view that objectivity in the human disciplines is infeasible because the observer himself is part of the phenomenon he is observing—are Wilhelm Dilthey's, Max Weber's, and Karl Mannheim's influential works in history and theoretical sociology. For Mannheim in particular, the cruelest paradox is that the social scientist's attempt to define an objective world process can only occur through his own subjective perception. The detrimental effect on criticism is that ideology understood to be such an unavoidably subjective prism has led to total acceptance of *everyone's* hypotheses, or Mannheim's "relationism," in which there are no objective standards for measuring validity but an unlimited number of equally valid viewpoints.[6] At the opposite but also potentially damaging extreme of Marx and Engels, the subjective partiality of ideology is a "false consciousness" to be polemicized against and rejected at all costs in favor of the material processes which supposedly shape the world.

In a similar, partially generic sense, ideology is an integral element of structuralist, semiotic, and deconstructivist vocabulary frequently evoked to help remove the superficial layers of meaning ascribed by others to cultural phenomena and to explore the limitations of the critic's own subjective condition. Roland Barthes, Julie Kristeva, and Jacques Derrida frequently engage in two related tasks: disassembling the ideologies of others in their cultural range, and examining their own ideological presuppositions.[7] Although often inaccurately grouped with the fertile structuralist research of Claude Levi-Strauss in anthropology, Tsvetan Todorov in genre theory, and Lucien Goldmann in the novel, such critical praxis is at times guided by a nihilistic sensibility. On the one hand, the use of ideology to "deconstruct" old, widely accepted meanings or cultural superstructures can become an end in itself rather than a way of defining a text; on the other, an extreme critical self-awareness threatens to create a condition of diffusion and infinite regress where the ideological glance inward proceeds through an endless multiplication of meanings with no epistemological first source possible in our despiritualized age. An instructive example is Roland Barthes's much discussed reading of Balzac's *Sarrasine*, in which any central or organizing meaning created by the writer is totally submerged (or "covered" in Barthes's terms) under the critic's own unconfined response to every conceivable nuance and origin of the text's elements.[8] The strong threat in criticism of this sort, regardless of the frequently impressive talent and insight shown by its proponents, is a methodology in which not only the object but also the subject of humanistic study is lost. "La recherche semiotique," writes Julia Kristeva, "ne trouve rien au bout de la recherche que son propre geste ideologique, pour en prendre acte, le nier et repartir a nouveau."[9]

Awareness of how ideology is used in such instances brings to mind the kindred literary malaise of locked-in metacriticism which neglects the definition of literary works created by others in favor of an endless sharpening of one's own methodological tools.[10] For purposes of concrete textual interpretation, however, the concept of ideology has to be extended beyond reminders of narrowly methodological preoccupation. By selectively using the familiar polemical models we have outlined, the critic aware of ideology can clear away rather than indulge in cultural dogmas and pervasive formulas which have set up barriers around a writer's work. He can also use recognition of ideology to control the subjective biases and ideas he brings to the text and, by making adjustments for the material he encounters, to change his hypothesis to bring it closer to its object. The term approaches its fullest potential when such checks and balances are not ends in themselves but the means to another goal: the definition of the *writer's* ideology and its literary function. If recognition of the ideological-subjective factor in culture is to avoid critical Babel, then, it should impel critics to legitimize and understand the individual cultural formulations of others rather than to license self-indulgence, political self-projection, or disassociation from the literary work's own reality.

Such an other-directed critical concern is most obviously endangered when critics and writers hold opposite sociopolitical convictions, whether the example is the relationship of Vissarion Belinsky and Nikolai Gogol, or of American critics and Ezra Pound. Less jarring but as open to abuse are instances when critics are *too* close to their subject's attitudes and beliefs (a pertinent example would be a Soviet scholar's reading of Nicholas Chernyshevsky's fiction). But the problem of how to approach cultural material objectively and how to control the observer's own ideology in defining the ideology of others is larger than political loyalties and involves basic questions of literary perception. For our purposes the modern involvement in inductive reasoning provides a particularly instructive example of attempts to control subjectivity. It is of special interest that an inductive approach is frequently praised or implied to have superior possibilities—within literary scholarship and literature itself—on the presumption that an uninvolved observer, dependent entirely and without prior bias on empirical evidence outside himself, has the greatest honesty and factual sense to offer. In a typical academic reference to a favored, supremely "objective" writer, Helen Muchnic has defined Pushkin's aesthetic logic as a process in which "universals are deductions from concrete instances";[11] while in a highly influential work, *Anatomy of Criticism*, Northrop Frye has provided a similar argument for inductive technique and empiricism in critical method.[12] An important source of appeal, often more assumed than examined but in Mr. Frye's case explicitly stated, is that the use of inductive logic in literary reading seems to afford the closest possible approximation of scientific analysis for critics interested in clarity and objectivity.

In reviewing related literature, however, it is suggestive to note that the theoreticians of scientific methodology themselves have recognized the infeasibility of a totally inductive approach. As Carl Hempel points out, it would be impossible, as proposed in the naive inductive model, to consider all empirical data.[13] Furthermore, even if the scope of the evidence is limited in some way, in effect already introducing a bias of subjective origin, the data in question will not coalesce by itself into some meaningful pattern. Without the observer's active personal participation, expressed through his creative imagination and hypothesis, in short, one cannot determine what natural phenomenon means at all.

The acceptance of a subjective organizing principle in the scientific community approximates the recognition accorded ideology in the social sciences and humanities. The ideological nature of hypothesis, a frame of reference and organization shaped out of the entire cultural range of ideas, attitudes, beliefs, and myths individually received, is impossible to avoid. What has been avoided more successfully by scientists than critics, however, is the notion that a hypothesis creates rather than interprets the world or texts. The inevitability of ideology does not mean that it is necessarily valid or in fact coincidental with what is there.

To take the step suggested by this conclusion and to advocate that ideology be measured against its experiential context is nothing more than to suggest that hypothesis be checked against the evidence. Certain twentieth-century theoretical works, ranging from Wittgenstein's essays to Thomas Kuhn's *Structure of Scientific Revolutions* have complicated such validation procedures by postulating the independent reality of a hypothesis in its basic denotations of linguistic and cultural paradigms.[14] Wittgenstein's influential shift of emphasis from metaphysics to the definition of word use is subject to mistreatment because providing language with its own existence based solely on the uses of whatever linguistic game is played by the public threatens to legitimize empirical distortion. Ernest Gellner uses the concept of "miracle" to make the point. "Miracle" might be accepted and used by a group of people, but that is no guarantee that miracles indeed exist.[15] Mr. Kuhn's widely praised argument that the dominant scientific paradigms of any historical period make up the reality of that particular cultural era points to a similar problem with empirical validation, for the idea of scientific hypotheses shaping reality makes it difficult to prove that the sun did not in fact revolve around the earth in the pre-Copernican period.[16]

Ideologies and paradigms of perception are fallible, in short, and such fallibility suggests a modest incorporation of induction into textual exegesis—in spite of the untenability we noted of a *totally* inductive criticism—to provide a check on critical formulas and hypotheses. In particular, a sensitivity to subject-object relationships brings to the foreground those inductive values of objectivity, flexibility, and openness to empirical data which can help mitigate the effect of our subjective biases. Indeed, the recognition of an ideological prism and its possible distortion indicates both the subjective problem and a way of confronting it with the aid of an inductive method. For the impulse to measure hypothesis and subjective perception against external evidence can only come out of one's own ideology. While total induction is unattainable, the critic can decide to view his antecedent hypothesis inductively—that is, as a dynamic and open formulation to be adjusted and refined in light of external evidence and a posteriori discovery. A practical optimism of this sort is offered by René Wellek when he writes that "men can correct their temporal and local limitations, aim at objectivity, arrive at some knowledge and truth."[17] The acceptance of such critical procedure makes it possible to measure the validity of a critical ideology through its relationship to literary material. Is it a rigid mold which deforms the text, or does it adjust to its elements? Is it self-serving, or directed at the object of study? These are pertinent questions for evaluation.

Critical theory in this century has laboriously moved toward evolving such standards of validation. Of special promise is a widely felt impulse to develop historical-contextual approaches which would incorporate cultural evidence without falling prey to the reductive categories and abstractions of past Marxian, history-of-ideas, and *Geistesgeschichte* criticism.[18] Such critical traditions have most frequently been hampered by the view—deriving largely from Hegel—that writers and their texts are victims or reflexes of sociocultural forces rather than aesthetic identities to be studied in their own right.[19] The familiar uses of ideology already noted are related to this attitude and indicate its typical deficiencies. The retrospective imposition of a conceived historical pattern which claims an empirical or scientific reality beyond ideology or "false consciousness" most often neglects the complexity and nuances of the writer's world-response in favor of the critic's own metaphysical and social preferences.[20] Following Wilhelm Dilthey's or Arthur Lovejoy's models, the use of ideology to designate prevalent ideas, or *Zeitgeist*, in its secondhand formulations tends to produce a leveling effect which is appropriate for the popular and the average in culture but inadequate for the innovations, peaks, and surprises of complex aesthetic discourse.[21] In both instances, writers who rise above the typically observed sociocultural patterns to create a literary work that is unexpected and subtle are subject to distortion or neglect. The rejection of subjectivity within such critical traditions thus creates an insensitivity both to the most interesting parts of the author's explanatory paradigms and to the critic's own ideological biases.

A measured ideological recognition which is open to the validation of external evidence requires other commitments. Rather than attempting to reject ideological subjectivity and allowing it to enter unexamined through the back door, the critic can find external and intersubjective confirmation or correction for his hypothesis by focusing on the author's individual response to his cultural referents. The culturally vital factors used in the writer's ideas suggest standards of validation for the reading of a text and allow some sense of its objective presence outside the critic's own ideology.[22] Such an interpretation of the other's ideological formulation is aided considerably by a historical approach attuned to literary genius and identity. The critic must be prepared both to recognize typical temporal and cultural boundaries and to break through them alongside the writer to grasp the individual creative formulations which occur.

The most productive ideological commitment for literary scholars, in this regard, is not to historical, social, and political issues, but to whatever organizing principle or system of values and ideas writers have used to shape their own textual meaning out of history, society, and politics. Ideology thus seen as the writer's individual literary response to his life situation allows use of the empirical material of culture for proof that an interpretation is not self-serving but a valid approximation of *another's* meaning.

Although there are any number of critics whose research provides us with an interaction between hypothesis and cultural data in which the reader does not impose and the authorial self is not neglected, for the best of them it is intrinsically difficult to delineate a paradigmatic method. Such work originates in the unique demands of the particular writer, literary text, or problem under analysis quite as much as in prior critical tradition or literary formulas. Indeed, in attempting to follow critical models of this sort, an appropriate modus operandi is a process contrary to the one often encountered in twentieth-century criticism. Rather than deconstructing the literary object and leaving one's own ideology in the controlling position before a textual mirror, it is the critic's ideology which should be guided by humility and the attempt to support the other cultural self's identity. The effort will always be incomplete, the reading never totally successful, and the analysis limited by one's subjectivity. Moreover, if it is to have true import, an interpretaion will take its place in the life of the reader; he will have to judge what a work offers and reject or accept it according to his particular circumstances. But the first emphasis must not be on this eventual place of the text, but on its own unique identity as an aesthetic realm of definition, concentration, and shape. Such an ethical act of attempting to understand another's meaning before using it for one's own purposes is a prerequisite for communication, and indicates one possible first step to breaking out of the subjective relativism threatening criticism in this century.

CHAPTER 2

The Ideology of
Russian Literary Tradition

THE THEORETICAL principles outlined are not meant to suggest an imperious method but rather to inspire some concern for the relationship between cultural context and individual ideological responses of writers. In the following sections of this work an attempt will be made to show why such a view of method is especially suited to Russian literature. The Russian writer, it is argued, tended to be profoundly ideological in the sense that he held to unusually intense cultural involvements and standards of subjective identity. This hypothesis—as suggested by the preceding examination of inductive technique—is offered in stages. The first includes a preliminary and deliberately tentative outline of past critical presuppositions and Russian cultural directions; the last and major sections are meant to supersede and refine initial conjectures by defining individual literary works.

Among the nuances of ideology I have noted, the most widely recognized in Russian literary scholarship is a tendency to create textual meaning out of strong sociocultural involvements. Western critics—beginning with the pioneering E. M. de Vogüé's essays in *Revue des Deux Mondes* (published 1873–86; separate edition *Le roman russe*, 1886)—have often written on the intensity of the Russian commitment to the intellectual milieu and vital human issues. Russian writers, it is frequently pointed out, took Western ideas that were discussed in abstract terms and shaped them into a literature dealing with experientially felt extremes of action, emotions, and values. As Erich Auerbach notes in *Mimesis*, "It seems that the

Russians have preserved an immediacy of experience which had become a rare phenomenon in western civilization of the nineteenth century."[1] The vitality of this aesthetic tradition is explained in a number of different ways; most interpretations, however, can be traced to a core historical judgment or assumption which provides a measure of their validity.

One such hypothesis is that government censorship and a form of political sublimation are executive factors within the culture. Readings which depend on this cultural model postulate that a repressive government, in conjunction with the upper classes' access to Western notions of enlightenment and civic responsibility, produced an explosive yearning for political action which could only be expressed in art. As a related factor, the pre–1917 censorship is often seen to have forced political, religious, and philosophical ideas into unique literary concentration and intensity.[2] The Russian aesthetic involvement in the "cursed questions," and the culmination of this involvement in literary phenomena such as the "superfluous man," or the great novels of the nineteenth century, then, can be explained as the result of literature's unique potential for civic self-expression in the midst of social repression.

A review of actual historical conditions, however, hardly supports the idea that Russian censors in the nineteenth century (unlike the twentieth) were influential enough to have a decisive literary effect.[3] The almost comic inefficacy of the pre–1917 censorship is well known and easily illustrated by the various strategies through which men of letters disseminated ideas unacceptable to the government. At the height of Nicholas I's reactionary regime in the 1840s, for instance, books by Fourier and St. Simon were prohibited, although their notions were easily circulated because books about them were not. During the same period texts on the forbidden-titles list found their way into print by the simple expedient of serialization in journals, and, by a similar circumvention, dramatists such as Nikolai Ostrovsky who had difficulty putting their plays on the stage could bring them to the public by having them published. Sidney Monas has estimated that "half of the personnel of the Main Administration of Schools (entrusted with the powers of censorship) were themselves either active contributors to or on the staff of the periodical press."[4] Unlike Soviet conditions in which such professional crossover has served the subversion of letters by the KGB and other political organs, in the nineteenth century the reverse was true, with censors such as Ivan Goncharov subverting political control of literature in favor of the independent endeavor of writers.

Literature and literary criticism, it is true, served publicists such as Chernyshevsky, Vissarion Belinsky, Dmitry Pisarev, and Nicholas Dobroliubov as a means of outwitting government policy and reaching a large public. The societal involvements of the radical intelligentsia, however, should not obstruct or be confused with the independent aesthetic aims and perspectives of Russian writers. In their regard, the censorship—when it *was* effective—did not produce a creative stimulus for social involvement through literature but, in case after case, served to hinder or irritate the expression of sociocultural commitments already formed. Such examples of literary repression as Pushkin's difficulties with *Boris Godunov*, Dostoevsky's with *The Notes from the Underground* and *The Devils*, Tolstoy's with *Anna Karenina*, or the minor tactical evasion of Turgenev making Insarov a *Bulgarian* revolutionary illustrate damaging, secondary effects rather than any core explanation for the organic force of Russian fiction.

The hypothesis of Russian political sublimation into art also suffers if one considers the social position of most Russian authors at the time their best-known works were written. Russian fiction up to the twentieth century, after all, originated largely in the *dvorianstvo* (landowning class), whose broad civic and political powers were codified in 1785 through the Charter to the Nobility. This is not to say that ultimate power lay anywhere but in the hands of the monarchs. But political action and the feeling of civic participation and power could be expressed by the upper classes in a number of local ways: ownership of land or serfs; central roles in the decision-making processes of the bureaucracy, the army, and diplomatic service; positions of control in government projects.[5] Tolstoy, in any case, voiced his civic inclinations to the fullest both in his writings and his life; Goncharov was himself a censor, and Zhukovsky, as Kantemir and Karamzin before him, a tutor and advisor to the czar. Dostoevsky, at the height of his most creative period of work, was the editor of an influential journal in which he stated his heartfelt opinions on pressing political issues, while Griboedov, Tiutchev, and Constantine Leontiev were high-ranking diplomats.

The notion that various forms of repression were not of vital importance in nineteenth-century Russian culture may appear to be heresy because both Soviet and Western literary scholarship have traditionally emphasized other examples such as Pushkin's troubles with Nicholas I, Herzen's and Turgenev's exiles, Dostoevsky's mock execution and prison term, and Lermontov's "Death of a Poet" and its aftermath. A close look at each of these instances, however, shows that government intervention into the writer's life either affected no change in essential ideas and literary procedures or, at best, contributed a secondary influence to a sensibility already formed. It is not hard to demonstrate that Shakespeare is more important than the Romanovs for Pushkin's texts. For Herzen and Turgenev Western exile only provided additional evidence for a sense of existence long formed in conjunction with German and French ideas. In Dostoevsky's case the mock scaffold and Siberia stimulated a reappraisal of his views of life and men—the impressions of death and imprisonment were too strong—but these views were already implicit in earlier works and were motivated, at the core, by other cultural factors. For Lermontov's poetry it was not government intervention into his and Pushkin's life which was of paramount importance, but romanticism.

Moreover, readings which place an overly strong emphasis on political-literary interaction imply an impossible situation. If censorship and the absence of civic outlets are indeed the determining factors in Russian literature, one can draw the implication that *stronger* repression would produce an even more favorable environment for the intensity and organic merit of Russian texts. The Russian experience in the Soviet period is totally at odds with this conjecture, of course, and suggests the dangers of proposing a positive function for inhibiting cultural processes. The most injurious effect is that by placing the emphasis on what prohibited or irritated Russian writers, such hypotheses do nothing to explain what inspired them. Perspectives of this sort, finally, tend to overlook the typical subversion of political issues in Russian texts by a strong religious and ethical bias.

Another common premise, with a tradition dating back both to long-standing Western prejudices and to the anguished self-derisions of Chaadayev, Pecherin, and the Westernizers, is that Russian literature was stimulated by cultural underdevelopment. In some typical variants of this view—dependent, as in the case of the preceding hypothesis, on a supposed deficiency—it is suggested that the absence of a native philosophical tradition and the relative naivety of the Russians in matters of Western civilization, contributed to the elemental force, youthful vigor, and intensity with which writers received Western ideas.[6] The exuberant experiential-ethical motifs of Russian fiction—its unembarrassed impulse to confront and explain basic issues—can thus be seen to have been made possible by the late arrival at an already mature cultural process. Unencumbered by the sophisticated nuances and inhibitions of more developed countries, untroubled by the worries and skepticism produced through a long and complex intellectual tradition, the Russian writer, in this view, could shape his texts with a fresh, crude force no longer possible in the West.

No serious student of Russian literature, of course, can afford to neglect the two major issues raised in such interpretations: the Russian relationship with the West, and the relative underdevelopment of the native tradition. The principal danger of this perspective, however, is that a core value judgment—the assumed superiority of one cultural history over another—can lead to an underestimation of the native element and produce a distorted and condescending view of the subject. Related observations on the unoriginality of Russian texts, or on their extreme dependence on Western literary models, thus tend to neglect evidence that modern cross-cultural interaction, whether in respect to genres such as the novel, or entire literary periods such as the Baroque, has made it exceedingly difficult to define *any* totally original or independent literary process in the West.[7]

The gravest problem, however, is that readings based on a judgment of Russian underdevelopment are inevitably deficient or one-sided when it comes to explaining the culture's inner strengths. The native aesthetic heritage, it should not be forgotten, was over seven hundred years old by the time of Peter's reforms; and Western ideas do not in themselves account for the preconditions and creativity of the Russian response to Europe. It is only recently that the underlying principles of old Russian culture, more than adequately explicated by Dmitry Likhachev, Dmitry Chizhevsky, N. Gudzi, and others, have begun to be examined as important factors in nineteenth-century Russian literature.[8] The range of work still to be done extends beyond the historical period of this study, but one direction for research can be given particular emphasis and a tentative outline. Hypotheses of intellectual and cultural immaturity are most frequently made possible by a particular condition of Russian historical studies: the neglect or disvaluation of the native religious component.[9] Indeed, because of the paucity of modern analytical works and the depreciation of Russian Orthodoxy in those instances when it has been noted by Western and Soviet scholars, the few balanced studies of the religious culture available to us suggest some of the more promising, unexplored passages to the heart of Russian literature. It is not merely a question of delineating local influence such as Dostoevsky's reading of Tikhon Zadonsky, Tolstoy's biblical exegeses, or Gogol's fondness for Father Matthew Konstantinovsky, although these are important symptoms, but of understanding a vital, organic process which affected basic intellectual formulations and directions.

The analysis of religious factors in literature—particularly in the Russian instance—traditionally has been marked by its own ideological pitfalls. A great deal has been written on the Russian Orthodox heritage—most tellingly in self-challenging reappraisals such as the Russians' own Vekhi ("Landmarks," 1909) and Iz-pod glyb ("From under the Rubble," 1974). Because of the very vitality of the topic, however, critics have invariably taken positions showing extremes of antipathy or empathy. During the past century and a half both Russian and Western literary attitudes toward religion have been affected by different varieties of materialism and by hostile liberal and radical impulses, typified in Belinsky's famous letter to Gogol.[10] On the other extreme, much of what the West knows about Russian literature originated in the works of E. M. de Vogüé, Dmitry Merezhkovsky, Nicholas Berdiaev, Vasily Rozanov, and Vyacheslav Ivanov, whose involvement in religious problems led them to use literary texts for their own spiritual explorations rather than to develop a properly distanced perspective.[11] Particular care, therefore, must be taken to separate religious ideas and historical factors which had an actual or highly probable literary significance from self-serving or extraliterary notions of both these extremes.

Studies of government policy, education, and printing provide such relatively dispassionate critical material by illustrating basic, formative processes in the modern period. Prior to Peter I, organized elementary education was almost entirely dependent on parish schools or on teachers from religious backgrounds.[12] Well into the nineteenth century, parish priests, using church books as primary texts, bore the greatest burden of instructing the mass of the people in reading and writing. Alphabet books—first hand-copied, then printed and distributed in large quantities—used predominantly religious subjects to illustrate lessons. When the radical secularization of the early eighteenth century occurred, it did not profoundly change the church's importance in the schools. Peter introduced a new government policy that was kept vigorous by numerous decrees and statutes up to Pobedonostsev's time. But its intention was to use and even stimulate church involvement in education rather than to mitigate religious input. Initially, even in a secular society in which Orthodoxy was considered to be but another administrative arm of the central authority, it was impossible to disregard the clergy's position as the social class with the most literate members. Peter's famous *tsifirnye shkoly* (cipher schools), through which he hoped to develop the secular sciences of mathematics and engineering in Russia, relied entirely on the children of clergy for their student bodies.[13]

Various statistics compiled during the eighteenth and nineteenth centuries testify to the results of this policy. During the first half of the eighteenth century almost all books were of church origin; in the second half—with secularization in full swing—out of 8,000 texts printed, 60 percent were still totally religious in content. At the middle of the following century (1855), out of 19,060 educational institutions counted in a census, more than 70 percent (13,600) turned out to be parish schools. With the twentieth century seven years away, new statistics show that the various zemstvoes and ministries together list 25,978 schools and are almost equally matched by the parishes (25,501).[14]

Two alumni of Russian elementary education who figure prominently in their culture in different historical periods illustrate perhaps better than can statistics the unexpected endurance of religious influence in key places. Peter himself and Maxim Gorky (Alexey Peshkov), in addition to stimulating secular cultural changes, share one other similarity: they both learned to read and write through the time-honored church books. Gorky's basic texts were the Orthodox breviary and psalter, while Peter, it was said, enjoyed singing the church service and knew the Gospels and the Acts of the Apostles by heart.

While the Orthodox church helped shape literacy in its fundamental sense, religious influences also affected higher education and the development of more complex cultural values. The history of

abstract. For religious experience occurs on a deeply personal level that requires some psychological sensitivity to understand. The implicitly accepted values or explicitly formulated standards of life that influenced the development of Russian literature, in short, were most likely to have an emotional dimension and appeal that directly interested or affected Russian writers.

One of the most persistent of such motifs in literary and cultural histories is the kenotic syndrome and the special Russian emphasis placed on suffering.[23] In critical writings, especially it seems, in studies of Dostoevsky, suffering has turned into a terminal value that can be read as another masochistic form of murky Slavic excess. In reality, of course, suffering as expressed by the early saints Boris, Gleb, Theodosius, and throughout Russian theological history, could hardly have reached its preeminent ethical position or acquired any of its strong psychological attraction if it were taken to be an end or goal in itself. The kenotic values—not only suffering but humility and love as well—are much more convincingly interpreted as forms of material self-renunciation put into the service of spiritual self-assertion. With Christ's Passion as a supreme metaphor, the appeal of kenosis is to a complex, two-sided impulse: on the one hand, the acceptance of the most crushing of material circumstances and one's victimization; on the other, the rejection of material standards with the knowledge, as St. Theodosius put it, that one will be "placed . . . on the right hand of the Father." The demotion of material goods, comfort, and secular power in favor of beggar's clothing, pain, humility, and death becomes a triumphant expression of man's God-related nature and the awareness of larger, nontransitory rewards. The kenotic saints, in the same pattern, traditionally asserted their moral freedom through humiliation and suffering in the face of the worst posible circumstances of the temporal world; even as earthly victims they triumphed spiritually because "God hath chosen the weak things of the world to confound the things which are mighty" (1 Cor. 1: 27). Indeed, it is only the immanent element of fulfillment and spiritual victory over aggression and secular power which explains what suffering alone cannot: the popular veneration of Boris and Gleb as the Russian patron saints of national defense.

The kenotic morality is complemented by a constant religious attraction to acts of charity, sacrifice, and social concern. A frequently noted element of this traditional Christian ethos—extending from Kiev-Pechersky monasticism to the climactic Slavophile notion of "sobornost' "—is the tendency to view personal, moral obligation as a part of a large collective pattern. It would be a mistake, however, to define the Russian sense of cosmic order and universal involvement as an assertion of group prerogative at the expense of individuality. In the less-exalted form expressed bluntly by Constantine Leontiev, Orthodox moral commitments are sustained by an egotistic hope of one's redemption in the afterlife. On a higher plane, felt forcefully at the end of the eighteenth century and the early part of the next in Freemasonry and idealism, the ethical-social breadth is supported by a metaphysical and emotional projection of selfhood into universal categories. Such social commitments are marked by a refusal to view oneself on anything but the largest of scales; a characteristic response is moral measurement of oneself in ultimate rather than local terms combined with an adherence to principles of free will and irrationality, as in Slavophile doctrine, that express and sustain human personality on a supernatural scale. In a period when biological and utilitarian notions of egoism would attain maximum importance, transcendent values of this sort offered writers a more complex and emotionally rewarding sense of the self's moral-social fulfillment than could be gained by materialistic reductions.

There were two distinct levels of transmission in the first half of the nineteenth century that allow us to speak of religious value systems in concrete terms. At the cultural apex, the Russian man of letters was exposed to the intellectual movements of Freemasonry, idealism, and utopian socialism which reworked religious motifs and issues into the language of contemporary secular thought. On another more popular level, the church and its ethos made itself felt in broadly based social mechanisms and rituals which provided cultural groundwork. We have already noted the strong church presence in elementary and higher education. There were certainly different degrees of response and exposure to catechisms, tutor-priests, and holy books; and in the worldly, upper-class education of a Turgenev or a Tolstoy such influences must be balanced by other, equally important secular factors. Even the works of both these men, however, show another form of daily religious involvement through a strong modal presence in mass culture. The Orthodox *narod* (people)—as is shown in *The Sportsman's Sketches* and by Platon Karatayev—was in itself a frequent object of veneration for educated

Russians. The commonly stressed feelings of guilt elicited by serfdom and privilege explain only part of this preoccupation, for the
image of moral balance arising out of the peasants' unquestioned
faith—frequent demonstrations of drunkenness and vulgarity not-
withstanding—was an equally strong reminder of the personal dignity and emotional stability of religious commitment.

It is certain, in any case, that at least five major authors—
Dostoevsky, Leontiev, Gogol, Leskov, and Goncharov—were exposed to substantial religious influences not only through observing
the lower classes but by experiencing religion directly in their homes
or schools. Gogol, Dostoevsky, and Leskov came from families with
strong clerical traditions, and the fathers of the latter two writers
were educated in seminaries. Goncharov attended a boarding school
run by the clergy, and Leontiev's education, as Gogol's, was begun by
a deeply pious mother. Joseph Frank's admirable biography of Dostoevsky reminds us that in such instances the religious, mental world
of the parents could not but have had a profound effect on the
intellectual formation of their children.[24] The legacy did not have to
be an actual belief in Christian doctrine to affect later literary work;
conventional piety could produce unconventional—even impious—
results in fiction by providing questions to be answered, language and
symbols to be used, issues to be examined, and ethical norms to be
explored or defended. On the other hand, a roundabout course of
religious contact should not be discounted; the young Alexander
Herzen learned parts of the Gospels by heart, although his father was
an agnostic with no firm belief in anything but imitating the French
manner of sarcasm and *bon ton*.

In addition to sharing the religious conventions of family and
school, almost all Russian writers—particularly when young—took
regular part in one socially mandated set of church procedures: the
various Orthodox services. The aesthetic appeal of Byzantine ritual
has always occupied a special place in Russian culture; according to a
frequently repeated legend, it was the reason for conversion to
Christianity. Whether or not the legend is true does not alter the
status of the church service as the most basic and durable of native
aesthetic processes. "Judged solely in terms of . . . artistic qualities,"
the distinguished German scholar Ernst Benz suggests, "the Eastern
liturgies can be compared only with Greek tragedy."[25] Indeed, the

powerful internal mechanisms of Orthodox rituals are a particularly rich source for the aesthetic-emotional sustenance religion provided to the values we noted above.

Orthodox theologians are fond of pointing out that Christianity is a liturgical religion which can be understood only through the total experience of worship.[26] Father Pavel Florensky defines the service as an "aesthetic sensory synthesis," and Fedotov points out that "from early Christian times to the present the Russian has been finding his way to God through the bodily senses, all five of them. . . . "[27] This process of sensory immersion begins outside the church with the sound of bells and the impressive architecture of cupolas and multi-colored walls reminding the believer of an extraordinary and non-mundane presence in life. It continues with the serene beauty of icons, the smell of myrrh and incense, and the harmony of the choir. The Orthodox ritual deliberately incorporates sound and light effects to express doctrine: candles are lit and doused at appropriate moments of sadness and joy; the key prayers of each service are sustained with the most beautiful melodies; and the priest changes his vestments from dark to light to mark Christ's alternately tragic and sublime journey. The culmination of every liturgy, as Gogol points out, is the moment of supreme mystery when bread and wine are transformed into Christ's flesh and blood; the believer is invited to participate not only in a mystical leap of faith but in the literal taste of divinity.

It is hard to agree with Fedotov that such rituals could produce a religious psychology based on fear of God. The Orthodox service is more likely to appeal to a positive frame of mind stressing hope and emotional-moral fulfillment rather than fire and brimstone. It affords, on the one hand, a medium for withdrawal into oneself and quiet contemplation away from everyday reality. On the other, it reflects the "Eastern pathos of heaven on earth" and constructs a microcosm of universal concord out of aesthetic devices and the optimistic resolution of life and death issues. The aesthetically pleasing structure of color, sound, and Christian doctrine extends to ritual acts outside church walls and is designed to convey harmony on a concrete socioethical plane. Orthodox ideas of mutual responsibility and love are communicated in vibrant, experientially felt gestures such as the traditional three kisses of Easter, and the custom, still followed by pious Russians, of asking forgiveness of friends and acquaintances for any wrongs caused them before the rites of confession and communion are undertaken.

In A Portrait of the Artist as a Young Man Joyce describes a similar effect of religious ritual when the recognition of "a beautiful and peaceful" universe expresses itself in the wish to lead a life of "grace and virtue and happiness."[28] Young Stephen's epiphany approximates the common emotional condition after confession when the unburdening of guilt stimulates a feeling of personal moral worth and the understandable impulse to preserve one's state of peace and gladness through virtuous acts. Fasting undertaken in preparation for confession, and the difficult and embarrassing act of admitting the worst deed or thought provide ego-reinforcement by demonstrating one's strength of character. In a more extreme form, the same elements of self-control and will-assertion can be seen in traditional church writings based on the lives of hermits and ascetics. Such emotional fortification is crucial to the core ethical imperative of Orthodoxy; it functions as psychological confirmation of the reality and fulfillment of free will.

Most of the other aesthetic and psychological devices in Orthodox services similarly complement an affirmative religious sensibility. The rituals tend to emphasize two motifs of Christian doctrine: theosis, the deification of man; and eternal life, the joining of man and cosmos beyond time. Theosis is expressed throughout the services with all the drama and emotional attractiveness of the Christ story, traditional components of Western religious practice and literatures. The ritual uses of eternity, on the other hand, are more narrowly characteristic of the Russian religious sensibility and reveal its unusual emphases. Cultural historians, in this regard, commonly point to the importance Russians attach to Easter. Christ's Resurrection, it is generally agreed, is the key holiday of the church calendar both in a doctrinal and an aesthetic sense. The most beautiful Orthodox melodies figure in the midnight matins, and they complement ritual acts which sustain the joy and hope of an eternal life.

A no less important and psychologically effective emphasis on immortality, however, is an integral part of another, less-commonly mentioned service: the Orthodox funeral. The Russian last rites still retain the lyric beauty of St. John Chrysostom's poetic talent and incorporate two of the most melodic and expressive chants in

Orthodoxy: "So sviatymi upokoi" ("Rest with the Saints") and "Vechnaia pamiat' " ("Eternal Memory"), the prayer Pasternak put at the beginning of *Dr. Zhivago*. Just as in the Easter ritual, the shock of mortality is transformed with the aid of doctrine and musical harmony into the hope and consolation of a spiritual existence. In the funeral service, however, the believer is much less likely to be affected on a purely symbolic level; the ultimate issues are too immediate in the death of an acquaintance or relative to be resolved with a detached perspective of eternity.

There are, of course, numerous biographical and textual examples of Russian writers confronting death and afterlife in close proximity to religious ritual or experience. Dostoevsky's reappraisal of ideas while sitting before his first wife's open coffin is a typical instance; it is at this crucial moment that the writer looks to his vital convictions and reveals his most intimate thoughts about ethics and personality. *The Death of Ivan Ilyich* and *The Brothers Karamazov* offer comparable critical material. Tolstoy arranges the banality and indifference which surround Ivan Ilyich's funeral so that they reflect the short-sightedness of the living; the moment of death and the glimmer of another existence transform Ivan Ilyich into something more serious than his earthly form and suggest our proper concern. In *The Brothers Karamazov* Dostoevsky creates the first important test of his great sinner Alyosha through Zossima's funeral. The absence of a miracle and Zossima's decaying flesh shake Alyosh's beliefs and allow an initial formulation of the key questions in the book: is religious faith possible without concrete proof? Can the spiritual perception of life survive on its own terms without material evidence? And if not how will men like Ivan react?

Such examples point to larger literary patterns in which religious attachments can be seen to affect textual directions. Three peculiarities of Russian literary history provide useful preliminary clues to the complex tensions and interractions involved. The first involves the late arrival of one of the most important Renaissance literary types: the picaro. A persuasive interpretation of the picaresque tradition in its original Spanish context is that a basic function of early rogues such as Lazarillo de Tormes and Guzmán de Alfarache was to undermine the didactic religious motifs and false piety of the Counter-Reformation. The work of Marcel Bataillon, a leading authority on this branch of literary history, suggests that a predominant aesthetic tendency of the Renaissance and Erasmian humanism was to introduce a new secularization into Western literature with the help of the picaro's deliberately alienated perspective.[29] In Russia, on the other hand, when the rogue finally arrives (after some negligible early attempts and Vasily Narezhny's primitive immitation of Le Sage) he appears in the form of Gogol's Chichikov—not a counterpoint to religion, but, in the author's intention, the means to a revitalization of the spirit and a fresh sense of religious values. Much of the original literary structure remains: the scoundrel-outsider's intrusion into society used for satiric purposes, the sense of journey, and the erratic plot formed through unrelated characters, settings, and chance events. The rogue, however, is placed in a Russian troika, the journey taken by Chichikov is a spiritual quest leading to ethical rebirth, and the typical secular environment of the picaresque is transformed into a supernatural realm by Gogol's sense of moral grotesqueness and religious vision.

A second distinctive feature is indicated by the differences between Russian and Western naturalism. In spite of sharing Western sources from Jules Janin to Herbert Spencer, the more gifted Russian writers who inclined to sordid detail and the portrayal of the urban poor were predominantly hostile to the clinical eye and determinism of the Flaubert-Zola-Dreiser line. With the exception of minor talents such as Nikolai Pomialovsky, Gleb Uspensky, Peter Boborykin and Alexander Kuprin, the course of literary history begun with the natural school and the physiological sketch was always marked by strong ethical-emotional commitments impossible for the detached Western perspective. In Russian naturalism, the human image and its destiny, it can be suggested, could not be brought down to earth by the weight of the scientific knowledge and cold objectivity found in its European and American counterparts.

A third literary particularity has been noted in scholarship by the unique conjunction "romantic realism," a term most persuasively employed by Donald Fanger.[30] Such a genre designation focuses the continued attraction of writers to romantic motifs and literary procedures in a post-romantic period. In the Russian instance it is significant that persistent romantic notions tend to be expressed in the various forms of individualism and the transcendental vision of man noted previously. Examples for a normative literary process of this sort are Dostoevsky's use of the romantic gothic element merging into questions of personality and ethics; Tolstoy's Tiutchev-like view of historical chaos eliciting the question of a personal, ahistorical happiness; Constantine Leontiev's Byronic sense of beauty and dignity finding expression in a "transcendental egoism"; Herzen's fascination with heroic types culminating in a passionate sense of man's moral freedom. The selective use of older literary forms on such a pattern, it has been argued, occurs as the result of religious factors affecting the entire tradition of Western romanticism. "Romantic philosophy and literature," M. H. Abrams suggests, "are a displaced and reconstituted theology, or else a secularized form of devotional experience." Romantic writers, he concludes, "undertook to save the overview of human history and destiny, the experiential paradigms, and the cardinal values of their religious heritage, by reconstituting them in a way that would make them intellectually acceptable, as well as emotionally pertinent, for the time being."[31]

On the whole, this is as apt a generalization as can be found to describe the nineteenth-century Russian writer's work. To it, however, must be added the elements of creative literary stress which occur when emotions and values learned in childhood and reinforced by sociocultural tradition come into sharp conflict with secularization and the "time being." Both the reformulation and the defense of native cultural impulses affected the special intensity with which Russian writers approached the craft of fiction.

Such an overview of literary tradition brings us back full circle to the initial meaning given ideology in the first few pages of this study. For romanticism, defined in terms of religious-secular tensions, is one literary expression of the ideological condition in history; it is that moment when there is still belief, commitment, and ritual, but in a culture in which God is no longer sacred. As has been frequently pointed out by social theoreticians and historians, the process is clearest of all in the nineteenth and twentieth centuries when ideology replaces religion.[32] The cultural transformation brings a new vitality to accepted belief systems by putting to question key supports and by activating an emotional dimension in the struggle of ideas. A strong stimulant to post-Enlightenment literature, then, is that it does not belong to theology and philosophy but stands much closer to an ideological condition in which ideas are not allowed either didacticism and abstraction, or uninvolved contemplation.

Ideology, interpreted in such ways, serves both a methodological and a historical function in the explication of Russian fiction. In the first instance, the concern for subject-object relationships and the validation of hypotheses in terms of the writer's cultural interests help to challenge external, self-serving readings and to focus on the critical approach necessary to understand the literary work's actual identity. Although each author under consideration in the following pages presents methodological difficulties arising out of his own particular literary and critical history, the suggested use of ideology offers a common strategy for clarifying and resolving these individual problems. In the historical sense, ideology defines a period when the persistence of religious factors in conditions of secularization creates an unusual creative opportunity to address cultural tensions and to explore values emphasizing subjective identity and commitment. Both the methodological and the substantive sense of ideology thus suggest that writers be approached as separate identities responding to a particular cultural context. The following sections of the work are each based on the attempt to define a core essense of one such distinctive literary world.

PART II

CHAPTER 3

Herzen's Fiction:
An Affective Verity

A MAJOR PROBLEM of Russian literary scholarship, found typically in studies dealing with the crucial decades of the 1830s and 1840s, is that readers have viewed the fiction of Gogol, Dostoevsky, and Herzen in one way, while the writers themselves have insisted on different interpretations. Indicative of this discrepancy are several well-known instances of authorial bewilderment over the response accorded texts, such as that unhappy series of misunderstandings between Gogol and his public, and the unexpectedly negative reaction to Dostoevsky's early fiction after *Poor Folk*. In Alexander Herzen's instance, the problem is perhaps most glaring since his intellectual history includes ideas and beliefs that are fundamentally opposed to attitudes and stereotypes usually attributed to the cultural milieu and his own literary work. Such differences do not occur by chance, it again should be noted, for nineteenth-century Russian literature has been persistently analyzed by readers who appropriated fiction for their own ends.

Literary theory of the 1960s and 1970s dealing with the reader's role in determining textual reality suggests, on the one hand, an unmanageable relativism in which a piece of fiction is anything any reader chooses to make of it, and, on the other, the writer's own intended meaning as a guide to what can be called the affective verity of a text, if we reverse W. K. Wimsatt's well-known term.[1] The location of affective verity, or responses to literature which are appropriate to original meaning, is indicated by J. L. Austin and other language philosophers who have argued that the comprehension of any speech act requires understanding not only of what words commonly mean but also comprehension of what "the speech agent saw himself as doing in issuing that particular utterance."[2] In the instance of Russian literature such language postulates are of special relevance because its writers were profoundly involved in shaping a specific, hoped-for interpretation of texts; the expectation of creating certain reader responses was one of the most intense and focused processes of their literary endeavor and a key part of what they brought to their culture. Although a similar concern for personal meaning could be argued for general critical application, in the Russian context, then, it is *particularly* clear that the validity of subsequent textual reactions is measurable against the original cultural impulses which went into a piece of fiction. Such a critical standard suggests that the later attribution of certain effects to texts is most likely to approximate non-self-serving, objective meaning if the writer's own basic hopes and values are given preeminence in interpretation. The primary obstructions to understanding Herzen's fiction— not unlike the critical condition of Gogol's and Dostoevsky's work— is its proximity to readers who neglected these core ideological meanings in favor of affective attributions creating other textual realities.

According to the most frequently encountered explanation of late 1830s–40s literature, Russian writers chose to place particular emphasis on man's victimization by the environment. The major evidence for this point of view rests on what W. K. Wimsatt called affective fallacies, emotive echoes in the audience that exist separately from the objective meaning of a work. In these emotive constructs, referred to, it is true, for many different critical purposes and in varying degrees of acceptance, the depiction of total environmental determination and debasement galvanizes compassion and pity for protagonists, narrows the distance between reader and character through sentimental empathy, and shapes the sociophilanthropic purpose of the text. As is suggested in a frequently repeated critical cliché, characters such as Gogol's Akakii Akakievich and Dostoevsky's Devushkin are thus meant to elicit not only "laughter" but most importantly "tears," with the ultimate reference being the impulse to social reform which is to be inspired by sympathy for the oppressed.[3] In the main, Herzen's characters have been taken to belong to this tradition, although the literary model of social victim is actually quite incongruous in the light of his ideological history.

Indeed, the dominant motif of Herzen's thought throughout his life was the image of man as an individual heroic being. In a sense he never outgrew the adolescent fascination we all feel for Robin Hood, D'Artagnan, or Douglas Fairbanks, except that he turned daydreams into a serious and lifelong philosophical concern. The components of this impulse were varied and did not stem from one cultural source. Herzen was undoubtedly influenced by the exalted human image of the Enlightenment. The play of Voltaire's wit and the daring rejection of dogma and system that D'Alembert expressed in his introduction to the *Encyclopédie* figured strongly in his intellectual formation. Rousseau, of course, contributed his share of individualism, and no less important was the related influence of the flawed, yet still noble protagonists of romanticism. Herzen knew the works of Byron, Griboedov, and Pushkin, and he grew up in intimate contact with the proud figures of Aleko, Eugene Onegin, and Chatsky. He was also inspired by another conception of heroic man, that of German idealism, particularly as it was formed in the works of Schiller and Schelling. The central characters of Schiller's plays—the Marquis Posa, William Tell, Karl Moor, Wallenstein—represented, in the words of Martin Malia, "The aspiration to individual dignity and independence of the Enlightenment in German conditions." Malia suggests, with particular reference to the Russian intellectual environment, that Schiller, the "poet of pure ego, of the limitless aggrandizement of self in fantasy," created a model of the human personality "exalted in fantasy and made to seem great and sufficient unto itself by aestheticizing . . . all its passions."[4] But no less important in Herzen's intellectual development was the heroic, even divine role that the artist played in idealism. Schelling, in one classic formulation of romantic aesthetics, wrote that the artist through his genius and intuition provided the vital link to the other world of ideas. He established man's most vital contact with the true essence of reality, the Absolute, and through this function attained virtual divinity.

Leonid Piper, Raoul Labry, Malia, and other students of Herzen largely examined such cultural sources and the image of man that evolved out of them while excluding or diminishing intellectual processes and tensions caused by religious impulses.[5] Vital points of stress in Herzen's intellectual development, however, arose from two particular circumstances: the dependence of nineteenth-century Western thought on religious ethical and metaphysical ideas and Herzen's direct contacts with Christian doctrine. Although his education and home life were typical of the young nobility of the day—largely secular and uncommitted to extreme varieties of religious experience—he knew the Gospels intimately from childhood, went to Lutheran services with his mother, and regularly fasted, confessed, and received communion in the Orthodox church during the Easter holidays. It would not do justice to a long and complex process of ideological growth to view this early exposure to religion narrowly or exclusively, but it does suggest the adumbration of lifelong directions and intellectual involvements. For Herzen's readings in Western philosophy and literature brought to intellectual maturity concepts of free will, moral prerogative, and the divine origins of man which already had a personal function and meaning for him in the core values of his native religious practice.[6]

Early Directions

Herzen's preschool education shows two points of direct contact with religion. Before attending Moscow University he was instructed in basic theology by a priest. At approximately the same time, Ivan Protopopov, a graduate of the Ryazan Seminary, gave him lessons in "slovesnost'" (philology). Protopopov was a liberal with a distinct preference for romanticism and the progenitors of *samizdat*, Pushkin, and the Decembrist Ryleev. Herzen's first introduction to literature and political rebellion, therefore, was made through the prism of one of the many young men who entered Russian culture by way of the ecclesiastical schools of higher education. The former seminarian disdained classical rhetoric as "the most barren branch of all the branches and twigs of ... good and evil," and preferred to arouse moral sensitivity and adolescent enthusiasm.[7] His impact on Herzen can be judged by the noble image of Monsieur Joseph, Bel'tov's tutor in *Who Is to Blame*; more important, the writer himself would retain a similar religious-moral depth of enthusiasm in literature and politics throughout life.

It is true that in the retrospective analysis of *My Past and Thoughts*, Herzen deemphasized such contacts and denied having any particular faith. This attitude, however, was not antireligious at the core; in keeping with Western liberal thought of the 1830s and 1840s, it combined criticism of the church as an institution subject to the graft and corruption of secular society with respect for the basic values of

Christianity. A vital indicator of Herzen's true impulses is that even at the late date of his memoirs his self-portrayal of a proud young rebel who is supposedly above all religious formulas is full of religious language and symbolism. He describes Nikolai Ogarev and himself as "the chosen novices" of a "mutual religion," who place their political heroes on an "iconostasis" and who "anoint" themselves to do battle with tyranny. In *My Past and Thoughts* the various examples of moral oppression and political injustice that occur in Nicholas I's reign are frequently condemned in similar terms, and one chapter dealing with the persecution of Herzen's acquaintances ends on an impressive note of Biblical incantation: "May the reign of Nicholas be damned for all eternity *(vo veki vekov)*, amen."[8] The interjection of religious fervor into political concern was not simply a stylistic matter, however, but an expression of deeper religious-moral commitments.

Such a religious center of gravity can be measured by a number of crucial events in Herzen's life when social manners tended to break down and real emotions tended to burst through. One telling and stressful moment occurred when the gendarmes came to arrest the young man before his first exile. In his autobiography Herzen recounts what followed in vivid detail. His father, the cold and withdrawn aristocrat who felt that religious belief was necessary only to keep up social appearances, could think of nothing else to give his departing son than a family icon; on his part the arrogant young rebel and admirer of the Decembrists, faced with the first really dangerous situation of his life, knelt in the old time-honored fashion to receive the parental blessing and the holy image.[9] Herzen relates a number of other such moments filled with religious significance when youthful pride and the newest progressive theories were overwhelmed by the onrush of deeper feelings. The best known is that classic scene, repeated in most histories of Russian culture, when he and Ogarev, while on Sparrow Hills overlooking Moscow, vowed to "sacrifice their life for our chosen struggle." The passage in Herzen's memoirs describing this place of "pilgrimage" is only matched for emotional intensity by a description of the two friends' reunion after their exile: throwing themselves down on their knees before a crucifix on Herzen's table, the young men and their wives embraced and tearfully offered a prayer of thanks for being together once again.

The crucifix was not an incidental prop, for any latent religious feelings Herzen might have had as a youth came out into the open during his Viatka-Vladimir exile of 1835–40. He was aided in this upsurge of faith and moral exultation by Natalia Zakharina, his deeply religious future wife, and by the architect Alexander Witberg with whom he lived for two years in Viatka. Witberg brought all the intricate symbolism and hieroglyphics of eighteenth-century mysticism and masonry into Herzen's intellectual world. Buttressed by Jacob Boehme, Swedenborg, Eckartshausen, and Paracelsus, the two men, in traditional masonic fashion, examined the symbols of history and relived the moral obligations which pointed to man's heavenly links and eventual reunion with the divine.

Herzen had earlier read the utopian socialists; Zakharina and Witberg thus added a vigorous supernatural element to Saint-Simon's and Fourier's vision of social paradise. The New Christianity and masonic mysticism overlapped with Protopopov's teachings in moral intensity; it is understandable, therefore, that the Gospels, "mystical-social" ideas, and Pierre Leroux would be later remembered in My Past and Thoughts as the components of one intellectual movement. Brought down to earth, however, socialist plans seemed less attractive; within the phalanstery Herzen felt "crowded," as he wrote in June 1840.[10] The discomfort resulted from an incompatability of his core sense of individualism with the blueprinted regimentation of Western socialist theory. Most of his work in the 1830s and 1840s, in fact, would show a similar key conflict: he would be drawn to the newest progressive theories of science, history, and society, yet time after time would respond to them by defending a spiritual image of man based on free will and the attributes of a human divinity.

"The Legend"

The young writer's first serious essay, "On the Place of Man in Nature" (1832), is a blunt defense of Christian standards and idealism against scientific devaluation.[11] "The creative ability to act freely," Herzen writes, "is the surest proof of the high origins of our soul."[12] The problem raised by natural science is whether to rank man among the animals of the species or somehow above nature. The properties of "freedom and will" clearly set mankind apart, he decides, even if measured against the theories of Linnaeus, Bacon,

Joseph Priestly, and Lorenz Oken. For "the creator shapes man in his image and likeness; without man nature would not express itself fully." "Pale, cold materialism" is attacked for turning the individual into a "corpse" without a soul; and Helvetius is made fun of for suggesting that humans would live in the woods and be cattle "if they had hoofs insead of hands."

Soon after completing this essay Herzen reread the Gospels once again and wrote to Natalia about those "divine examples of self-sacrifice," the Russian saints (letter of 10 December 1834). One result of this religious preoccupation was "The Legend," his first work of fiction, and a largely unnoticed attempt to bring an older genre tradition of Russian Christian culture into nineteenth-century literature. The principal source of "The Legend" was a *Cheti Minei* or church calendar reading of saints' lives. Herzen's particular choice is St. Theodora; he does not leave the original structure of her vita intact, however, but adds a surprise ending, mysterious flashbacks, and other narrative devices meant to liven up the genre's rigid form. The stylistic changes, designed to appeal to a modern reader, reinforce the short story's intellectual purpose by making contemporaneous the moral intensity of religious values expressed in St. Theodora's noble sacrifice and spiritual heroism.

One such contemporary technical innovation—suggested, in all likelihood, by prior readings in the autobiographical styles of Rousseau, Heine, Goethe, and Karamzin—was the use of the first person in combination with an omniscient point of view. The narrator of the first part of the story, as Herzen himself during the writing of the primary draft, is in a prison which overlooks Moscow. Glancing down into the city he thinks of the constant polarity of good and evil, "holy minutes of ecstasy" and "the poisonous essence of licentiousness," which affect the urban life of the present. The ringing church bells of Simon Monastery remind him of the derisive "whistles and laughter" which greet religion in the nineteenth century and lead him to think of past spiritual heroism which could provide examples for the present.[13] A lengthy footnote at the conclusion of the passage explicitly formulates Herzen's intentions. In it he asks why it is necessary to retell the life of a saint already available in the old church text and suggests a response which clearly postulates the need for bringing a religious message into the contemporary world: the compiler of saints' lives did his work in the tenth century, while "it is now the XIX."

The latter part of the narrative shifts into a third person acount of St. Theodora's life. The plot is full of flashbacks and interruptions at key moments; a number of puzzling questions are answered only in the shattering dénouement when it is finally revealed that the humble monk Theodore is really Saint Theodora. (Malia as Lemke inaccurately refers to the story as "The Legend of St. Theodora," a title which would make superfluous all of Herzen's efforts to create suspense). Initially, the reader is faced with the enigma of Theodore's motives and origins before entering the monastery: the youth is noble and handsome but deeply troubled by something. At about midpoint in the story Herzen adds a second key puzzle when the half-naked daughter of an abbot attempts to seduce Theodore and the passage is tantalizingly interrupted before we find out if she succeeds. Soon afterward, however, a newborn child is brought to the monastery; accused of its paternity, Theodore is ostracized by the monks. Suspense is maintained by the implicit question of why a character till then portrayed as the noblest and purest of men would fall into such extreme temptation, and, moreover, why he would lie to his mentor about his sins. The last is a particularly heinous act on the face of it, because Theodore and the Abbot establish a near sacred friendship in which they set out together on a spiritual quest to find the true meaning of religion.

The intellectual motifs of the story are expressed mainly in the protagonists' theological dialogues. Theodora, as much in action as in words, stands for kenotic values; she willingly accepts suffering and martyrdom to achieve a moral triumph over injustice and humiliation suffered at the hands of the monks. The abbot, on the other hand, defends a metaphysics based on theosis; through Christ, he argues, man has the means of expressing his free will and divine destiny. Close as such ideas are to the ones offered in "On the Place of Man in Nature," Herzen does not allow Christianity to be idealized. The failings of the church (in addition to the monks' shortsightedness and the potential for religious corruption represented by the seductress) are hinted at in a passage on the Inquisition and in the overly heated rejection of women and sensuality which the abbot—all ironic ignorance—proposes to Theodore. The abbot also notes a more positive religious role, however, by pointing to monastic life as a model of brotherhood and equality for the future. The direction indicated is toward the religious foundations on which utopian socialists would build their plans. At the same time, by having the monks reject Theodora, the writer suggests his favorite dilemma of the individual standing against the crowd. Socially progressive as it may be, monastic life thus indicates the future concern for uncomfortable conditions in the phalanstery that Herzen would later show in his defense of individuality.

"Elena"

The progression from religious motifs and values to a contemporary literary perspective continues in Herzen's second complete work of fiction, "Elena," written during 1836–38. Shortly before undertaking the story, the young exile concluded a brief affair with Praskovia Medvedeva—a married woman soon to become a widow—living in Viatka. In rough outline the new work duplicates biographical incident: a young nobleman, not unlike Herzen, after seducing one woman proceeds to fall in love with another and suffers pangs of conscience after leaving the first for the second.[14] Nevertheless, in "Elena" the abandoned woman, unlike Medvedeva, dies from unrequited love, and other parts of the narrative are considerably less obligated to Herzen's affair than to his reaction to the intellectual-literary tradition of the day. His literary evolution is out of a direct dependence on the native religious genre of "The Legend" to more complex nineteenth-century fictional modes responding to moral and supernatural motifs.

"Elena" unites three narrative tonalities, repeating in a somewhat less successful fashion the fictional experiments begun by Alexander Pushkin and Nikolai Gogol in the 1830s. The primary stylistic line involves wordplay, sudden reversals in meaning, cutting metaphors, satire, and irony. Not unlike Pushkin's "Little House in Kolomna" (1830), Gogol's "Nose" (1836) and "Nevsky Prospect" (1835), a jocular and often mocking narrative voice jolts the reader's sensibilities and expectations. The opning sentence, "In a small house on Povarsky street lived a man who was of small height," establishes an irreverent tone which continues throughout.[15] The description of a room is made in these terms: "The whole study was a continuation of this table, or better, the table was an abbreviation of the study." A bust of Socrates with an "upturned nose" stares at a bust of Cardinal Richelieu with "drooping cheeks." The life of one protagonist is described as "peaceful," but a phrase is added to the effect that cemeteries are peaceful too. An old woman's face is described to be a "coffee-pot," while her neighbor's face "did not even have the appearance of a coffee-pot." The major character, who is to become thoroughly mad at the end of the story, declares in his first dialogue that "[he] is not mad," and so on. In contrast, a second narrative line provides a straightforward description of the protagonists' strong passions and tragic destinies. The Prince's "gnawing conscience" is declared to "tear asunder [his] soul." When he begs his mistress to be calm in the face of their impending separation, the argument used is that "every tear falls as molten lead on my heart." Sensing the inevitability of her lover's departure the young woman exclaims in all seriousness, "Is it not happiness to die now on your chest remembering our [first] meeting!" A servant is described praying before an icon of the Holy Mother with a comment that "the simple girl was so noble at this moment." From the narrator's point of view, in short, there is nothing funny in such prayers, in the high seriousness of true emotions, or in the fate of the abandoned Elena.

The two narrative modes evolve out of separate literary traditions. The mocking, satirical treatment is partially reminiscent of Voltaire's short fiction, partially indebted to Pushkin's irreverence, and partially written in the style of 1830s "clerk" literature of which Gogol created the most talented examples. The description of high emotions, on the other hand, extends back to the genre based on saints' lives and the sentimental and romantic writings of Rousseau, Karamzin, and Goethe. A further complication is a third influence—evident in the Prince's madness and in some hints of the supernatural—of romantic writers such as Hoffmann, Zhukovsky, and Novalis. "Elena" is among the first Russian works after Gogol's to raise difficulties of interpretation arising from the use of such different literary traditions in one text. As a result of the narrative mixture the reader is likely to be uncertain where the author himself stands.

One cause of this uncertainty in perspective is the abandonment of a protagonist—similar to St. Theodora—who can directly present the writer's ideas and who can be used as an example of moral heroism and dignity. Herzen's growing awareness of literary craft undoubtedly suggested to him the clumsiness of the straightforward argumentation of the earlier pattern, although as we shall see in the later "From Roman Scenes" and "William Penn," the genre of drama, with its classical rhetorical component still strong, allowed such a treatment. An increasing familiarity with new fictional modes led the young author to introduce his beliefs not in the speeches or heroic acts of a central, positive character, but through experiments with different prose situations. Because of its rough edges in fact, "Elena" can be said to be most interesting for its probative nature; Herzen appaises and reformulates various literary traditions in the course of the narrative and tentatively starts off on an independent course appropriate to his own maturing thought.

Although the Prince comes from a long line of romantic heroes, and Elena suffers the fate of a typical sentimental character, neither is allowed the luxury of remaining within their literary tradition. A pivotal scene which can be expected to jolt and frustrate expectations of readers accustomed to established narrative schemata occurs at the story's end. The Princess comes to Elena's grave to beg absolution for her sick husband. Her touching speech—" ... forgive him, he is suffering, tormented, unhappy in my embraces, and I do not dare to console him without making up with you"—is answered by a beautiful chorus of women's voices heard through an open church window. Apparently the prayers have some effect, for "a small cloud which had covered the sun dissipates." In the next scene the Prince indeed awakens a changed man; it would seem that a miracle has occurred. "He again felt his strength and his health," comments the narrator, but in this case from a deliberately unreliable and ironic perspective: the change is really in the direction of total madness. The Prince jumps out of bed only to start composing insane projects and to receive his wife, just arrived from Elena's place of repose, as a petitioner for government favors.[16]

The ending mocks a number of conventions. Those readers who tended to view Elena as the innocent, suffering victim out of sentimental fiction are now faced with the unpleasant possibility—hinted earlier in her rather self-centered outbursts—that she is dispensing revenge rather than meekness and forgiveness from beyond the grave.[17] Beguiled by the deceitful narrator, those readers who had placed their hopes in the efficacy of prayer and in some form of divine intervention are now confronted with a jeering providence that ridicules their expectations. Finally, the readers anticipating a noble or tragic resolution of the Prince's grief are left with a ludicrous madman scribbling incoherent projects.

The mocking narrative construction is not an end in itself, however, but serves a larger purpose supported by Herzen's feelings of guilt over Medvedeva, his contacts with Natalia and Witberg, and the attempt begun in "The Legend" to reformulate certain religious values in contemporary literary terms. Most of the traditional literary meanings of the characters and their actions are made unsteady by the narrative perspective, with one notable exception: the moral reality of the Prince's madness. By invalidating peripheral literary situations the narrator concentrates attention on the central motif which he does take seriously. Herzen's ideas on free will and man's dignity, as we have seen, would predispose him to view unfavorably either a simplistic religious faith in divine intervention or an elevation to heroic proportions of sentimental characters who do not control their fate. Since the element of moral triumph shown by St. Theodora is practically nonexistent in Elena, and since there is nothing of high exemplary value in her suffering or in that of the Princess, it is fully in keeping with his vision of individualism to maintain a narrative distance between himself and these characters and to have a bit of fun at their expense. The protagonist's madness, on the other hand, is neither the simplistic hope of supernatural intervention felt by his wife nor the sentimental fate of his mistress, but rather an expression of self-generated feelings of guilt. The importance of this internal spiritual process is hinted at from the very beginning. At the outset of his illness the Prince suffers a horrible nightmare, full of laughing skulls, dwarfs, and bloody gore, which concludes with the narrator's comment that it is all a result of bad conscience.

The literary precedents for depicting a moral struggle in such terms were noted by Herzen in a short essay on Hoffmann written in 1833-34.[18] In addition to the German romantic, the writer mentions Balzac, Eugene Sue, and Jules Janin as representatives of a new "psychological" tradition in fiction which is destined to replace the "syrupy sentimentalism" enjoyed by *Stubenmädchen*. The narrator of "Elena" essentially repeats these literary preferences by deflating sentimental literary components and reformulating gothic and romantic supernaturalism into psychological categories. The Prince's madness is thus in the pattern of narrative evolution followed by Pushkin's "Queen of Spades" (1834), Gogol's "Notes of a Madman" (1835), and Dostoevsky's "Landlady" (1847) in which romantic-religious motifs are given fresh life and verisimilitude through a shift of emphasis to man's mind. The supernatural is no longer viable on its own in this fiction but evolves into new literary situations marked by the use of psychology to explore moral involvements.

Sketches and Notes

In subsequent works Herzen continued to look to religious material not only for moral reference but also for historical subject matter and for reinforcement of his sociocultural theories. The extent of his religious commitment can be judged by "From Roman Scenes" (1838) and "William Penn" (1839). Although the original texts are lost, two remaining sketches of these verse dramas include a number of telling rhetorical passages.

The first piece is set in pre-Christian Rome and consists mainly of a debate between the down-to-earth Meveii and his visionary friend Licinius. Licinius anticipates new eras not yet clearly seen and agonizes over the influence time and space have on human destiny: "The consciousness of my moral freedom, my eternal life lies in (my) heart, while I am limited on all sides by my body."[19] In a formulation reminiscent of "On the Place of Man in Nature," he argues for the absurdity of putting a soul in man if he is only a "hairless monkey." Feeling himself to be a disbeliever in pagan religions he senses, nevertheless, that "man must be connected to God, [must find] peace in him, [rise] up to him in love." At the sketch's end a fulfillment of this vision is hinted in the coming of Christ. Plebians brought on stage to explain the new era give it both a social resonance in keeping with French progressive theories—"God sent his son to save the world, to save the oppressed and poor"—and a supernatural meaning—"and the blind have begun to see, and the dead are resurrected."[20] Many of the same religious motifs are present in "William Penn." The Quaker, in Herzen's interpretation, is reminiscent of the heroic kenotic image of St. Theodora brought close, it is true, to utopian socialist standards. Moreover, the protagonist and his mentor, George Fox, show the visionary qualities of Licinius;

they too are willing to sacrifice their lives for "social, progressive religion."[21]

In "The Notes of a Certain Young Man" (1840–41) elements of the "clerk" literary tradition are combined with autobiographical, romantic, and sentimental components. As in the prior pattern, a core motif is the high spiritual destiny and the importance of the individual. "Life is my natural right," Herzen writes from the first person, "I am the master in it. I press forward with my 'I.' ... I struggle. I open my soul to all. Through it I suck in the whole world."[22] In large measure the reference here is to the pantheistic corner of German idealism in which the ultimate attainment of personality was understood to be the merger of man with nature. The tone of the quotation, however, is more indicative of authorial intent than the pantheistic message in the abstract. For throughout the sketch Herzen's core argument is not for subjugation to nature or to anything else, but for the assertion and spiritual fulfillment of the "I" to be brought about by a frontal attack on the obstacles to its existence.

Herzen's style, therefore, is again sharp with irony, bright with sarcasm, and colored with youthful exuberance; he is full of insolent jokes, puns, and slapstick incidents which explode in all directions. The principal target is the town of Malinov, through which, in the manner of Gogol's rollicking caricature of sentimentalism, the landowner Manilov, the narrator cruelly satirizes some of the hallowed affectations that arose out of La nouvelle Héloise and "Poor Liza." In a characteristic scene a teacher's wife invites the narrator, obviously Herzen's alter ego, for tea and parades her refined feelings by complaining of ennui and expressing her wish to die. Her glances at the young man with eyes that are so "near to death" tell him another story, however, which has nothing to do with dying, and his supposition is soon confirmed, we assume, while the husband is away.

The lady in question, as the rest of Malinov, is shown to lead a shallow existence without dignity or depth; the mimicry of sensibility replaces real emotional substance for her. In part, Herzen reverts to animal metaphors reminiscent of Gogol's symbolic technique to indicate such spiritual inadequacy. As Dmitry Chizhevsky's essays suggest, Gogol's expectation in using literary devices of this sort was not to gain the reader's empathy with the characters or sympathy for their social victimization, but precisely to encourage the opposite response of ridicule and rejection.[23] The narrative tone in question strips sentimentalism of its cherished pathos; the characters described become objects of laughter and outrage rather than pity. "One is truly sorry for them," Herzen writes in his work, "and yet it is impossible not to laugh." For both writers the main vehicle for such an effect is a cruel, grotesque caricature of the baseness, whining servility, and blind obedience of an archetypal petty man, the Russian clerk. Herzen, in short, is agonizingly aware of the low thing that human beings make of themselves, and his principal intent is to force the reader to confront and reject this type of personality.

The one positive character to be found in Malinov is an eccentric landowner named Trenzinsky who is given the calm dignity, mystery, and world-weariness of a romantic hero. In the traditional romantic manner Trenzinsky rejects society; and while Herzen is critical of the defeatist element in such a life, Trenzinsky's proud figure is obviously to be preferred to that of anyone else in the province. The central failing of this protagonist, however, is that he along with the rest of Malinov is unable to live up to the free and glorious human image of Orthodoxy and German idealism. He cannot make his "inner world," that which is the "spark of the divine," independent of external circumstances, and Herzen clearly indicates that such spiritual freedom is man's noblest goal.

In the best known Soviet study of Herzen, Professor Iakov El'sberg is obviously unhappy with a philosophical construction of this sort and uses a key passage out of context to suggest that Herzen is arguing for the "impossibility of making 'the inner world independent of the external.' "[24] In the context of the work itself, however, it seems clear that Trenzinsky is there to show that man *should not* let himself be a victim of the environment and the "nature of things." The protagonist, it is true, stands for "materialistic" human qualities such as skepticism and common sense which Herzen endorses. Trenzinsky is useful, in this way, as a means of criticizing idealists who dwell too long on abstractions without bringing the individual's spiritual dignity into play in the real world. At the end of the sketch, an obvious romantic example of such active heroism is presented by contrasting the supposedly abstract German school of thought to Byron. But the principal cultural communication of the work has little to do with philosophical materialism as such; Herzen hopes to indicate the "divine spark" in man, to stimulate his sense of sublimity, and, as is suggested in a telling passage, to encourage "the proud spirit [which] rejects all external influences."

Who Is to Blame?—Cultural Background

In the early 1840s the young writer returned from exile and picked up considerably the tempo of his intellectual life. During 1841–42 he once again was sent to the provinces for an indiscretion but his absence from Moscow and St. Petersburg was not of long duration and he managed to remain in contact with new cultural developments. This was the "remarkable decade," in P. V. Annenkov's apt definition, when a vast complex of ideas and social theories opened exciting vistas for the creative energy and literary or intellectual talents of Russian young men. Herzen began to publish with regularity and established himself as one of the more promising men of letters of the new generation. His reading matter included philosophy, theology, natural science, anatomy, church history, social theory, and mathematics. In the midst of this frantic intellectual pace he sat down to his longest and most ambitious fictional work, Who Is to Blame?, which was serialized during 1845–46 and published in a separate edition in 1847. The novel continued the narrative technique and thought of his earlier prose fiction, but also showed the tensions and discoveries of continuing literary and intellectual growth. Two written sources of this period are of considerable benefit in clarifying essential directions and in sorting out the important ideas which went into the text: a diary kept by the writer from 1842 to 1845, and the philosophical essays—Dilettantism in Science, Letters on the Study of Nature, and "Whims and Reflections"—he brought out at approximately the same time.

Not surprisingly, a large number of passages in the diary involve religious issues.[25] As already noted, Hersen would later say in My Past and Thoughts that he moved away from his religious beliefs at the end of the decade. We know of the disillusionment experienced after the death of his children and of his contact with Left Hegelian attacks on theology after Ogarev introduced him to Feuerbach's Essence of Christianity in 1842. The actual response to religion in the diary, however, is far from outright rejection. On the one hand, the writer criticizes the religious "formalism" of fasting, ritual, monasticism, and pietistic "cruelty"; remembering the funeral of a friend, he notes the inadequacy of religious dogma in contemporary society and describes, as an example, a widow's revolt against her old beliefs after her husband's death.[26] On the other hand, he reads Augustus Gfrörer's *Geschichte der christlichen kirche* and comments, with a glance backward to utopian socialist doctrine and "From Roman Scenes," on an "amazing" likeness between the contemporary era and the years immediately preceding the appearance of Christ. Several passages on church debates of the past are included; Bishop Feodor and St. Augustine are quoted with approval, and the importance of Arianism is noted. The critique of religion, in short, does not present a total break with past beliefs, but repeats an ongoing internal debate in which certain doctrines and traditions of the church are attacked while other basic values are not only left intact but reaffirmed.

The diary is of inordinate interest for the internal view it provides of such an intellectual state of transition, felt as it must have been by many other young Russian men in the 1830s–40s. The major element of this cultural experience involves a projection of old moral values and ideas into new, secular conditions brought about by thinkers like Feuerbach. In Herzen's instance the criticism of ritual, fasting, and unquestioned faith is simply a new, more intense variant of his objections to limitations placed on the individual. His most pointed attack is on the notion of divine intervention; theologians, he points out, do not recognize that "not only Christ's passion, but all of history is a prepared comedy from their point of view." At the same approximate time, however, he suggests the opposite idea of free will in a form no less familiar to theology: that of "Christ-man, Christ-God, godman." The process of thought is characteristic for him: on the one hand we see an attack on religious predeterminism and other prohibitions on human centrality and dignity; on the other, the formulation of a defense against these prohibitions using equally religious concepts and symbols such as free will and Christ. It would not be farfetched to say of such notes in the diary that they represent a type of theological debate using competing religious ideas.

The pattern of thought is no subconscious evolution in old beliefs, moreover, but a highly reflective appraisal of religious cultural sources and their implicatons for one's cherished values. In the notation of September 1842, Herzen writes: "Christianity has amazingly prepared individualism for the present. Submersion into oneself, the acknowledgment of eternity within oneself, purified egoism that is yet developed to the highest level, and, therefore, the development of one's dignity. And on the other hand, the idea of self-sacrifice for the common good, love, and so on. This . . . created all the riches of the human soul."[27] The paragraph concludes with the comment that Christianity has only "murkily seen" what is brought to fruition by "Tsar Reason" in the contemporary world. But such an adjustment does not minimize the recognition of religion's importance; for it is the same core ideas of an individuality that triumphs over space and time, of "purified egoism," "dignity," "self-sacrifice," and "love," that continue to be Herzen's basic points of reference in his philosophical writings and ficton.

In another such reflective entry, Hegel is characterized as "the last link of Christianity and a Columbus of philosophy and humanity" (December 1843). As numerous commentators have pointed out, Herzen's major essays of this period—*Dilettantism in Science* (1843-44) and *Letters on the Study of Nature* (1845-46)—are written with the great philosopher in mind. The Absolute Idea indeed frequently replaces the Christian God in these works but not in exact imitation of the original Hegelian model or in the materialistic prism of a Marx or Herbert Spencer. Rather than arguing for either patterns of reason or material forces that impose a historical determinacy on existence, Herzen interprets Hegelianism to express a fulfillment of the self in universal form. The coming to consciousness of the Absolute Idea, in his view, creates the conditions for "intelligent, morally free and energetic action [in which] man arrives at the actuality of his personality and immortalizes himself in the phenomenal world."[28]

Since nineteenth-century progressivism—whether of Hegelian or of other origin—usually includes a sense of its own historical inevitability, however, it would tend to conflict with such a hard standard of free individualism. Herzen faces up to the dilemma implied by his ideas and goes to some lengths—although not always consistently—to argue that modern social and philosophical thought need not degrade man's spiritual dignity and free will. In the diary he expresses his defense in notations on Fourier's "deadly prosaity" and "sad pettiness," in that remark on the utopian socialist predilection for crowding the communal structures, and in some guarded appraisals of scientific hypotheses. One significant entry deals with the work of Louis Agassiz, the American naturalist who opposed Darwin. Herzen points out with great satisfaction that every geological period is unique and unrepeatable according to Agassiz's findings, a hypothesis similar to the one used in the twentieth century to argue against genetic and biological determinism.[29] In another set of notes made while he was auditing a course in anatomy, the dissection of a live dog leads not to materialistic skepticism but to a sense of wonder over the "secret compartment of life" and "the mystery of existence" which "will not fall [but will] instill geater and greater pious respect for itself." Anatomy reveals an "abyss of new facts" and the natural scientists "know a lot," Herzen remarks; but there is still "something that they do not know, and this something is more important than all they do know."[30]

The major concepts of Hegelian thought are adjusted to the same standards of morally free action, individual uniqueness, dignity, and respect for the spiritual side of existence. The following passages of *Dilettantism in Science* and *Letters on the Study of Nature* show a characteristic concern:

> Forgotten in science, personality has demanded its rights, demanded life, passions, and is only satisfied with actual, free action.... Man demands [personality] and science ... confirms his right to it. [Science] does not hold back, it gives its blessing to personal life, to a life of free action....

> History is the passionate, dramatic epos of transition from nature to logic ... its agents are not general categories, not abstract norms ... they are personalities ... [who] struggle with indifferent fate.

> Nature without man, to give it a name, is something mute, incomplete, a failure, an *avorte*. Man has blessed it by giving meaning to its existence.[31]

The vision of human dignity and centrality can be seen to lead Herzen to a subversion of metaphysical premises taken out of materialism and idealism alike. On the one hand, he came to reject the external influence of God or the Absolute; on the other, economical, political, or biological conditions failed to impress him as ultimate causes. As a reader of Schiller and the utopian socialists, to be sure, he recognized the degrading effects of social oppression and poverty; but he could not bring himself to make the environment an ultimate determinant of human destiny, nor could he admit an imposed logic of history. The intellectual tension of this position is that it affords no material or transcendental referents to support the values of free will and dignity that Herzen carried over from idealism and Christianity. One possible resolution, as we have seen, is the literary shift in "Elena" away from the supernatural to the moral-psychological characteristics of the Prince. Changes in fictional modes, however, are usually given depth and stability by ideological evolution, and Herzen found such new intellectual support in the writings of Ludwig Feuerbach and the Left Hegelians grouped around Arnold Ruge's *Deutsche Jahrbücher*.

The primary subject matter of Left Hegelianism, of course, was religion; Feuerbach, David Friedrich Strauss, and Bruno Bauer rejected the divine origins of the Biblical message and undermined religious metaphysical concepts such as God and the soul. Curiously enough, however, in one sense it is more accurate to interpret the basic premise of Feuerbach's seminal *Essence of Christianity* to be more idealistic than materialistic in nature since he defines the preeminence of an intellectual-psychological process of the mind. God, the Left Hegelian argued, was a result of human aggrandizement and egoism, a self-projection of man into the divine; the point was to bring the abstract into the real world through a shift in human understanding. Social and economic factors were important parts of this secular deification of man, as Marx and Feuerbach himself would come to view it; however, the unmistakable conclusion could be drawn that a state of mind leads man to his condition in life, and it was this keynote which was most likely to influence Herzen's own ideas of human centrality and dignity.

In "Whims and Reflections III. New Variations on Old Themes," published in *The Contemporary* during 1847, such a psychological condition is the major theme:

> The love for subjugation, for authority which is based on self-ridicule and the destruction of one's dignity is so widespread, so epidemic [that it] afflicts entire generations.... Is a virtuous man really one who considers himself stupid, incapable of understanding truth, weak, despised ... one whose existence is entirely a function of something external? "I am a complete orphan, without mother or father," a clerk of fifty told me. At his age ... he considers himself to be *an orphan*, without mother or father, and not a self-sufficient man capable of standing on his own two feet! Do not laugh at him; a large number of the most mature individuals are as lacking in self-sufficiency.[32]

Quite out of keeping with the emphasis usually placed on Herzen's

social interests, the key issue here is clearly not the "external"
oppression of Russian society, but the internal oppression that man
imposes on himself by his feeling of inadequacy. In Left Hegelianism
Herzen found the antidotal psychological means to cure self-
degradation: "Man is endlessly on his knees before this or that. . . .
The need to respect, to worship is so strong in people that they are
constantly worshipping something outside of themselves . . . they do
not have the slightest notion that there is something inside of them
which is worthy of respect, that they are equal to anything that is to
be respected. . . . A man who has attained the awareness of his dignity
is acting in a human manner because it is more natural, easier, more
characteristic, more pleasant, more reasonable for him to act
thus. . . . "[33] The idea of subjugation to "outside" factors is a direct
imitation of Feuerbach's hypothesis that man sets up gods alienated
from himself without realizing that his own inner drive for self-
assertion is the key element of this process. The recognition and
fulfillment of egoism is the first step to dignity; it is "the core of
everything human," for "to tear egoism out of the human heart
means to tear out his living core, the leaven and salt of his personality." This psychological imperative, in short, suggested a contemporary, practical means for putting man in the center of things.
Throughout his work from now on, Herzen would consistently turn
to self-interest as the inner state that best supports the individual's
centrality, power of will, and dignity.

Who Is to Blame?—Text and Readers

It is possible in such a frame of reference to speak of an affective
meaning in Herzen's novel based on specific cultural material and his
response to the important issues of the 1830s and 1840s. The moral
and anthropological terms of Herzen's cultural sources suggested to
him the importance of what the individual feels, and in particular
what he feels about himself. Such emphasis on emotions is natural
for an intellectual system in which the free will and dignity attributed
to man allows for few prime movers of human destiny more crucial
than one's own spiritual world (the works of St. Augustine, the
mystics, and Goethe are pertinent Western examples of kindred
literary traditions known to Herzen). The important aesthetic
conjunction occurs when the ideas of individualism and the self's
vitality are, quite naturally, applied to the literary text's audience.

The reader's response suggests a focus of interest because it represents a potential fulfillment of cherished ideas and, in specific instances, a test of the latest theories of individuality found in Feuerbach's psychological model. Moreover, the Left Hegelian stimulus to such an affective concern is complemented by a skillful and inspiring literary technique of audience address already available to Herzen in the work of Gogol. In such passages as the mayor's concluding monologue in *The Inspector General* and the direct address to the audience of *Teatral'nii raz"ezd* Gogol made it quite clear that the major meaning of his art was in the moral change he hoped to elicit in his public. In fact, when Ogarev came to visit Herzen in 1842 with *The Essence of Christianity* in hand, he also brought the first part of *Dead Souls*, which had just been published. The two books can be seen to mark, respectively, intellectual and technical directions. For if Feuerbach pointed to a new, fresh definition of man's spiritual vitality for Herzen's fiction, Gogol suggested a literary method of galvanizing it in the real world.

Both the substantive and technical issues of an approach to readers are explored in the diary. Herzen is quite aware that rhetorical address or exemplary heroes are no longer suitable literary devices that will produce a serious emotional effect. He notes that Pushkin's only possible solution for the noble Lensky in *Eugene Onegin* is to have him shot. On the other hand, Gogol's negative heroes—the "dead souls"—suggest to him the type of a convincing literary protagonist that can elicit results. "Do we not all ... live the life of Gogol's heroes?" is his strongest response to Chichikov, Korobochka, and Plyushkin.[34] By combining such an anticipated personal effect produced out of the audience's self-recognition in negative fictional characters with Left Hegelian ideas of self-interest, we can anticipate literary directions. In *Who Is to Blame?* Herzen will use literary types that are all somehow lacking in Feuerbachian egoism and individualism to attempt to arouse these very moral-psychological qualities in his audience.

Of particular help in confirming this hypothesis are Herzen's remarks on a now-forgotten drama by Auguste Jean-François Arnould and Narcisse Fournier, *Huit ans de plus*, which he happened to see after beginning *Who Is to Blame?* Scholarly commentary, on the whole, has not proceeded beyond establishing the similarity of plot outlines in the two works. Both are constructed around a love-triangle: wife/husband/wife's lover, in the instance of the novel; wife/husband/mistress, in the drama. Herzen, however, goes much further than the common plot, although not in the sense of showing any direct imitation since he recognized Arnould and Fournier's mediocrity. In the diary and in a review written in 1842, he uses the play as an occasion to clarify essential conceptions of aesthetic catharsis, religion, and psychology. The opening quotation of the review, taken from Feuerbach's *Essence of Christianity*, immediately suggests the frame of reference of his thoughts.[35]

What occurs on stage in the play, Herzen notes, creates a "strong, organic link" with the stalls through action which "entices the spectator after itself." The point of enticement, the important effect of drama, is to project viewers "no further than [their] own hearts." In *Huit ans de plus*, protagonists indicate this inward direction for the audience by suffering tragedy as a result of insufficient psychological awareness. Confined to a narrow sense of love and family duty, they are unable to attain the "vital religious feeling" in which personality "rises up to the universal, without ceasing to be personality," and reaches "the greater development of one's individuality in the generic." The religious and the generic, it should be recognized by now, refer to Feuerbach's psychological delineation of the individual's self-projection into universal categories. Such fulfillment in the world through "love for one's country, art, science" (and, we must assume, the political action Herzen is unable to mention directly) affords ultimate forms of self-expression and of man assuming his proper role at the center of things. The problem of the characters and thus of the audience, Herzen adds in his diary, is that they are not such "heroes, giants, or better, egoists."[36]

Who Is to Blame? reflects the major premises of the essays and private writings. Herzen's characters are all psychologically inadequate in some way, and their respective failures to rise up to high levels of "egoism" provide readers with clues to the novel's meaning. The first important clue, of course, is the unusual title. The personal pronoun evokes a sense of individual responsibility—precisely "who" and not "what"—while the form of a question shapes the entire text into a response invited from the audience.[37]

As in the case of his earlier fiction, Herzen uses a number of different prose traditions. Each of the protagonists—the teacher

Krutsifersky, his wife Liubon'ka, and the nobleman Bel'tov—derive from a separate literary world. Krutsifersky belongs to the clerk and natural schools of writing; Liubon'ka to sentimentalism; and Bel'tov to romanticism. The literary styles and motifs are not inviolate, however, but are juxtaposed for purposes of parody, irony, and the expression of Herzen's own literary ideas. In a more complex version of "Elena's" literary structure, the narrator stands outside the characters and events he describes. It is largely through his intervention that the different literary traditions are used to focus the intellectual presuppositions Herzen wants to criticize and to establish the principal sources of responsibility for what occurs.

Initially, the action centers on Krutsifersky, a shy and browbeaten student who stumbles into the household of Colonel Negrov to tutor his son. There he meets Liubon'ka, Negrov's illegitimate daughter and a ward of the colonel's sentimental wife. The young people fall in love and marry. They live happily until the arrival of Bel'tov, a man of noble intentions and unfulfilled promise, who becomes a close friend of their small family. Liubon'ka falls in love with him, Krutsifersky responds by becoming a drunkard, and Bel'tov, seeing the unhappiness he has caused, leaves both Liubon'ka and Russia.

This unsatisfactory dénouement—which stands in a much closer polemical relationship to the plot Nicholas Chernyshevsky selected for *What Is to Be Done?* than the source usually mentioned, Turgenev's *Fathers and Children*—is a result of the respective literary and intellectual qualities Herzen chooses for each of his protagonists. Of the three, Liubon'ka is the *least* to blame (and condescending as he is, Herzen's portrayal of her would still probably be of direct interest to the modern feminist). Liubon'ka is to blame because she, a woman with all the inhibitions of the nineteenth century, is unable to live up to the glorious vision of humanity and female freedom advocated by George Sand.[38] The tragedy of the character is that she is well on the way to achieving this high ideal but is unable to take the final step of breaking with a narrow sense of family obligation and wifely duty.

Herzen cleverly highlights the new issue of women's rights by refracting it through an older literary tradition based on feminine helplessness. The circumstance of Liubon'ka's background—a peasant mother, illegitimacy, the insults she endures in Negrov's household— place her in the typical victim role of the emotionally high-strung and suffering heroine favored by sentimental writers. Such a literary destiny is impossible in her case, however, because it is anticipated and caricatured through another character, Liubon'ka's stepmother. Madame Negrova comes out of a similar mixed-class marriage between a merchant-woman and a count. Her father is a hopeless drunkard who despises his wife for her social origin and who finally ejects the woman from their home. Both parents eventually die and leave the child—again anticipating Liubon'ka's lot—to be a ward in the household of a spinster aunt. The girl grows up on romantic and sentimental fiction such as *La nouvelle Héloïse* leading to daydreams of pistols, dashing men, and passionate abductors who exclaim "you are mine forever." She finally finds her hero in the person of Negrov (a far from dashing forty at the time), adopts Liubon'ka in an effusive gesture, and settles down to country life. Her charged emotions continue to produce overly stimulating daydreams which find an outlet in poor Krutsifersky, but Negrova becomes a sad parody of the sentimental heroine. She grows fat and indolent, to the point of hunting for mushrooms out of a carriage while accompanied by peasant children who do the actual picking.

Herzen uses the common background of Liubon'ka and Negrova to show the younger woman's potential triumph over the sticky and degrading female role played out in her stepmother's caricatured sentimentalism. Liubon'ka, the narrator takes pains to point out, is unaffected by sentimental and romantic fiction because she develops intellectually on her own. The "barren environment" of country life, rather than being a hindrance, contributes to her mental and spiritual development by throwing her back on internal resources. She feels a sense of alienation, and this independent perspective enables her to rise above the laziness and vulgarity of the Negrovs. The one sentimental, romantic expectation she does share with Negrova, however, proves to be decisive. In this regard, Krutsifersky performs the same damaging function for her that her father earlier served for his wife, for the men are a form of escape that turns into another, ultimately defeating loss of freedom. In irritation over her husband after comparing him to Bel'tov, Liubon'ka experiences the Feuerbachian insight that "humility [is] fearsome pride." that "the greatest self-renouncing love, [is] the highest egoism," but is unable to follow through on her own behalf and break away to a new life.

Some time before undertaking his novel, Herzen wrote to Natalia Zakharina about the psychological quality he expected women to show in their relationships with men. "Why do you submit to my will?" he remarks. "I hate submission in friends . . . I [do not] want to see myself in you [but] to see *yourself in you* . . . submission lowers a person."[39] Such condescending concern for feminine self-assertion would undoubtedly haunt him later when Natalia actually sets off on her own to become Georg Herwegh's mistress. But at this point at least, the frustrated human dignity of women could be expressed unequivocally in Liubon'ka's failure to live the ideals of George Sand and Feuerbach to the fullest.

In Krutsifersky Herzen combines philosophical and psychological concepts he explored in his essays with the clerk and natural-school literary traditions. Krutsifersky's "blame" goes deeper than Liubon'ka's, for although he has none of the disadvantages of women, he nevertheless turns himself into a "girl." The pejorative attributes of the female, in this instance, are the same as those negative traits of man that Herzen delineated in his earlier work. Meekness and day-dreams place Krutsifersky in a position in which he is totally incapable of self-assertion, and such a failure of egoism in turn leads him to the debased life of an alcoholic. A complementing factor is Krutsifersky's ponderous fatalism; Herzen has him constantly parading the belief that all things, including his marriage (and assumedly Liubon'-ka's affair with Bel'tov) are predetermined and cannot be controlled by human beings.

Krutsifersky's life, not unlike Liubon'ka's, follows the narrative heritage of his parents. The father, a poor doctor, is aged prematurely not by "passions" but by an "endless, crushing, petty, humiliating battle with need." In such conditions "the soul fades away" and "forgets that it has wings." Three out of five children in the family die, an older sister runs off with a soldier who abandons her, and Krutsifersky's mother suffers some terrible illness. It is not surprising, therefore, that Krutsifersky becomes an alcoholic in compliance with a traditional pattern of the natural school, the literary world most reminiscent of such misfortunes. Any pathos or compassion that could be evoked by the young teacher's fate, however, is deliberately undercut by the comical and absurd tone of the narrative voice.

Part of this effect is created through the ironical juxtaposition of Krutsifersky with sentimental and romantic predecessors.[40] Madame Negrova is very close to the truth when she compares the young man's love for Liubon'ka to something out of *La nouvelle Héloïse*.

Krutsifersky's emotions are worthy of a Werther or a Vladimir Lensky, the narrator points out, except that he exists in a naturalistic, desentimentalized environment in which such sensibilities are incongruous in a man. What is required from Krutsifersky for survival, it is made plain, are action and daring rather than the bouts of crying and readings from Zhukovsky of which he is fond. Liubon'ka, the sentimental heroine who rises above her literary prototype almost to the point of a complete break, can only note with bewilderment her husband's fixation in a similar role of a helpless, unmanly victim. She never thought a man could cry so, she writes in her diary.

The mockery of sentimental effusions is, at times, quite cruel. In one characteristic scene, the boorish and dim-witted Negrov acts as a tool of deflation when he accidentally receives Krutsifersky's love note to Liubon'ka. His slow reading, in a "heavy, bookish pronunciation" of Krutsifersky's poetical outpourings ("Be my Alina [Zhukovsky heroine]. I love you mindlessly, passionately, with exultation; your very name is love ...") provides one of the more humorous scenes in the novel. In another such incident the mockery reaches slapstick proportions. Krutsifersky's growing love for Liubon'ka is matched by her stepmother's desire for him; the stepmother, as we have seen, is a rather fat, middle-aged woman who is subject to overly stimulating daydreams. Krutsifersky receives a perfumed note calling for a rendezvous and blissfully rushes off to keep the appointment. It is night, the setting is romantic, and our young hero, "swallowing air like a fish," is so overwhelmed by tears and emotions that he dares to attempt his first "kiss of love." The kiss is successfully given but Krutsifersky suddenly utters a scream. His beloved, thinking he is overcome by passion, urges him to calm down; but the real source of his distress is, of course, his discovery that he has been making love not to Liubon'ka but to her stepmother.

The mockery and victimization of the unhappy tutor in such passages would be a senseless cruelty on the part of the narrator if the character was indeed shown to be helpless and crushed by the environmental circumstances which affect his family. Krutsifersky, however, has more than ample opportunity to break out of the sad degradation of his life. In Part II Herzen gives him and Liubon'ka the means to a happy if not luxurious existence supported partially by her dowry and partially by his teacher's salary. Constricting environmental conditions are casually dismissed by the narrator as "external history," and emphasis is placed on the inner drama of ego and morality played out by the Krutsiferskys and Bel'tov. In this situation, the major issue is clearly Krutsifersky's character, and it is in such a realm of spirit and personality that he is conclusively shown to be inadequate; he can neither defend his rights to Liubon'ka's love, nor sustain attempts at noble self-sacrifice (labeled "unnatural" by the narrator). The core of his failings, as we have already seen, is inadequate self-assertion and a fatalistic acceptance of his lot. The "blame" for Krutsifersky's degradation, therefore, can be traced to his own intellectual suppositions as well as to a deficiency of will and character; and the mocking narrative voice, in this frame of reference, far from being pointless, is directly germane to the ideas Herzen expresses in his essays and earlier writings.

Bel'tov, Krutsifersky's rival for Liubon'ka's love, continues the evolution of the romantic hero begun in Herzen's earlier works. On the whole, critics have tended to place him among the "superfluous men," in keeping with the character typology developed out of Pushkin's term by the radical publicist and editor of The Contemporary, Nicholas Dobroliubov. According to the major component of this still-popular interpretation, the central male figures of mid-nineteenth-century Russian literature—Bel'tov, Onegin, Pechorin, Oblomov, Rudin—are understood to be social types reflecting the oppressive state of society. As Georg Lukács puts it, such protagonists, in Dobroliubov's conception, were "specific, objective forms" of reactionary conditions rather than products of the "mental peculiarities or biographical circumstances of their authors."[41] "It does not matter at all," Lukács argues in regard to Dobroliubov's reading of Turgenev's Asya (1858), "what Turgenev himself wanted to express" (p. 121), as long as one is able to grasp the objective social factors illuminated by the fictional characters.

The dangers of such interpretation—with specific ramifications in the instance of Bel'tov—is that "objectivity" threatens to be located solely in the eye of the critic with little respect accorded the writer's own formulation of reality. In a classic moment of Marxian aesthetics, the very similar "victory of realism" Friedrich Engels saw occurring in Balzac's work over the French writer's religious-romantic vision and conscious intentions, can actually be taken to be a triumph of the reader's imagined sociopolitical preferences over the very real process of the author's creative response to literary-intellectual tradition.[42] *This* objective process of aesthetic conceptualization in Herzen's instance, meanwhile, suggests that the principal "blame" for Bel'tov's superfluousness lies in a particular moral-fictional stance the character is made to assume, rather than in class position or social structure.

This is not to say that Herzen disregards social class either as a factor in human affairs, or as a means of character description in the new literary manner of Balzac. The structuralization of blame in the novel depends on both components of society and protagonists. In the first instance, human failure and inadequacy are expressed through the narrator's satirization of various minor social types—landowners, clerks, peasants—such as the Negrovs; in the second, the internal mechanisms of this inadequacy are revealed through the spiritual world of the central characters. Bel'tov's positioning outside of the less important social narrative line, however, allows Herzen to accent the moral-psychological factors which he considers to be of ultimate significance in human affairs.

Herzen's principal contribution to Russian literary characterization through Bel'tov, in fact, lies in his development of the "superfluous" protagonist's spiritual qualities. We know that the literary origins of the superfluous man lie partially in a stock situation of romanticism, a positioning of central hero against social milieu or "the crowd" that can be seen in Byron, Goethe, and Pushkin.[43] In original form the romantic hero—mystic, poet, artist, or madman—stands outside of society or mere social categories since he represents the much more important contact of man with the nontemporal and divine. Bel'tov, in fact, reads Lord Byron and has the dignity, pride, and capacity for intense passions that separate him from the everyday community and link him with his literary predecessors. But if Childe-Harolde's, Aleko's, Onegin's, and Pechorin's negative moral and psychological traits are partially diminished and blurred by the attractiveness of their separation from the crowd and by the meanness and vulgarity of the society they abandon, Bel'tov's ideas and conscious judgments are focused by Herzen and found to bear the major responsibility for his condition. The perceptive Russian scholar, L. Ginzburg, writes that for such new literary characters:

> A greater complexity in psychological analysis, made ethical values more complex as well.... It is impossible to imagine an ideological hero ... without moral responsibility and the freedom to choose his

actions. The primary conflict of the nineteenth-century's ideological, intellectual protagonist is no longer a conflict with hostile, external conditions, or a pre-formulated, uniform conflict based on the opposition of personality and society (romanticism), but it is an *idependent* conflict in the sense that it develops out of the intellectual hero's reason and conscience.[44]

The new literary situation also supersedes the sentimental-romantic pathos of characters such as Werther. Bel'tov, in this regard, stands in roughly the same relationship to Krutsifersky as Liubon'ka stands to her stepmother; the sentimental typology is preempted in both instances by its caricature in the clearly inferior characters. Krutsifersky's maudlin nature, absurdly passionate letters, and readings of Zhukovsky make it impossible for Bel'tov to be received as an idealistic, pure soul ruined by fate and society, just as it is impossible for Liubon'ka to be read sentimentally after the satiric depiction of Madam Negrova. An example of pertinent literary composition was readily available in Pushkin's work, for Lensky, the character who had to be shot according to Herzen, presents the reader with the same German romantic idealism and sentimental effusion which make it impossible for Eugene Onegin to occupy his ground. The internal competition of the characters in both texts—although psychological and moral components are less distinctly formulated by Pushkin—is not only a matter of plot and theme, then, but involves a process of literary evolution in which one type of protagonist replaces another.

Bel'tov's life, in the same way as Liubon'ka's and Krutsifersky's, is flawed by an inability to project and express his personality in the world. Educated by a Genevan tutor, a hopelessly idealistic and impractical man, he fails to pursue any one activity to its end. His biography is a succession of defeats, first in government service, then in medicine, art, local politics, and finally in love. The chief intellectual source of these difficulties, along with the sentimental-romantic literary typology, is anticipated and caricatured in Krutsifersky. Just as the tutor, Bel'tov does not believe in free will and refuses to recognize an independent sphere of action for man; but unlike Krutsifersky, Bel'tov is provided with unusual intelligence and talent so that the pathos of unfulfilled promise stands out in much stronger relief against his consciously accepted fatalism. The narrator directly belittles his attitude—"Bel'tov confronted reality . . . and again he

cowardly backed down before it"—and makes clear that a break-
down in spirit and will is the principal source of his failure.[45]

In the pattern of the other protagonists, Bel'tov is thematically
linked to family history. Of particular interest, because it indicates
what Bel'tov himself could have undertaken in the affair with Liubon'ka given a more resolute frame of mind, is the life of his father.
The reader first encounters Bel'tov's parent, a profligate nobleman,
during his attempt to seduce Sofia, a governess in his mother's
household. Although she manages to escape his advances, gossip that
arises out of the elder Bel'tov's careless remarks dishonors the young
woman and makes it impossible for her to find a decent source of
livelihood. Having reached the point of extreme poverty and despair,
she decides to spend her last few pennies on a letter to vent her
outrage over Bel'tov's dishonorable behavior. Bel'tov, who has
entirely forgotten his unfortunate victim, is deeply affected by this
correspondence and it generates an intense moral crisis in him. He
radically changes his sense of values, goes off to find Sofia, and finally
marries her.

The point of this key episode is that the elder Bel'tov's life is
redeemed by his moral conversion; having served his function, in
fact, Bel'tov dies soon after his marriage. It is not the society or
economic forces that transform this protagonist, but an inner struggle and his own will to change his life. Such a moral confrontation,
with oneself suggests, in turn, the proper solution to the dilemma of
Bel'tov's son and Liubon'ka Krutsifersky. Bel'tov and Liubon'ka
are at fault much more than the society they inhabit because they
allow themselves to be victimized by the social institution of marriage
instead of asserting the moral prerogative of their love. The absence
of such assertion lies at the heart of their tragic separation and
indicates that "blame" and responsiblity, in Herzen's view, must rest
finally with the individual, his internal makeup, and his ethical
choices.

The Last Fiction and Reprise

Herzen completed two more substantial prose works, "The Thiev-
ing Magpie" ("Soroka-vorovka," 1848) and "Doctor Krupov"
(1847), before his departure from Russia. The first is based on the
life of a serf-actress told him by the famous actor, M. S. Shchepkin.

This story is undoubtedly the most "social" of his published fiction in that it focuses on the abuses of serfdom and the brutal treatment of peasants by the infamous Prince Kamensky. A central motif is the triumph of human spirit and dignity in noxious conditions of oppression. The second work is more complex and interesting for it provides a synoptic view of the literary technique and ideas we have been observing. In compact form, the story includes most of the essential points of transition from Herzen's religious and idealistic influences to the aesthetic culmination of his fictional work.

The two protagonists of "Dr. Krupov" are Levka, a feeble-minded boy serf, and the doctor himself, a character Herzen had already introduced in his novel. Levka is the last transformation of the positive, religious hero that Herzen began with St. Theodora. Anticipating somewhat Tolstoy's Platon Karatayev and Dostoevsky's Myshkin, he is the *iurodivyi* (holy fool) familiar to the Greeks as a *salos* and encountered frequently in Orthodox saints' lives and the kenotic tradition. In original form the *bozhii chelovek* (person of God), as he is also known, provided a reminder of nonearthly involvements and a divine moral standard for laymen through his rejection of material goods and commonsense pursuits of happiness. The *iurodivyi's* saintly disorientation and prophetic talents, as demonstrated by the holy fool who jolts Boris Godunov's conscience in Pushkin's play, served to suggest the presence of a transcendental measure in the universe; and Herzen, while hardly believing in prophecy or miraculous forces by now, uses Levka in essentially the time-honored fashion. The character's madness is really a form of moral worth and the means to indict the "banal ritual" and "same dull repetition not leading anywhere" of everyday, mundane life.

Herzen, it will be remembered, used madness in "Elena" to depict the importance of conscience in personality. Although Levka is constructed on a similar pattern of the supernatural's secularization and evolution into moral-psychological exploration, new allusions to madness became available as a result of several notable events in Russian culture. One such nuance was provided by the official declaration of Peter Chaadayev's insanity after his belittlement of Russian history in the 1830s. Chaadayev was joined by two fictional lunatics—Pushkin's Eugene of "The Bronze Horseman" (published posthumously in 1841) and Gogol's Poprishchin from "The Notes of a Madman" (1835)—who figured prominently in the development of Russian prose. All three protagonists, whether historical or literary, reflected the pathos of the individual's failed rebellion against Russian society and history. The failure, of course, would not be considered a virtue by Herzen—we know that Chaadayev served him as a model for the inactive romanticism of Trenzinsky, in one instance—but the opposition itself between madman-individual and society could not but appeal to his sense of literary structure.

The key to Levka's madness is his individuality; he refuses to follow the norms and conventions of society and the humiliations and mockery he suffers result from a reluctance to abandon his own inclinations for a common measure. The people who surround Levka, Krupov decides, are as weakminded as he is, but they dislike the boy because he is "weak-minded not in their way but in his own." This independence, as we last see Levka, takes a traditional form of moral positioning found in the saints' lives; he retreats to the forest, lives on fruit and berries, and is befriended by animals whose natural state enables them to respond to the innate spiritual worth rejected in civilization. An added, still-vibrant intellectual nuance of such withdrawal from society, of course, was provided to Herzen and his readers by Rousseau's exploration of secular sainthood.

If contemporary social and literary motifs in combination with religious prototypes suggested the metaphor for a positive spiritual condition in an ostensibly unbalanced mental state, madness also offered a technical resolution to the problem of depicting a positive hero in the desentimentalized and deromanticized conditions of 1840s literature. By separating Levka from the normal course of events—his withdrawal to the forest is not unlike that of another sublime idiot type, Prince Myshkin, who can only survive in the ethereal heights of Switzerland—Herzen is able to make his protagonist bear the burden of positive qualities without disturbing the skeptical and unsentimental narrative tone. Levka's incorruptible and timeless attributes are thus not imposed on the way things are understood to be in reality, and are used to measure the real against the ideal without didacticism or overly rhetorical gestures on the author's part.

The intermediary between Levka and society is Doctor Krupov, who serves as narrator and a figure of deliberate historical and religious reference in his own right. The two roles are interconnected: as the narrator, Krupov's function is to contrast Levka's timeless spiritual dignity to the society at large; as a character with his own literary meaning Krupov represents one concrete social form of the transition from religious to secular moral values. He is a priest's son who receives his higher education in a seminary, a fictional model of those many teachers, radicals, and men of letters who entered Herzen's cultural milieu by way of ecclesiastical training or background. Krupov's decision to interrupt his study of "spiritual subjects" in order to turn to the "earthly subject" of medicine is undoubtedly a form of commentary on the shifts of religious-moral impulses in Russia. Krupov realizes the "unimportance" and impermanence of earthly things before the ultimate, perennial issues of his early suroundings, and he infuses the secular pursuit of medicine—a thinly disguised dissection of the social corpus—with the intensity and moral maximization of religious training. His role as a narrator and intermediary, in short, is not only a fictional expediency but a historically accurate interpretation of the way in which Levka's symbolic religious message acted on Herzen's contemporaries.

The thematic structure is closely related to this underlying sense of movement in ideas from religious to secular concerns. If the work's first section includes Krupov's clerical background and a description of Levka's spiritual state, in the second Herzen shifts to a madhouse in which Krupov works and then to society at large. The narrative line incorporates, in miniature, the course of Herzen's writing from directly religious subjects, to supernatural-ethical issues explored in psychological form, to the secular sociopolitical expression of core religious moral standards. An essential omission in literary reference is perhaps as telling an indication of this fictional evolution as what is included. For both "Dr. Krupov" and the larger pattern of Herzen's literary development show a progression out of religious subjects and modes without the typical Western recourse to the picaresque. The structure of the picaresque—a series of unrelated characters and events connected by the secular point of view of the rogue—was certainly well known to Herzen through the related depiction of world madness in Voltaire's *Candide* and through the works of Fadey Bulgarin and Alexander Vel'tman. It was this structural arrangement which was used by Gogol in *Dead Souls*, although the religious crisis planned for Chichikov in Part II of the novel called for a moral transformation of the picaro which appears to have been unsuccesul. Rather than attempting such an awkward change in the rogue's essential secular properties or using the picaro at all for a thematic center, Herzen rejects the rogue's outside positioning, it can be hypothesized, because he recognizes that the totally alienated and cynical perspective could not adequately express his own strong commitments. Krupov, however, provides such a required narrative center by expressing native standards related to spiritual dignity, individualism, and moral vitality through his seminary-student-turned-doctor point of view. The character expresses both criticism and conviction, and thus allows Herzen to formulate his disagreements with the way things are without falling into complete disillusionment.

Although Krupov's examination of madness is the uniting thread of the two sections, in the second part a potential source of confusion is that instead of representing the positive attributes of Levka's individuality, madness is used to describe the *negative* qualities of various social types Krupov encounters. The reason for this transition from positive to negative nuances is not at all obvious in a superficial reading and has not really been explained in literary scholarship. It is one key, however, to Herzen's fictional treatment of the moral-psychological condition in modern society and opens his principal address to his readers.

In the lunatic asylum the causes of madness are still as clear as in Levka's case: madness originates in the inadequate recognition and nourishment which the committed are able to find for their "proud individuality." By humouring the inmates—i.e., addressing one as the Chinese emperor he imagines himself to be rather than administering the prescribed treatment—Krupov is much more successful than his medical colleagues. His cure, as can be expected, involves the acceptance of each patient's right to a particular existence and vision of self. In the outside world, however, lunacy is as prevalent as in the asylum, although the causes are much less clear to Krupov. One example is familiar to readers of *Who Is to Blame?*: a husband and wife who insist on living together although they hate each other. In other instances—officials who demand an unnatural deference to their rank, a woman who stays with her husband although he is a hopeless drunkard, the mean submission of clerks in a government office—madness is given the same negative tonality.

Ostensibly in such instances Herzen is using madness purely for purposes of social caricature. The underlying explanation of the new negative shades of meaning, however, comes out of a continued exploration of psychic imperatives, particularly the drive to assert and fulfill one's individuality, dignity, and moral worth, that we have already observed. For if in the instances of Levka and the psychiatric ward patients, madness is presented as a clearly symbolic and abstract statement of such spiritual needs, in the everyday world the same moral-psychological forces are shown to prevail but in the actual self-defeating forms created for them by Herzen's contemporaries. The literary formulation in question approximates Left Hegelian theory and particularly Feuerbach's suggestion that all human problems—religious, social, and political—are generated by the inadequate recognition of human psychological makeup. As in the case of Levka and the mental patients, each social type Krupov describes is guided by impulses of self-aggrandizement and projection, except that each invariably chooses a degrading and short-sighted form of their expression. The metaphor of madness in both sections is addressed to self-interest and individuality, thus, and its negative denotation represents those instances when individuals veer away from the high norms of dignity and morality that Herzen envisions to be the proper form of self-fulfillment.

Herzen's intellectual future is prefigured in the remaining observations made by Krupov. Among other modern forms of madness he mentions religion and romanticism, and characterizes the last as a "spiritual scrofula" that fosters "revulsion for everything real (and) practical." The remark anticipates Herzen's total shift from core Orthodox and romantic ideas to new sociopolitical interests. In later works, he would abandon entirely religious subjects and motifs, although their influence would remain in the deep-seated values and moral intensity of his memoirs and his political and historiocultural writings. One such metamorphosis would be evident in the writer's defense, undertaken in the court of Western liberal thought, of Russia's unique spiritual destiny. Herzen would never give up his conviction that the native Russian sense of communality and brotherhood offered the best hope for a historical model of morality and goodness and, at the same time, he would remain adamantly opposed to the notion that history is predetermined to some such inevitable future. The vision of a free and irrational world evolution in which the individual's sphere of action is of primary value would form the basis of his historical and political speculations, and would be accompanied by an unbroken faith in moral choice and individual dignity, even in the face of the high-powered materialism and utilitarianism that would prevail in the 1850s and 1860s on the Russian political left.

Continuity would be preserved between Herzen's fiction and later political essays in one other constituent element of his writing. His abandonment of literature as a medium, in fact, was most likely made in response to an intensification of the long-active impulse to confront and affect his readers; the shift to total political rhetoric and historical argument was part of an attempt to reach the audience even more directly than in the earlier prose. Before the balance and distancing required of fiction was lost, however, (although not entirely, since a full range of important narrative skills were clearly put to work in *My Past and Thoughts*) Herzen once again signaled his particular concern for readers in the introduction to a novel he left uncompleted, *Duty Before All* (1851). "I do not know what goal could be nobler for an author than to educate and improve morals," he writes. "This is the duty of everyone who takes pen in hand, for what can be more pleasant than to teach others and to raise them up to *our* level of perfection."[46] Characteristically, the ironic tone is complemented by a serious literary purpose, for what follows is a differentiation between "dry" didacticism and a morality decorated by "fancy" which Herzen proposes "to develop in a tale of moral education." The hoped-for spiritual education of the reader proceeding through literary fancy can be seen to be a core meaning of the fiction we have examined from its beginnings. It is in terms of such an aesthetic catalysis of the readers' responses to the transcendental standards of their selves, then, that we can discard affective fallacies and speak of Herzen's own affective verity.

CHAPTER 4

Dostoevsky:
The Christian Ego

FEW BODIES of literary criticism have been more sensitive to problems of ideology and identity than interpretations of Dostoevsky. Commentators such as Nicholas Berdiaev, André Gide, Albert Camus, Hermann Hesse, Sigmund Freud, and Martin Buber have made Dostoevsky's fiction an integral element of modern consciousness, but in the process they have also created conditions in which it has been almost impossible to separate his ideas and values from their twentieth-century denotations. The psychoanalytic, theologic, and philosophic constructs are so varied as to suggest a total loss of conern for personal authorial meaning. Indeed, the danger of Dostoevsky slipping away completely into the empty and frivolous role of a relativistic intellectual game gives new urgency and vitality to explorations by scholars of the Russian historical-literary context.[1]

In order to move beyond twentieth-century sensibilities and our commitments, I suggest that we sustain scholarship defining anew Dostoevsky's own ideological center, and that we check the validity of our definition against the increasingly complex stages of his career. The process of verification is not difficult to formulate because standards of validation are provided by such widely accepted points of critical reference as Dostoevsky's attraction to romanticism and Ivan Shidlovsky, his reading of utopian socialism, his first literary endeavor in *Poor Folk*, his response to Gogol, his relationship with Vissarion Belinsky, his statement of ideas and values in the Petersburg feuilletons, and his creation of the "dreamer" type.[2] Although a comprehensive study would have to include the Siberian prison term and other vital life experiences, the essential measure of any definition of Dostoevsky's ideology is available in these crucial instances of the early formative period. The ground so covered should not be expected to yield startling new discoveries; it has been explored many times over and is familiar to most students of Dostoevsky's fiction. But a fresh effort to define in cultural context the original emotional and intellectual meanings of Dostoevsky's values and beliefs and to check the validity of the definition against the accepted evidence of his early literary formation can suggest ways of resolving some long-standing critical difficulties and of producing a close view of his work's deep-seated nuances.

The Ideological Core

The most influential premises of Dostoevsky's initial intellectual formation are not found in literary scholarship at all but in the work of a pioneering psycholanalyst, Sigmund Freud. Freud's writings, including the often-cited essay "Dostoevsky and Parricide," were ideological in the best sense of the term; his goal was to clear away the *false* ideas or "manifest content" that appear to influence man and to discover the true psychic imperatives that affect human behavior. In the specific instance of Dostoevsky, however, breakdowns in key elements of Freud's hypothesis have been convincingly demonstrated to allow a much simpler interpretation of the writer's relationship with father and family than the Oedipal syndrome.[3] On the basis of available research, we can postulate with a high degree of certainty that rather than inspiring Oedipal neuroses, the truly decisive ideological function performed by Mikhail Dostoevsky and his wife Marya was to provide their son with a very thorough introduction to native religious ideas and values. Indeed, if Freud is abandoned, the most attractive hypothesis available to us is that Dostoevsky's ideological center was shaped out of his Russian Orthodox background. And while the history of Dostoevsky scholarship provides model examples of the sort of neglect or abuse, both well intentioned and not, of the religious cultural tradition that we have already noted, almost all serious readers have followed Dmitry Merzhkovsky, Nicholas Berdiaev, Konstantin Mochulsky, and other Russian émigrés in at least recognizing Dostoevsky's *mature* response to the religious issues of free will, faith, theodicy, and theosis.[4] The problem is that the majority of critics have slighted the initial, deep-seated meanings of these cherished religious principles as they affected the basic, childhood formation of the writer's sensibilities, and as a result readings of his work have habitually lacked the true depth and intensity of both his cultural and emotional commitments.

All the historical and biographical material at our disposal points to one major source of values in Dostoevsky's childhood: the Russian kenotic tradition. The most likely schema of his ideological formation is an initial acceptance of such kenotic standards as humility, faith in a spiritual victory over the ways of the earth, charity, love, suffering, and poverty, followed by the development of an increasingly complex mental-emotional world responding to these same values. The second stage is brought on by internal paradoxes within kenoticism itself as well as by the questions raised through Dostoevsky's own maturing intellect. Early intermediaries for such a process of value formation in family life, religious literature, and forms of religious experience generated by socially common church rituals and personal emotional response, are thoroughly documented in scholarship.[5] In the first instance, Dostoevsky's father is clearly of key importance in making firm standards of conduct an integral part of the way his children viewed the world. He is the type of patriarchal moral center whose gradual disappearance from the family structure Dostoevsky would bemoan at length in his mature work. But Marya Fyodorovna, Dostoevsky's mother, exerts an equally, if not more crucial influence by directly demonstrating a strong relgious faith and by showing her son an active, everyday expression of Christian values of love, humility, and charity. If Mikhail Dostoevsky provided the structure for an initial sense of values, then his wife helped contribute its emotional substance and example of practical fulfillment.[6] In addition to peasant beggars and "holy fools" the Dostoevskys encountered in their regular visits to churches and monasteries, two female kenotic types were also familiar presences for the family: the nanny, Alyona Frolovna, a devout and charitable spinstress who sacrificed marriage to be a "bride of Christ," and Agrafena, a half-mad woman who lived in the Dostoevsky village. It is likely that the abject other-worldliness and rape of the latter provided the model for Lizaveta Smerdiashchaia's life in The Brothers Karamazov.

Dostoevsky's familiarity in childhood with the various church rituals is also documented with some precision in critical literature. The family attended services regularly and observed the important periods of fasting. Doctor Yanovsky, a close acquaintance of Dostoevsky's in the 1840s, was not simply indulging in professional terminology when he noted that the writer's "most certain medicine was always prayer."[7] The first pieces of prose the young Dostoevsky memorized were prayers and the pious conditions of his early milieu suggest that this was not merely a formal ritual, but a deeply felt emotional experience taken for granted in the family. Prayers undoubtedly provided moral-emotional fortification and acted as a daily form of reinforcement of religious values for the Dostoevskys.

No less important were the periods of Lent and the rites of fasting and confession that accompanied the celebration of holidays like Easter. As we noted earlier, passage through the discomforts and trials of the rituals was likely to provide psychological support for a rudimentary sense of important Orthodox values such as free will. In Dostoevsky's particular instance, the stimulus of an ethical impulse in taking the Eucharist and going to confession with the accompanying feelings of joy and emotional well-being are suggested through biographical material. When Dostoevsky was two years old his mother brought him to church to participate in the sacraments and during the ceremony a dove flew through the place of worship. Whether the dove left an immediate impression on the young boy or not is hard to determine, but clearly the ritual itself was associated by the Dostoevskys with this traditional symbol of purity, gladness, and spiritual quality and given that connotation in family discussions. Nicholas Lossky is probably correct in his supposition that the effect of such church experiences on Dostoevsky is reflected in his depiction of Father Zossima's religious awakening during the Lenten services.[8]

In any case, focusing the effect of church worship on moral-intellectual formation provides an important dimension of Dostoevsky's response to his parents. While the usual critical emphasis has been placed on the death of Mikhail Dostoevsky, his son was far away at that particular time and throughout his life showed little if any reaction to it. The death of Marya Dostoevsky, on the other hand, although it does not significantly aid the Oedipal hypothesis, *was* a profound emotional stimulus which was felt by the entire family, and which, there is very good reason to believe, left a traumatic imprint on the life of her sixteen-year-old boy.[9] No small part of the deep emotions and anguished questions that the tragic event raised must have come out of the three funeral services with which the Dostoevskys paid their last respects. It was during these most terrible and acute of experiences that the young writer first had the questions of transcendent realities brought home to him, and it was then, through the skillfully structured harmony of Orthodox melody and doctrine, that the hope of eternal life and the joyous affirmation of faith even before the most real limitations of human existence were first made available. In any case, it was Dostoevsky and his brother who chose the epitaph for their mother's tombstone; it expressed precisely the Orthodox hope and consolation of eternal life, although formulated in the contemporary language of Karamzin's sentimental poetry: "Rest, dear deceased, till the joyous morning. . . . "[10]

If family and church provided Dostoevsky with an elementary ideological structure and various emotional supports for it, a more complex source of symbols and ideas was made available to the young man in his education. Two favored books in the Dostoevsky family are of particular interest: Marya Dostoevsky's primer entitled *One Hundred and Four Holy Stories from the Old and New Testaments* used to teach reading and writing, and Metropolitan Filaret's short catechism which was used for religious instruction. The first text introduced the Dostoevsky children to the key biblical events and characters; the effect on the reader, as Joseph Frank points out, was that "the very first impressions that awakened the consciousness of the child were those embodying the teachings of the Christian faith . . . the world thereafter for Dostoevsky would always remain transfigured by the flow of this supernatural illumination."[11] The catechism has been more neglected and it is no significant mark of the deficiencies in Dostoevsky critical literature that no one has closely examined its role in his intellectual formation. This was the work, after all, from which Dostoevsky memorized his lessons *word by word*, according to his brother, and which was his first introduction to a skillful interpretation of the religious values that were an integral part of family life. Although it is unlikely that all the intellectual intricacies of Filaret's doctrinal statement stimulated a response in a boy of eleven or twelve, the catechism must have left its mark on a rudimentary structure of first principles. Dostoevsky's exposure to the catechism coincides with the key period of mental development, as Jean Piaget's work suggests, in which adolescents experience a turning point in their thinking towards construction of theories of reality and formal intellectual systems. It is at this crucial stage, when "thinking takes wings," in Piaget's words, that the young Dostoevsky encountered one of the more talented interpretations of Orthodox tenets available in the first half of the nineteenth century; and it is then, if we further follow Piaget's hypothesis, that he consciously began to deal with his own role in the world in terms of the values and ideas available to him.[12]

From Andrei Dostoevsky's memoirs we know only the first few phrases taught to the brothers from the catechism—"The One God worshipped in the Holy Trinity is eternal, that is, has no beginning or no end to his being, but always was, is, and will be"—and there is no evidence which would show what passages Dostoevsky himself emphasized or memorized. But Filaret's religious message was not confined to the catechism alone for his various writings provided active conceptual stimulants for Dostoevsky throughout the Russian cultural milieu. The catechism itself went through 252 editions in its short version, while a longer format was reprinted some 91 times.[13] Filaret—the man who drafted the Russian Emancipation Proclamation—was, in Vasily Rozanov's words, "the last (perhaps the only?) great prelate of the Russian Church . . .";[14] his sermons were widely distributed through frequent reprints and they certainly must have been known to the deacon who taught from the catechism in the Dostoevsky household. A central theme emphasized throughout this large body of theological work was the Christ story interpreted with a strong kenotic orientation. Filaret's frequent exhortation, as Nadejda Gorodetzky points out, was, "Let meekness and simplicty, [let] condescension to those lower than yourselves ... let quietness in humiliation [and] patience which no offence could overwhelm, let all this become your mind as it was of Christ Jesus."[15] Through a fortunate coincidence, moreover, the deacon who tutored the Dostoevskys was equal to his material in the energy of his rhetoric and in his ability to touch the audience profoundly. Andrei recounts in his memoirs how the "inspiring teacher" would hold the children and their mother spellbound for an hour and a half to two hours of lessons.

And yet while such intermediaries to the kenotic tradition are undisputedly present in Dostoevsky's youth, and while kenotic values—as implicit standards against which to measure the latest theories of egoism and self-aggrandizement, or as overt character-

istics of Sonia, Myshkin, Makar Dolgoruky, and Zossima—can be
seen to provide key points of reference for all of Dostoevsky's
fiction, to define kenoticism in a narrow sense suggests a paradoxical
view of his life and work. It is quite obvious, on one hand, that
Dostoevsky was anything but meek or humble during the early part
of his mental-emotional development. Reminiscences of family and
friends, such as his parents' characterization of him as a "real fire,"
suggest a highly energetic boy moved by all the normal ego demands
of childhood. Moreover, as Dostoevsky grew older the kenotic perspective understood *only* as humility and meekness becomes harder
and harder to equate with his ideas and actions. In the 1840s he was if
not a radical, at least a firm opponent of the *status quo* and an
outraged, active enemy of social injustice. In later life he became an
advocate of Russian nationalism and of political aggrandizement,
leanings which show little concern for Christian docility or forebear-
ance. Interpreting the kenotic syndrome of suffering, love, and meekness to be a terminal ideological position thus only widens the
puzzling gap that appears to exist between Dostoevsky's life with all
its sociopolitical involvements and the values we see expressed in his
fiction.

When placed in their cultural context, such apparent incon-
sistencies are explainable as the writer's own complex way of partici-
pating in the long-standing dilemmas of the native religious tradition.
The paradoxical elements of kenoticism are evident even in a superficial definition: on the one hand, there is the Russian emphasis on
quietism, humiliation, and suffering; on the other, the supreme value
given to free will, spiritual dignity, and ethical action. In sociopolitical refractions the same paradox underlies the strange combination
of humility and imperialism in Slavophile doctrine and in the motifs
and ideas of Vladimir Soloviev. In Russian theology the seemingly
disparate motifs are explicitly brought together. For Tikhon
Zadonsky, "union in suffering leads to likeness in glory," while for
Metropolitan Filaret, the humiliated Christ points to the surest road
to reach "the throne of Majesty." Dostoevsky's own moral-
psychological use of the kenotic paradox in terms of such models is
shown, in one late instance, by his notes for "The Life of a Great
Sinner": "Tykhon. About humility (As more powerful than humility). All about humility and free will."[16] Even at the early stages of
life, however, the cultural superstructure we outlined must have

suggested that suffering and humiliation provided the means to attain a transcendent greatness and divinity rather than being the terminal points of religious sensibilities. Unless we stop at that unpromising and silly presupposition of an ingrained psychological trait which somehow inspires all Russians to bouts of masochistic indulgence, the attraction of kenoticism to any relatively healthy Orthodox youth was not some fatalistic self-abasement but an assertion of the prerogatives of a spiritual view of self through the rejection of earthly standards. The point is that in such internal terms of Russian culture, humiliation ultimately served self-affirmation, and the appeal of kenoticism to Dostoevsky is difficult to explain unless such nuances of the native heritage are clear.

Just as values of humility and meekness expressed in the kenotic story of Boris and Gleb were brought together in Russian tradition with affirmative motifs of national defense and political triumph, so Dostoevsky's own value system must have found room to grow through native cultural outlets available for an adolescent's ego and the natural impulses to assert one's presence in the world. The emotional supports of the religious services are a case in point; as one student of Russian thought has pointed out, in the apparently self-effacing Orthodox rituals such as communion the "individual as a *person* participates with God: the individual retains his individuality. . . . Man does not simply reach out to an unknowable absolute: he absorbs this unknown absolute into himself."[17] Dostoevsky's sense of his "I," we can surmise, went through these projections of the self into a timeless universalism; moreover, acceptance of God's will did not lead to a fatalism or a quietism which would disappoint an energetic young man because in the simplest doctrinal and emotional terms of the religious culture, the divine presence was equated with an affirmation of man's own potential greatness and will: his freedom of choice. The humiliated Christ was also God; the pious martyrs spiritual heroes; and the backward, long-suffering masses of believers—the *narod*—models of dignity and eventual historical triumph precisely for their backwardness in the evolution of sociopolitical doctrines, of Westernizer and Slavophile alike, which coincided with Dostoevsky's youth.

Important as they are for defining normative patterns of thought and belief, such public cultural impulses can only suggest vague outlines to specific textual interpretations. Dostoevsky's own evidence, however, submitted through a fictional alter ego, enables us to move the hypothesis of his ideological formation away from general perception of context to the concrete details of personal literary response. "In my youthful fantasy," he writes in 1861, "I loved to imagine myself sometimes as Pericles, sometimes as Marius, sometimes as a Christian in the time of Nero, sometimes as a knight in a tournament, sometimes as Edward Glendenning in Walter Scott's *The Monastery*, etc., etc. And what did I not live through with all my heart and soul in my impassioned golden dreams—exactly as if from opium?"[18] One of the less complicated ways of finding the values and ideas that are of particular importance in an adolescent's developing emotional-intellectual world is to focus on the qualities emphasized in such heroic role models.[19] The interesting symptom of Dostoevsky's role-playing is his apparently instinctive combination of triumphant historical and fictional characters with the spiritual victors of Christian martyrdom. We can postulate that the common ground he saw was the heroic attributes that struck his adolescent imagination in both sets of characters, and the congruence of these virtues with the kenotic values we have already noted is readily apparent. In part, such protagonists offered confirmation for Dostoevsky's rudimentary sense of free will in their ability to overcome all obstacles. But most important, they all expressed courage, dignity, and moral triumph through their kenotic-like acts of sacrifice and devotion to some noble cause.

As Dostoevsky's reading expanded to include more of Karamzin, Scott, and the German idealists, such heroic types not only served as outlets for adolescent ego-affirmation in role-playing, but also provided the first material for literary expression. Karamzin's history, a favorite book throughout adolescence, was a particularly important source for such heroic models, and it is the combination again of piety and suffering with courage and triumph which provides us with some of the deep-seated implications of its preferential status in the young man's mental world. As we know from biographical data, one of the more memorable occasions for the Dostoevskys was their regular pilgrimage to the Trinity-St. Sergey Monastery. After reading Karamzin, Dostoevsky would have undoubtedly responded to the Zagorsk *lavra* not only as a religious shrine, but as a metaphor for Russian historical affirmation, in which the religious and the secular came together in one glorious victory of self-sacrifice, spirit, and arms. Without the martial nuances there was one other such heroic model, of course, that Dostoevsky knew intimately from his earliest childhood: it was the story of Christ's spiritual triumph in poverty and humiliation which attended the transformation of religious values to literary commitments in the initial stages of his career.

Transitions I

The vital process in which Dostoevsky moved from childhood's unquestioned acceptance of basic values and ideas to the use of moral-intellectual material in literary texts was governed by several, well known agents. They were active in the period of roughly 1833–41, and included his exploration of writers like Scott, Schiller, Pushkin, Gogol, and Balzac, his exposure to the romantic idealism of I. I. Davydov in Chermak's boarding school, his friendship with Ivan Shidlovsky, and at the beginning of the 1840s the gamut of beliefs that went into his attempt to write two romantic tragedies using Boris Godunov and Maria Stuart as models. Of the biographical data available to us from this transitional period, none is more important than the letters Dostoevsky wrote to his brother Mikhail in 1838 and 1840. Through them it is possible to establish how the kenotic concepts we outlined were integrated with new cultural motifs and what core ideas entered the first fiction.

In large part the transition was accomplished through Dostoevsky's reformulation of religious premises and beliefs into the languages of German and French romanticism. The influence of Davydov's readings in Schelling, or Dostoevsky's own direct contacts with the texts of Schiller, Hoffmann, Pushkin, Balzac, Chateaubriand, and Hugo has been thoroughly explicated and needs only brief mention here. Related key concepts formulated in the letters are the transcendent referents of nature, soul, and God on which Dostoevsky depends, as well as postulates of the emotions' superiority over reason and the artist's divine mission which he outlines for Mikhail. Much less attention, however, has been accorded the image of human personality that is also touched upon in the correspondence and that provides a fulcrum for earlier beliefs and values. Dostoevsky's characterization of Shidlovsky is fairly typical in this regard; the young friend of the two brothers is described both as an emaciated "martyr" of love and as a "marvelous, exalted being, the correct form of man depicted for us by Schiller and Shakespeare" whose "spiritual beauty" increases in proportion to "physical decline."[20] The kenotic motif is clearly present in this imagined martyrdom and is joined with the sentimental-romantic character's usual predilection to suffer over unrequited love or other earthly discomforts. Of added significance is the emphasis placed on spiritual elevation out of bodily deterioration; clearly Dostoevsky envisions some form of spiritual triumph of individual personality over life's physical limitations and humiliations, and he uses Shidlovsky, with whom he attends church services in the period of their friendship, as a convenient metaphor to express the nonterrestrial dimension he values in man.

In other passages of the letters Dostoevsky explores his early high vision of the self using a specific literary language referring to familiar protagonists of fiction and drama. The impulses we have already noted—to assert the prerogatives of free will and to project oneself into the Absolute—are now expressed in terms of romantic egoism: man's soul is "the fusion of heaven and earth," and "an explosion of will is enough . . . to merge with eternity," he writes.[21] In letters to his father, it is true, Dostoevsky piously and conventionally refers to the fulfillment of God's will on earth. On the other hand, in writing to Mikhail, an interlocutor in debate rather than a parent to be humoured, earlier religious convictions appear largely as a belief in the power and spirit of the individual *human* will, and the idea of providence and God's control of things is deemphasized and even treated somewhat sacrilegiously. Writing on Hoffmann's heroic seeker of the divine, Alban, Dostoevsky points out, "It is terrible to see a man who has the unattainable in his power, a man, who, not knowing what to do, plays with a toy that is—God!"[22] The idea of the Absolute is clearly no longer a matter of naive worship in such passages, but is viewed in romantic terms suggesting the divine powers of heroic types. Indeed, much of the importance of these remarks lies in the emphasis placed on human will as a determining factor of life, as distinct from those factors that can be located outside of personality. The perception of individuals enveloped in such an aura of exalted qualities in all likelihood channeled Dostoevsky's earlier religious education into his mature conviction that the self plays a key role in shaping a suitable spiritual existence for man.

A significant clue to the overriding importance of these first literary paradigms is that Dostoevsky interprets dissimilar literary traditions and writers in the same romantic-heroic light. In another letter to Mikhail he defines Corneille's Octavius and the Cid as "gigantic characters," while Corneille himself is praised because he is "almost Shakespeare" in his "romantic spirit."[23] Although we have very little evidence for anything but an unverifiable hypothesis, it is probable that the first texts to come from Dostoevsky's pen—the dramas "Maria Stuart" and "Boris Godunov"—were inspired by similar romantic notions of the heroic and given added impetus by the kenotic inclination to emphasize moral triumph in the midst of martyrdom and suffering. Such an image of Mary was already available to Dostoevsky in his reading of Schiller, while the martyred child Dmitry, who acts as a moral catalyst to the tragic story of Boris, was provided by Karamzin.

There are additional circumstances in the course of Russian culture which suggest reasons for emphasizing Dostoevsky's interest in will and individuality in preference to other ethical categories, particularly of a sociopolitical nature. Ever since Joseph Volokolamskii's teachings and the adjustment made by the Russian church to the demands of power and politics in Ivan the Terrible's reign, the idea of striving for a religious moral life through sociopolitical involvement was largely discredited for the Russian intelligentsia through the concrete examples of what happened to moral values in the church's compromises and corruptions within the secular state. An integral and unquestioned sense of values, on the other hand, was created in Nil Sorsky's opposing suggestions for ascetic withdrawal, contemplation, and union with God. Indeed, it can be postulated that it was this Hesychast-inspired mysticism rather than sociopolitical programs which was the real subversive force in Russian culture right up to the early nineteenth century.[24] And while Dostoevsky's contact with the fiction of Balzac and Hugo, among other Western and Russian texts, undoubtedly led him to think of the important effects that class distinction and oppression have on human destiny, a sensitive Orthodox mind such as his was unlikely to look to social categories for solutions because it was the individual, self-generated ideas and acts that retained most moral authority in Russian cultural history. This is not to say that Dostoevsky found himself in an intellectual-literary tradition in which, as Richard Pipes inaccurately suggests, it was considered entirely futile to change the social and political environment.[25] The literature we have been discussing is noteworthy for the intensity of its involvement in the full range of human experience, including the social and political, rather than in a quintessential other-worldliness. But the most attractive emphasis of the native religious heritage was always on the self as both the beginning and end of any attempt to restructure society, and it was this first, basic belief in priorities, means, and goals that accompanied the evolution of Dostoevsky's literary sensibility.

Such cultural mechanisms combined with Dostoevsky's own response to the vital issues of his day suggest that he followed two major procedures when he began to select values and ideas for his fiction. First, he assumed the defenses indicated by romanticism and his own native religious culture against secularization and moral debasement and, consequently, accepted and refined an internal view of the human image which integrated his awareness of transcendent qualities and spiritual heroism. Second, he honored his own psychological needs by expressing what was a perfectly ordinary defense of self-image, except that in this instance its particular meanings were also affected by the values and ideas we noted. The somewhat speculative and abstract nature of these conjectures is considerably ameliorated by concrete evidence found in the letters. In several passages Dostoevsky shows an extreme sensitivity to those things, largely internal or moral-psychological, that are detrimental to the high image of man he envisions, and in other instances he indicates methods for defending this image in terms of the spiritual heroism that will eventually figure in his fiction. One such example of budding literary formulation occurs when he introduces Hamlet to express his frustration with "petty-souled man" who does not assert his will and break out from banal, everyday existence to the Absolute but only declaims "stormy, wild speeches in which are echoed the groans of a chained world." In another letter he takes to task Mikhail's somewhat constrained circumstances and points out: "How sad is your life ... when man ... recognizing unlimited powers in himself, sees them wasted ... and from what? From life worthy of a pygmy and not a giant, a child and not a man."[26] In both these letters the fulfillment of man's spiritual destiny is implied through internally generated acts of will and the self-expression of mankind's God-related powers.

Two other passages in the letters are of considerable interest because they show Dostoevsky's early concern for moral-psychological assertions of the self, as well as his recognition, even at this early date, of the *dangers* of self-assertion when it is not complemented by other moral values. In one letter he argues that Byron was an "egoist" whose idea of fame inadequately expressed the romantic ideal because of its "worldly" (*suetnaia*) component.[27] In another letter, dated the first of January, 1840, he responds to his brother's request for intellectually stimulating argument and criticism by refusing any such polemical role. "Your egoism (which we sinners all have)," he points out, "would force the most favorable conclusions about the other, his opinions, rules, character, and intellectual limitations." Such criticism would remain "forever the excuse for dissension between us" rather than serve any useful purpose because it would only stimulate natural ego defenses and self-serving interpretation.[28] The value of these remarks is that they show Dostoevsky consciously reworking the core motifs of his cultural milieu into the dilemmas of personality that would become prime issues of his fiction. Ego-assertion, after this first tentative formulation, is always recognized by him to be a basic human need which either leads to a truly heroic, spiritual quality worthy of the religious-romantic ideal, or degrades the human image by a narrow and distorting selfishness.

These two passages, added to the material we have already examined, suggest that by the end of the 1830s Dostoevsky's crucial ideas and beliefs were grouped in large part around an all-important balance that he imagined to exist between egoism and humility, free will and moral control, self-dignity and love. Such a symmetry of moral-psychological parts came out of the structure of native Orthodox tradition and the romantic works which offered a praxis of literary design in which to rethink and readjust the crucial balance. As Dostoevsky began to reach full intellectual maturity in the 1840s, however, and as romanticism began to decrease in importance in his milieu, new, suggestive constructs for transforming the vision of human spiritual equilibrium into the stuff of fiction appeared on his cultural horizon.

Transitions II

A common point of emphasis in literary scholarship in dealing with this period is that Dostoevsky read the works of Balzac, Hugo, and George Sand in the 1840s, fiction that focused on the poor, portrayed the plight of the downtrodden city-dweller, and ran parallel to the influence of the French utopian socialists in advocating social reform. According to the usual view, such literary sources in combination with Dostoevsky's exposure to the political works of the French left stimulated his feelings of pity for the oppressed and were among the prime reasons for a criticism of "the evils and injustice of society" in his early fiction.[29] "The basic characteristic of Utopian Socialism," V. Komarovich, one of the ablest Soviet proponents of this interpretation, wrote in an often quoted essay, "is a distinctive humanism expressed in a love for man developed to the point of worshipful ecstasy. . . . The writers whose subject was social utopia wanted to analyze suffering and they hoped to end it forever. Their primary aim was to arouse a feeling of compassion for the downtrodden."[30]

As in the case of Herzen, interpretations of this sort have put a disproportionate emphasis on one aspect of Dostoevsky's value system without consideration of its meaning in the total context of his views. Suffering and compassion, as we have seen, were not final, primary concerns but stages along an imagined journey to spiritual heroism and man's divine destiny. The harmful effect of defining Dostoevsky's "humanism" in the exclusive tonalities of pity and commiseration, meanwhile, has been to throw askew his delicately balanced perception of personality by the neglect of those elements of religious-romantic heroism that we noted, and the excessive emphasis on environmental and social determination.

The difficulty of defending interpretations that depend on Dostoevsky's supposed societal perspective is obvious as far as French utopian socialism is concerned, if only in that it is impossible to find a phalanstery, or even the hint of a commune, in his first literary efforts. Nor, for that matter, can one see in his correspondence or any other material that could bypass the censors consistent use of the terms and economic categories of Fourier, Louic Blanc, or Considerant.[31] In fact, instead of any form of social concern that would provide confirmation, however veiled, of Komarovich's hypothesis that philanthropic feelings were stimulated in the reader, Dostoevsky's basic character situations—the grotesque inadequacy of Devushkin, the madness of Golyadkin, the miserliness of Prokharchin, the alcoholism of Yefimov—deal with personal human tragedy that generates no readily apparent solutions outside of itself, in say shared labor or communal life.

The point is that the young Dostoevsky viewed the means and goals of social reform not so much in sociological or economic categories but rather in terms of the human personality. And while the oppressive society of Nicholas I troubled most young men of ideas in the 1840s, a large number of them believed in changing society by reshaping man rather than changing man by reshaping society. This is not to say that utopian socialism—the "New Christianity"—was not an important cultural source for Dostoevsky, but simply that it reinforced basic impulses that were already long active under the influence of the native religious heritage. To explain fully the juxtaposition of Christianity and the Russian left of the 1840s in the light of this native Russian condition, it should be clear that the theories of Saint-Simon, Fourier, Pierre Leroux, and George Sand offered not only the vision of a new society but reformulated an old religious theme: inner renewal, an upheaval in the soul and the personality, the creation of a new man. For Dostoevsky there was no contradiction in going to confession and helping to set up a clandestine printing press because the task, the spiritual tempering of man, was the same in both instances. In this light, the well-known remark Dr. Yanovsky made in his memoirs that Dostoevsky considered the "truths of the Gospel" and not the "1848 bylaws of social-democracy" to be the rightful basis of human morality does not have to be taken as evidence of Dostoevsky's total rejection of French progressive thought. Yanovsky knew that Dostoevsky was a religious man; he probably did not know the young writer's *specific* response to utopian socialism under the influence of his religious values.

Two other men, Nikolai Gogol and Ludwig Feuerbach, provided important stimulants for the religious sensibilities of thoughtful young writers in the early 1840s. Unfortunately, the critical tendency has been to read both of these major figures largely for the negative and critical perspectives they brought into Russian culture: Gogol for his description of the grotesque and the absurd in society and man; Feuerbach for his destruction of God. The writer, like the philosopher, meanwhile, offered equally powerful reinforcement of long-standing beliefs. For Gogol, one of the major frustrations of his life was that readers such as Vissarion Belinsky insisted on looking to his work solely to find material for their own critical appraisals of society. Gogol had studied the pietists and like them wanted to reform society, not by the kind of social revolution that Belinsky envisioned, but by a revolution of man's inner soul. He looked, first of all, for an upheaval in the human personality (starting with his own) on which later social reform could be based, and his Chichi-kovs and Bashmachkins were created to show the inadequacy of man in the hope of nudging the readers towards the vision expressed in Konstanzhoglo's personality. While this moral-aesthetic task was largely misunderstood and ridiculed, as it still is in the Soviet Union, there is room to wonder if Dostoevsky took up Belinsky's interpreta-tion of Gogol's work or understood what the writer himself was trying to do.

Feuerbach, too, while he offered powerful ammunition to the destructive and skeptical voices on the Russian left in their attack on church and state, was instrumental in giving Russians the psycho-logical material for creating a vision of man as the supreme being of existence. In short, if we emphasize such nuances in works like *Dead Souls* and *The Essence of Christianity*, it is not at all surprising that Dostoevsky would look to them for new ways of expressing the long-familiar ideas of will, dignity, and self-assertion.

Poor Folk

Such cultural stimulants to rethink old ideas and values ran paral-lel to the inner movement of the Russian literary tradition in the 1830s and 40s away from sentimental fiction toward a new realism. The pioneering study of this phase of Russian literature, as well as of Dostoevsky's role within it, is Victor Vinogradov's *Evolution of Russian Naturalism*.[32] Vinogradov interprets naturalism more as a body of literary devices used to approach the real or "natural,"—i.e., the common, vulgar, and cruel world of the city and its poorer inhabitants, as opposed to the pastoral, hazy colors of sentimental idealization—rather than as the philosophical fatalism of Zola and Dreiser that we in the West commonly associate with the term. Such critical differences in part reflect different patterns of literary history: the fiction of Zola and Dreiser rests on the notion of man's total dependence on his environment, while the Russian "natural school" under the influence of men like Gogol looked to change the nature of things, to reshape the environment and the personality of man. The central essay in Vinogradov's study focuses closely on *Poor Folk* and in it the critic shows how the naturalistic theme of the poor city clerk, a common source for Russian popular fiction of the time, was used by Dostoevsky in combination with sentimental procedures such as the depiction of poor or lower-class types in all the depth of their emotions. An essential part of the meaning of Makar Devushkin, according to Vinogradov, is formed out of the tensions arising between such sentimental components of the protagonist and the oppressive naturalistic background.

It is true that at an important moment of his study Vinogradov indicates the ultimate source of Devushkin's troubles to be psychological.[33] But in light of his extensive examination of the clerk's naturalistic environment, the major theme of the text can seem to be derived from the oppression of society and Devushkin's lowly position on the social scale. By placing the emphasis on the terrible burden of the social milieu in this manner, as was done in Komarovich's essay published five years before Vinogradov's study, Devushkin can be viewed as an object for pity and compassion. And indeed, this interpretation has been followed by latter-day critics such as Konstantin Mochulsky and Edward Wasiolek, so that the protagonist of *Poor Folk* traditionally has been taken to be the helpless victim of social injustice and pathos meant to touch the most unfeeling reader's heart.[34] Placing greater emphasis on Devushkin's psychological flaw—in the letter of 21 August he himself writes that his "fall" came about because he lost self-respect and abdicated his dignity—leads to an interpretation which brings to the foreground the high vision of human spirit and free will outlined earlier.

Dostoevsky, we know, made a particular point of separating himself from the characters of *Poor Folk*.[35] One way of measuring this distance that is maintained by the author is to place Devushkin in the mainstream of the other farcical clerks Vinogradov found in the literature of the day. In the context of this literary tradition, the hero of Dostoevsky's first novel should be viewed not only as an object of compassion but, more importantly, as the subject of ridicule, the catalyst for bitter laughter. Rather than taking seriously several outlandishly sentimental ploys that Dostoevsky resorts to in the work, such as the names of the servants Therese and Faldoni culled from Nicolas-Germain Léonard's popular *Lettres de deux amants* (1783),

Devushkin's own name (*devushka* being the Russian equivalent of
"girl"), his remark that François Ducray-Duminil's maudlin *Le petit
carillonneur* was one of the only two novels he ever read, or his
reference to Pushkin's "The Stationmaster," we can suspect that
Dostoevsky was having a bit of fun with Devushkin and the too
sentimentally inclined reader. Dostoevsky's frame of mind in this
period, which shows up clearly in the changed tone of his letters
beginning with 1843, undoubtedly contributed to this disillusionment with pure sentiment. In a letter to his brother dated 31 December 1843, he describes art not as the exalted substance of friendship, love, and poetry that he previously considered it to be, but as
something to be sold, using Eugéne Sue's *Mathilde* (1841) for the
commercial vehicle: "Let us talk business, my dear friend.... We
need at least five hundred rubles.... With this money we will print,
advertise and sell the book at four rubles a copy. It has already sold
well.... Three hundred copies will bring in enough to cover the cost
of printing.... Put out the entire novel ... and we'll clear seven
thousand."[36] No less telling is the plan made by Dostoevsky, Grigoro-
vich, and Nekrasov to publish a bi-monthly journal called *Zuboskal*
whose function, the writer points out in a letter dated 8 October
1845, would be to "make fun of and laugh at everything, to spare
nothing."[37] Dostoevsky later became so irritated with the overly
sentimentalized work of fiction that disregarding the clear imitation
of his much-loved George Sand, he would write of A.V. Druzhinin,
the author of the popular *Polinka Saks*, that he "makes me ill."[38]
Thus, Vinogradov was absolutely correct in pointing to Dostoevsky's tradition-breaking use of sentimentalism, except that the break
was probably more radical than has been usually suspected.

The uses of naturalism and antisentimentalism in Dostoevsky's
first works were organic parts of the ideological process that led him
to defend a heroic, spiritual image of man. If religious or romantic
heroes were no longer acceptable or believable vehicles to show the
contemporary audience what man should be spiritually—although
Dostoevsky, of course, in his mature phase would challenge that
assumption—fictional characters similar to Devushkin could be used
to show what man should *not be* in the important moral-psychological
aspects of his life. Dostoevsky's sure sense of literary development
and fictional methodology, we can hypothesize, led him to create the
essentially negative types acceptable to post-sentimental and post-

romantic readers, but the religious values he acquired in his youth remained in the implied reference to a human typology unattainable by his characters. Such an interpretation of *Poor Folk* is of direct benefit in resolving the long-standing problem in Russian literary scholarship of Dostoevsky's specific literary uses of Gogol. The usual point made about "The Overcoat" and Dostoevsky's novel is that Gogol made his clerk into an absurd and grotesque figure, while Dostoevsky, although he employed some of Gogol's literary devices, endowed Devushkin with more "human" characteristics partially on the basis of sentimental influence.[39] In the light of Gogol's religious intellectual history, however, it is clear that the absurd and the grotesque masks of his fiction were not meant to be taken as an end in themselves but served him as the vital forms for showing his reader the flaws in man's earthly image and for awakening an awareness of disharmony in personality and society. Dmitry Chizhevsky has described this artistic process as an "exaggeratedly disgusting, repulsive representation of everyday life in somber colors" which is meant to evoke a "longing for a higher, nonterrestrial world."[40] If this emphasis on the comical and inadequate in Devushkin is correct, then Dostoevsky can be seen as a writer who continued rather than broke the Gogolian tradition of catharsis. By eliciting the reader's negative response to society and the unmanly and ridiculous in his protagonist, Dostoevsky hoped to evoke an urgent and direct feeling for the necessity of change. And by giving Devushkin the means to struggle with the environment and then showing his inability to respond to it, Dostoevsky indicated that the change has to come not only in social institutions but especially in the spiritual structure of personality.

There are several indications in the novel that Devushkin, although poor, is not in a hopeless financial condition. He has his job, a gift of one hundred rubles, and the chance to develop extra income from the copying of manuscripts.[41] He is not, therefore, an entirely helpless victim of social circumstances. His real difficulty, a deficiency which is the key to his spiritual imbalance and degradation, is his lack of will and easy acceptance of fate, his self-subjugation to the passive role of a *devushka* and, as he himself indicates in the letter of 21 August, his loss of self respect.[42] The resemblance to Krutsifersky is direct, even to the adjective used to describe Herzen's protagonist ("girly"), and although *Who Is to Blame?* was published after *Poor Folk*, it does not seem farfetched to assume that Herzen's prior attack on dilettantes and dreamers in the journal that ultimately brought out Dostoevsky's first novel helped to shape both the distance of laughter kept by the author between himself and Devushkin, as well as the emphasis on personality, underlying the criticism of social injustice, which evolved into a crucial part of his fictional technique. Devushkin's degradation, his loss of respect for himself, his alcoholism, passivity, and belief that fate is to blame, were all major traits of a negative personality syndrome that Herzen used to point readers in the direction of the true glorious image of man.[43]

In this light it is not necessary to make the usual distinction between Devushkin's poverty and Iakov Golyadkin's obvious solvency, or to think that Dostoevsky only began working seriously with the stuff of psychology in "The Double." Edward Wasiolek defines the important issue of Dostoevsky's second work when he writes that "man's tragedy and his deepest problems do not spring from social and economic causes, but from his own insecurities and his own unquenchable drive for self-worth and dignity."[44] Although the interpretation may be a bit extreme in having Dostoevsky reject all social causality, it clearly touches on a vital factor of Golyadkin's madness. It is mainly within the native religious tradition, however, in which self-worth and dignity were absolute values, that Golyadkin's spiritual imbalance can be traced to historical fact and the actual cultural situation out of which Dostoevsky created "The Double."

Vissarion Belinsky: Early Tests

Belinsky's reserved reaction to "The Double," if this work does indeed stand close to *Poor Folk* in thematic structure, makes his relationship to Dostoevsky a particularly useful clue to the writer's first defenses of his ideology. There is no question that Dostoevsky agreed with Belinsky's acute sense of injustice, that Belinsky's praise of *Poor Folk* left a life-long impression on him, and that it was this praise which established Dostoevsky's literary reputation. Moreover, Dostoevsky knew that it was his reading of Belinsky's letter to Gogol which figured most in the events that led to his Siberian imprisonment, and his later assertion that it was Belinsky who strongly influenced the direction of his revolutionary youth must have been inspired in part by this bitter knowledge. Nevertheless, Belinsky criticized "The Double" for what he called its "fantastic setting," and this criticism indicates an important difference in the two men's view of fiction. "In our days the fantastic can have a place only in madhouses, but not in literature," Belinsky writes, "being the business of doctors, not poets."[45] The setting of Dostoevsky's second story actually is the same as his first: St. Petersburg. But Belinsky's comments clearly indicate that what he had in mind was not locale but Dostoevsky's description of the inner arrangement of Golyadkin's personality. This critical response was not inconsistent with Belinsky's first appraisal of Dostoevsky's work, for *Poor Folk* could easily be interpreted as an indictment of society without any regard for personality. In "The Double," however, environmental pressures are clearly relegated to a secondary role; Golyadkin is not at all poor and it is this choice of emphasis which irritated Dostoevsky's most important acquaintance and critic.

The explanation for such differences between the two men is that Belinsky and Dostoevsky saw different things in the progressive movements of the day, although they essentially responded to the same cultural influences. Belinsky, not unlike his young protégé, was well aware of the utopian socialists and respected their humanitarian mission. As the decade moved on, however, another Western school of thought, Left Hegelianism, assumed the predominant role in influencing Russian men of letters. In Herzen's instance Left Hegelians such as Feuerbach and Max Stirner offered a means of shifting emphasis from the type of social restructuring proposed by the French (although Dostoevsky, as we have seen, focused on the French moral-psychological component) to the restructuring of the self. The German thinkers not only wanted to inspire hatred of oppression, but also argued strongly for an inner trait of personality which could be used to change society from within. This new psychological force was self-interest, the idea of egotistic personality which left its imprint not only on young Russians like Herzen but also on the early sociopolitical theories of Western radicals like Marx.[46]

Pavel Annenkov's memoirs of the period provide an invaluable eyewitness account of the effect that egoism had on Belinsky's ideas. According to Annenkov, Belinsky primarily reacted to a specific Left Hegelian text, Max Stirner's *The Ego and Its Own*. While accepting Stirner's view of self-interest as a basic human imperative—"it is proven that man unalterably feels, thinks and acts according to the law of egotistic motives"—Belinsky rejected the distinction that

Stirner made between the interests of the individual and society: "Egoism will become a moral principle only when every individual personality will be capable of attaching to its own interests and needs the interests of strangers, its country, the whole of civilization. [The individual must be able] to view these interests as the same issue, devote to them the same care which is devoted to self-defense, self-protection and so on. Such a socialization of egoism is, in fact, its reformulation into a moral principle."[47]

Such a delineation of what came to be called "rational egoism" was a vital element of the personality syndrome that Dostoevsky encountered in his meetings with Belinsky during the second half of the 1840s. The crucial problem is to determine his response to this sociopsychological message, and a solution is offered to us in the way Belinsky and Dostoevsky related personality to ethics. In the meeting with Belinsky which Dostoevsky describes in the *Diary of a Writer* in 1873, one of the main arguments was whether or not "man is economically brought to commit evil acts."[48] Since Belinsky was arguing so vigorously for this position, it is most probable that his interlocutor, Dostoevsky, had said something to dispute it. Further on, however, Dostoevsky writes that by 1848 he was "passionately following all his [Belinsky's] teachings." The biographical evidence we have available to us indicates that this remark was most likely made for effect and should be taken as a euphemism rather than a solid piece of evidence proving that Dostoevsky was indeed a convert to *all* of Belinsky's ideas.

Belinsky's influence on Dostoevsky was strongest in 1846, the year of the meeting discussed above. From 1847 to 1848, the year of Belinsky's death, relations between the two writers gradually worsened and finally reached the point of a "formal quarrel," in Dostoevsky's own words.[49] It is likely that the quarrel was not only a personal one but dealt with literary and ideological matters that reflected a basic disagreement between Belinsky and several former members of the Petrashevsky circle of which Dostoevsky was a member. Between 1847 and 1848, in fact, Belinsky, now writing for *The Contemporary*, stepped into a direct polemic with those *petrashevtsy* grouped around his former journal, *The Fatherland Annals*.[50] The quarrel was reflected in Belinsky's criticism of "The Double" and "The Landlady" in the middle of 1847, and was based on his conviction that

such fiction led art away from "the poetic analysis of social existence" to a purely psychological emphasis.

The type of "socialism" that found its way into Petrashevsky's
gatherings had indeed a particular spiritual emphasis. Professor
Usakina describes Petrashevsky as believing that "the laws of historical development should be searched out not in a social entity but in
the nature of the human individual."[51] The most striking ideas of
Feuerbach ("*Homo homini deus est*") were given in Petrashevsky's
Pocket Dictionary of Foreign Words (published in 1846) and Petrashevsky himself wrote that "the favorite sphere of the poetic imagination must be the inner world of man." Clearly, there was something in this view of personality that Belinsky could not accept,
although as a disciple of the Left Hegelians he too had to confront
man's "inner world." The most likely hypothesis is that Belinsky
looked to Left Hegelianism for a purely materialistic view of things,
for an ideology that undermined rather than enhanced the spiritual
essence of man which was discussed so avidly in Petrashevsky's
gatherings. Indeed, this was the way that Belinsky viewed egoism: not
as an indication of man's spiritual dignity, but as a "law" of nature
that stood outside of all moral questions and that controlled all
human beings with the weight of the gravity principle. "It should be
noted," Annenkov remembers him saying approvingly in a further
remark about self-interest, "that love, compassion, respect and, in
general, heartfelt emotions do not play any role at all. . . ."[52]

Dostoevsky's memoirs in the *Diary* show the effect that this notion
of personality had on Belinsky's ethical views. On the one hand
Dostoevsky writes that Belinsky "valued reason, science, and realism
above all, but at the same time understood better than anyone else
that reason, science, and realism alone, could only produce ant heaps,
and not social 'harmony.' He knew that the foundation of everything
lies in ethics. He believed in the new ethical foundations of socialism
to the point of madness." On the other hand, the writer points out,
Belinsky "rejected completely the moral responsiblity of personality." When confronted with the "glorious personality of Christ
himself ... Belinsky did not stop even before this unconquerable
barrier" (p. 9). Dostoevsky, therefore, considered Belinsky's goals to
be highly moral, but he also understood that the critic did not place

any particular hope on qualities of personality as a means of attaining his goals. Belinsky's materialistic ideas about human nature developed in two important essays—"A View of Russian Literature in 1846," and "A View of Russian Literature in 1847"—indicate some further reasons for this rejection of the individual's moral strength.

In spite of his repudiation of the conservative implications of Left Hegelianism, Belinsky could never entirely tear himself away from Hegel's dialectic, a system of logic that helped him to define an inner process of causality that moved the world. "When the extreme of a principle is stretched to absurdity," he writes as late as 1846, "its only natural outlet is a transition to the opposite extreme. This is inherent in the nature of men and nations."[53] Not unlike Marx, however, the Russian critic abandoned Hegel to look for causality in matter instead of in the realm of ideas. The object of the following passage's sarcasm is typical, as are the alternatives Belinsky offers:

What constitutes man's sublime and noble substance? Of course that which we call his spirituality, i.e., feeling, reason, will, in which is expressed his eternal, intransient, essential substance. And what is considered man's lower, casual, relative, transient element? Of course, his body. It is well known that we are accustomed from childhood to despise our body, perhaps precisely because, dwelling as we do eternally in logical fantasies, we know so little about it. . . . You, of course, place great value on a man's feeling? Good!—then place a value on that piece of flesh which quivers in his breast, which you call the heart and whose quickened or slackened pulsation responds faithfully to every movement of your soul. You, of course, have great respect for a man's mind? Good!—then halt in awed wonder before the mass of his brain, the seat of all his mental functions, whence run throughout his organism by way of the spinal column the threads of nerves which are the organs of sense and are filled with fluids so fine that they escape material observation and elude speculation. Otherwise you will marvel in man at effect in lieu of cause, or—still worse—will invent your own causes, unknown to nature, and content yourself with them. Psychology which is not based on physiology is as unsubstantial as physiology that knows not the existence of anatomy. Modern science did not halt even at this: it wishes by chemical analysis to penetrate the mysterious laboratory of nature and by observations of the embryo to trace the *physical* process of *moral* evolution. . . . Mind without body, without physiognomy, mind which does not affect the blood and is not affected by its operation is a daydream of logic, a lifeless abstraction. Mind is man in the flesh, or rather, man through the flesh, in a word, personality.[54]

Such excerpts indicate that Belinsky at this stage and in spite of what V. V. Zenkovsky calls his "personalism," imagined personality in pseudoscientific and grossly empirical terms. The consequence of his ideas of placing all the weight on material forces was a view of the individual that lapses into pathos. We should not judge the unfortunate among us harshly, he writes; we should "pity him as a man, even if he himself is largely to blame for his fall."[55]

It is precisely this low opinion of human capabilities generated by respect for material causes that Dostoevsky remembers the critic expressing while he argued for the ethical impotence of personality: " 'Do you know,' he screeched out one evening turning to me, 'do you know that one cannot chalk up sins to a man or to weigh him down with responsibilities . . . when the society is so base. Man cannot help but commit evil acts when he is economically forced on the road to evil. It is silly and cruel to demand of man that what he, by the very laws of nature, cannot do even if he wanted to. . . .' "[56]

In examining this ideological syndrome we see that Belinsky's rejection of ethical choice naturally evolves out of the materialistic definition of personality. Since the individual is only matter, he, as all other things, is totally dependent on the "laws of nature," which are simply the economic or pseudoscientific categories offered in the latest progressive theories. Dostoevsky, on the other hand, based on all we know of him in the 1840s, never reduced personality to material substance or accepted the idea that chemical processes could determine morals. The two men responded in radically different ways to the ideas of Feuerbach, Stirner, and the other Left Hegelians, and a vital indication of their differences is that Dostoevsky, unlike Belinsky, integrated the Left Hegelian view of egoism into his vision of man as a proud, dignified being who retains specific moral tasks and obligations. Other evidence in Dostoevsky's biography supports such an interpretation, including his friendship in this period with Valerian Maikov.

Valerian Maikov: Confirmations

Maikov, the brother of the minor poet Apollon, at first belonged to the Petrashevsky circle, but broke off and formed his own group which met from 1846 till his death in 1847. Maikov was an admirer of Herzen and his interpretation of Herzen's ideas was either a factor in the rift between Dostoevsky and Belinsky or, at the very least, helped to fill in the void created in Dostoevsky's intellectual world when Belinsky took his powers of persuasion elsewhere. For we know that Dostoevsky visited Maikov's circle, and Maikov's work gives us a clear picture of what he encountered there: "A man in whom life's external circumstances, the entire panorama of his genesis and development, are reflected as in a mirror," he writes, "is this a free and reasoning being who is created in *the image of God?*" Man is "tsar of the world" he inhabits, and the best of men are most striking in "the power of their response to external conditions." Maikov accepts the idea that evil is produced through the improper arrangement of society but he does not admit that absolute environmental determination of human will is possible because his view of man as a heroic being does not allow it: "The true greatness of man stands in direct opposition to his dependence on external factors," he writes.[57] And as if in answer to the blasphemous and cynical Belinsky that Dostoevsky describes in the *Diary*, Maikov calls on Christ to act as a symbol of man's glorious spiritual nature, stressing that it is the inner essence of the Man-God that counts: "The greatest upheaval in the life of mankind was created by God himself in the image of man. Christ, in his human aspect, exemplifies the most perfect image of what we call the greatness of personality" (p. 58).

It was this sort of emphasis on the individual and personality which inspired Maikov to reject deterministic and social forces and to criticize the pseudoscientific ideas which Belinsky and others were then enthusiastically postulating. With the help of Maikov's writings, we can speculate that after the initial impression of Belinsky had worn off, Dostoevsky was not content to stay on the level of their mutual hatred of social injustice and turned away from attacks on society back to his old and never-abandoned involvements in the basic ingredient of all societies—the self. While the young writer was too well aware of environmental forces crushing the "insulted and injured" to neglect the criticism of Russian social conditions, it is probable that Maikov's respectful emphasis on personality helped confirm his basic distrust of the helplessness of the will or the hopelessness of the human condition. We have already noted the major stimulants to this defense of moral freedom, but the full story of Dostoevsky's continued analysis of man's "inner world" is best told in the writer's own words.

The Feuilletons

Dostoevsky's correspondence provides a logical starting point. In a January 1847 letter to his brother, the writer roundly criticizes the "despicable" and "faceless" men who advocate reconciliation with fate, "limitations in life, and contentment with their place."[58] "To be a *man* among men," he writes even when in prison (22 December 1849), "to always remain a man, not to lose heart or your human dignity ... no matter what misfortunes might befall you, that's what life is" (p. 129). It is possible that this optimistic view of man's strength of character and the winning battles of the self were reflected in a lecture that Dostoevsky gave in Petrashevsky's home entitled "About Personality and Human Egoism." We do not know the exact nature of the lecture but Grossman proposes the interesting hypothesis that it was based on Stirner's *The Ego and Its Own*, a book found in Petrashevsky's library.[59] The issues involved can be understood best of all through Dostoevsky's writings in the Russian press, specifically in the feuilletons he wrote in 1847 for the *St. Petersburg News*.[60] These short sketches make up the only nonfictional body of work that the writer published in the 1840s and they provide direct testimony to the ideological substance of his early prose. A number of critical studies, particularly the valuable analysis by Professor Frank, have demonstrated the feuilletons' importance as a source of evidence of Dostoevsky's literary intentions. But some puzzling passages have not been explicated in sufficient depth and it is they that most clearly suggest the complex moral-psychological nuances of personality he introduced into his early fiction.

In the first feuilleton, Dostoevsky gives us a hint of his reasons for abandoning Petrashevsky's gatherings for those of Maikov and then of Durov by ridiculing the circle where "one can ... finish off one's useful life between a yawn and gossip."[61] In a gathering of this sort the members calm themselves with endless arguments instead of concrete activity, and the activity Dostoevsky envisions, of course, is of a revolutionary bent. Significantly enough, he introduces his call to action with a remark about the familiar, romantic-heroic role that man should play: " ... to live means to make an artistic creation out of oneself.... " Such individualism, however, Dostoevsky once again suggests, must be accompanied by the moral balance of committing one's "good heart" to others, for its is "only through sympathy for the mass of society, for its direct and immediate demands, rather than in daydreams ... " that the man of good intentions will be truly worth something.

In his fourth and most important feuilleton Dostoevsky shifts into a direct analysis of the well intentioned but inactive dilletante types. Why, he asks, do we have the "most unpleasant habit of doing nothing but weighing our impressions," of being completely engrossed in "future delights" which have not yet come into reality. It is these daydreams which lead us to be content with fantasies, and "to be useless thereafter in real action." True happiness lies in the fulfillment of oneself in "eternal, untiring activity, and the practical development of all our inclinations and capabilities." The main thing is that we ourselves be active, that "our own individual creativity be brought into play." Man is not a real presence in the world unless he asserts his existence by moral action in the concrete life of society. The principal blame for the inactivity of daydreams and empty talk, then, lies not in sociopolitical prohibitions, but in the individual himself who is unwilling to undertake moral aggrandizement in the real world. The need for this type of self-assertion, Dostoevsky goes on, is a distinct psychological characteristic of man, a vital imperative of his personality, and its fulfillment depends on one's sense of dignity and egoism:

> When a man is dissatisfied, when he has not the means to show what is best in him (not out of vanity, but because of the most natural human need to realize, fulfill, and justify his I in real life) he at once gets involved in some quite incredible situation. He becomes a rummy, if you permit me the expression, or provokes duels, turns to gambling and cheating at cards, or finally goes mad from *ambition*, at the same time within himself totally despising ambition, and even suffering from having had to suffer over such trifles as ambition. And before you know it, you come to a conclusion, an almost unfair, offensive but seemingly very probable conclusion, that we have little sense of personal dignity; that within us we have little of indispensable egoism. ... .[62]

Two parts of this passage provide fairly clear evidence of the moral-psychological frame of reference I have proposed. Dostoevsky understands the natural impulse of self-aggrandizement ("realize, fulfill, and justify his I") to be a positive force and brings it together with moral quality, "what is best in him." The "means" to such moral self-expression is shown to be an internal, spiritual matter of "personal dignity" and "indispensable egoism," two categories that are combined to demonstrate anew the balanced, noble form of self-fulfillment that the writer imagines. There is, moreover, a suggestive psychological note in the remark about "suffering from having had to suffer" which points to the themes of the mature work.

The middle part of the passage, on the other hand, is unclear in meaning and seems to present an argument against the very ideas of the "I" and egoism stated at its beginning and end. The key term is "ambition" which must surely be taken to be an expression of egoism and self-aggrandizement, but which Dostoevsky uses to describe *aberrant* rather than positive qualities of personality. Fortunately, another biographical source, the testimony Dostoevsky offered to the commission investigating his arrest, suggests an explanation for the apparent contradiction. In it he summarizes the lecture he gave on personality and egoism in Petrashevsky's circle, and comments that he "wished to show that there is more *ambition* among us than genuine human dignity, that we tend to fall into belittling ourselves, into a pulverization of personality out of trivial self-love, egoism, and the aimlessness of our occupations."[63] The deliberate contrast of "ambition" and "genuine human dignity" indicates that under the first term Dostoevsky is thinking again of the improper and destructive expressions of egoism; ambition as is described in the feuilleton is part of the short-sighted "trivial" impulses of secular society such as getting ahead in the demeaning bureaucracy, drinking, or gambling, which stand in direct opposition to a true self-realization based on the individual's rightful dignity and eternal spiritual qualities. The crucial stimulus to this pejorative sense of ambition is the contrasting religious-romantic vision of a heroism which stands above the need for a transitory (*suetnaia*) and undignified projection of oneself in the world of clerks and everyday meanness, above the fatal flaw, in short, of characters like Devushkin and Golyadkin.

In the following, often-cited passages Dostoevsky uses his fictional language to describe the results of neglecting the spiritual heroism he imagines and to sketch the literary type of the dreamer that is so important for his texts:

And in the end the man is no longer a man but a kind of strange being of a neuter gender—a *dreamer*. And do you know what a dreamer is, gentlemen? It is a Petersburg nightmare, it is a personified sin, it is a mute, mysterious, gloomy and wild tragedy, with all its frantic horrors, catastrophes, . . . and unhappy endings—and we are not saying this in jest. You sometimes come across a man who looks absent-minded, with a pale, crumpled face, always busy with something terribly burdensome, some kind of difficult, abstruse problem, looking exhausted by some apparently hard work but actually producing absolutely nothing—such is the dreamer from the outside.... They usually live in complete solitude, in some inaccessible quarters, as though they were hiding from people and the world, and generally there is something melodramatic about them at first sight. They are gloomy and taciturn with their own people, they are absorbed in themselves and are very fond of anything that does not require any effort, anything light and contemplative, everything that has a tender effect on their feelings or excites their sensations. They are fond of reading and they read all sorts of books, even serious scientific books, but usually lay the book down after reading two or three pages, for they feel completely satisfied. Their imagination, mobile, volatile, light, is already excited, their senses are attuned, and a whole dreamlike world, with its joys and sorrows, with its heaven and hell, its ravishing women, heroic deeds, honorable acts always with some superhuman struggle, with crime and all sorts of horrors, suddenly possesses the entire being of the dreamer. His room vanishes and so does space; time stops or flies so quicky that an hour counts for a minute.... Gradually and imperceptibly the talent of real life becomes blunted in him. He quite naturally begins to believe that the pleasures that his uncontrolled imagination gives him are fuller, more splendid and more enchanting than real life. At last, in his delusion, he completely loses the moral judgment that enables men to appraise the full beauty of the present; he is at a loss, he gets flustered, he lets the moments of real happiness slip by, and, in his apathy, he folds his arms indolently and does not want to know that a man's life is continual self-contemplation in nature and actual reality.[64]

The distillation of the dreamer's qualities provides additional evidence that Dostoevsky wanted to emphasize that part of his religious heritage which argued for man's spiritual assertion and moral awakening from within. It can be suggested that the kenotic harmony noted earlier between such values as egoism and humility, triumph and suffering, inspired literary exploration of the emotional factors which upset it by throwing personality out of balance. In the dreamer's case the psychic tilt is produced by excessive self-humiliation and suffering and further affected by the loss of the compensating spiritual weight of dignity and self-worth. Dostoevsky begins with a delineation of human impotence and moral-psychological inadequacy ("neuter gender" and "personified sin"), then proceeds to a parodistic use of key literary schools such as gothic fiction ("mysterious, gloomy, and wild tragedy"), sentimentalism ("tender effect on feelings"), and romanticism ("heroic deeds," "superhuman") to describe the imagined results of spiritual weakness. Finally, the reader is given a hint of solutions and is brought back to earlier motifs of spiritual aggrandizement and indispensable egoism in the remark about the dreamer's inadequate "self-contemplation in nature and actual reality," as well as the references to "beauty" and "moral judgement."

In specific detail the passage beginning with "their imagination" and ending with "a minute" is an almost exact description of what happens to Ordynov, the protagonist of "The Landlady." In such instances, humility and suffering are depicted in terms of ascetic self-withdrawal and fatalistic lack of concern for one's active presence in the world. But the internal tilt and self-withdrawal of the dreamer as Dostoevsky describes him characterizes many other protagonists in his early fiction as well. In "The Double," "Mr. Prokharchin," "A Faint Heart," and Netochka Nezvanova, the writer makes a point of giving his central characters the material means to happiness—whether it be Golyadkin's solvency, Prokharchin's access to two thousand roubles, Vasya Shumkov's kind-hearted superior and beautiful bride, or Yefimov's talent and the way shown to him by the successful "B," who starts out in exactly the same environment as he. All of the protagonists in question wreck their lives not through any drastic imposition of external circumstances, but through some inner flaw. And in all of these instances, as well as in "White Nights," the psychological inadequacy can be related to a deficiency of dignity, a lack of will, the abdication of the glorious freedom of a man in moral control of his world. This is not to say that the bureaucratic world of Vasya Shumkov is not a factor in his madness, or that Yefimov's peasant origins do not affect him or his daughter; it simply means that Dostoevsky thought that adjustments in society must be preceded by adjustments in personality which would produce an unselfish yet self-confident, proud, and dignified human being with the will to achieve true spiritual greatness in the world.

Conclusions and Continuities

Dostoevsky's exploration of the self and reformulation of religious and romantic issues in the 1840s suggest, in turn, a perspective on his later fiction. The egotistical definitions of man remained a vital force of Russian culture throughout Dostoevsky's life. Most noticeably, it affected Chernyshevsky's passionate interpretation of Feuerbach and moved on to touch Mihailovsky and the populists, both instances, of course, of men that Dostoevsky responded to in his work. Even a brief glance at Dostoevsky's major novels, in fact, shows the results of this intellectual continuity on the left. The definition of self-interest, or advantage, is a crucial motif of *The Notes from the Underground*; egoism reappears in Raskolnikov's interpretation of English utilitarianism, and the most extreme, immoral form of it is a dominant theme of *The Devils*. In *The Idiot* it is egoism that Dostoevsky selects as the one tragic flaw of Myshkin, the most basic human element of his love for Aglaia which forces his earthly self into an irreconcilable conflict with the divine selflessness of his love for Nastasyia Filipovna. The crucial difference, of course, is that in such instances Dostoevsky looks to a reversal of the spiritual disharmony he imagined in his youth. The issue is no longer human abjectness and humility which are lacking in dignity and ego, but the opposite situation of contemporary secular egoism which is unmitigated by humility, charity, and love. There are some notable exceptions; Yefimov's personality as portrayed in *Netochka Nezvanova* represents an early criticism of egoism, while the character of Father Ferapont in *The Brothers Karamazov* is a late parody of holy-fool humility. The ideological frame of reference is the same, however, as is the literary energy and vitality which is inspired by the writer's use of the perennial Russian issues. Indeed, it is not a denigration of Dostoevsky's own textual meanings to say that he never abandons the core values postulated in his Orthodox heritage. For while the actual cultural context should not be taken to be an exclusive or reductive indication of fictional properties, neither can it be deemphasized if we are to understand the deep-seated nuances of this creative endeavor. In both major periods of work, the implied or explicit reference of a organic moral-psychological structure is at the heart of the fiction, and in both instances the creative tensions and problems of literary vision come out of those basic ideas about man that Dostoevsky learned in his family and childhood milieu.

CHAPTER 5

Leontiev's Prickly Rose

CONTEMPORARIES and latter-day critics of Constantine Leontiev have tended to emphasize his reactionary political views, homosexuality, and personality quirks. The eccentric psychopolitical image of Leontiev discussed in such instances has injected a paradoxical note of disharmony into the appreciation of a seemingly inverse grace and form in his fiction. The man has come to represent one thing, his literary work something quite different and unrelated. Part of the problem is that readers and acquaintances showed an almost uniform hostility to Leontiev's ideas or used them to argue their own convictions. Ivan Aksakov spoke of Leontiev's "voluptuous cult of the cane"; Turgenev thought that he surpassed Dostoevsky in fatuous self-satisfaction; Nikolai Strakhov suggested that "with him religion, art, science, patriotism . . . were so many excuses for his basest stirrings and his most depraved thirst for pleasure and self-gratification"; Vasily Rozanov, as in the case of Dostoevsky, managed to interject his own exotic tastes into a discussion of the writer's fiction; Masaryk in *The Spirit of Russia* attempted to maintain his usual insight and impartiality, but ended up being as hostile to Leontiev as Leontiev was to the Czechs; and Sergei Bulgakov considered him to be an "ethical monster."[1] Although scholars such as Nicholas Berdiaev, Georges Florovsky, and George Ivask have hinted at the ideological factors which suggest possible ways of bringing the man together with his work, no real organic interpretation explaining Leontiev's texts in terms of his own cultural situation, his ideas, beliefs, and ideological problems is available.[2] A review and definition of the writer's basic intellectual constructs rather than the

familiar delineation of the external features of his biography or
literary style would be a useful corrective both to Leontiev's extrava-
gant reputation and the neglect of his fiction. For if we interpret his
literary endeavor as part of a response to certain internal ideological
tensions and changes in the cultural tradition to which he belonged,
we see a complexity and subtlety in his art, the full range of which has
not been adequately explored.

Childhood and Early Fiction

Leontiev's ideological biography was broad and eclectic in scope
but its key can be located in the intensity of his Orthodox involvements. Although he shared a passion for native ideological commitments with Herzen and Dostoevsky, he was ultimately the only major
Russian writer who felt such passion strongly enough to become a
monk. Leontiev's ideological formation shows childhood religious
training, projections of religious values into romantic literary modes,
temporary distancing from Orthodoxy, and eventual return to
church doctrine, all of which provide examples in extremity of the
cultural processes suggested in the early chapters of this book. He
responded to the liturgy, thus, not indirectly, as part of the general
historical background of Russian literature, but as a specific formative influence on his aesthetic taste.[3] Moreover, he accepted romantic
doctrine with the full force of absolute religious conviction, and he
brought to his literary texts all the tensions and paradoxes of defending older religious values and concepts in a secular age. Not unlike
Herzen's and Dostoevsky's experience, the early stages of this ideological course involved family, church rituals, and long-standing
social customs.

Leontiev's father was not a particularly religious man but both his
mother and his aunt regularly attended Orthodox services with the
young boy.[4] In their everyday routine the family took part in all the
religious customs woven into the fibre of Russian society. The day
began with prayers which Leontiev would enjoy listening to while
still in bed; the meals were regulated by fasts and the church calendar;
visits to Moscow and St. Petersburg would be made memorable by a
particularly beautiful service in one of the many urban places of
worship. Such an everyday "poetry of religious impression," Leon-

tiev notes with obvious self-reference in his recollections, provided basic emotional-aesthetic sustenance; and although the adolescent "love of religion" was initially naive and unquestioning it would eventually nurture mature doctrine.[5] The periods preceding and following confession were especially important and solemn occasions. Toward the end of his life Leontiev still vividly remembered the first time he went through the stirring emotional act of asking one's acquaintances and relatives forgiveness before undertaking confession, and a second lifelong memory was the image of moral calmness and spiritual dignity his mother projected *after* she had gone through the ritual.[6] On the basis of Leontiev's own testimony the early stage of this religious experience can be separated into two major lines of ideological formation: an aesthetic concern and appreciation stimulated by the music, icons, and regalia of Orthodox services, and a moral imperative given special impetus by the Protestant influence he detected in his mother.[7]

As Leontiev grew into adulthood the religious-aesthetic side of his sensibility was gradually transformed through contact with romantic literature; the mature works he wrote came out of new cross-pressures of secular and religious values. His first fiction, however, largely responded to earlier moral standards and to the not unusual process of transformation in which childhood moral codes learned in catechisms are projected into hopes of social and political reform. After leaving his family to make his way in the world, the young man showed all the cultural mannerisms of a mid-century liberal landowner. He spoke French, dressed well, had a small income from his estate, and was concerned about the humanitarian notions in the air. He later admitted to having believed in a republic, although the most radical changes he advocated were based on nothing stronger than the feeling that the gentry and the government should treat the peasants better. That this fashionable liberalism was sincere, however, can be seen in his choice of a medical career, which then carried some of the same weight with the new generation that social service does now and which was made into a symbol of the progressive young in Turgenev's *Fathers and Children.*

Most important, Leontiev cared enough about a number of social issues disturbing the Russian progressive at mid-century to use them in his first literary efforts of the fifties. The short story "A Summer in the Village" (1855) develops familiar motifs, used by Turgenev in his early sketches, illustrating the high moral and aesthetic qualities to be found in the peasant.[8] Vasil'kov, a young student of the classics, comes to spend the summer in a serf's hut. He discovers that Masha, the daughter of his landlord, has an "inbred instinct for the lofty and the good" and falls in love with her. Some of Leontiev's later skillful use of colors and feeling for nature come though—Masha's eyes are grey in daylight and turn into "black satin" at night; a rainstorm "brings out a thousand strong, fresh smells from the fields"—but the story is essentially a sentimental pudding mixed with the banal message that a member of the nobility can find happiness in the arms of a commoner. If such green liberalism looks back to the moral concerns of Rousseau, Karamzin, and Zhukovsky, "Hard Times," a play written in approximately the same period, is more up to date and at least in part deals with the notions of George Sand. Published in 1858 in *Annals of the Fatherland*, the journal which had earlier featured the works of Belinsky and Herzen and which was for a time the only outlet for liberal writers, the drama is formed around a love triangle heavily slanted to the side of a young widow, Alexandra Sinevskaya.[9] Against the background of a Fonvizian characterization of the willful and immoral sort of eighteenth-century Russian aristocracy (in the main represented by the grandmother, Nastasya, and the *nedorosl'* Alexei), Leontiev focuses on the play of strong passions in Alexandra, whom we can assume is one of the new women. Although far from being a tract on female emancipation, the play clearly shows Leontiev's concern for the rights of feminine emotions and for the moral sensibilities of the Russian nobleman which are displayed in the rich landowner Sergei Nepriadov.

Perhaps most interesting of Leontiev's early works, primarily because it is so different in ideological orientation from his mature writings, is the short story "A Day in the Village of Biiuk-Dorte."[10] The piece itself is highly unsuccessful. Leontiev's syntax is awkward, the plot is muddled, and the soldier's jargon he attempts to use for military color comes out sounding suspiciously like the prattle of university-educated young men. But the political message of the story is developed in a spirit of Westernism and, considering Leontiev's later attacks on the West, this is striking testimony indeed to the radical change which was to occur in his ideas. Muratov, a well-meaning landowner, goes off to war because he hates the French and English; he is convinced that Russia must set the historical example for the rest of the world. On the front, however, rather than a holy, messianic battle, he encounters dirt, cold, cholera, drunken medics, and an old friend and extreme nationalist, Markov, who turns out to be a Peeping Tom. Leontiev does not draw outright conclusions, but he is heavily sarcastic at the expense of Muratov's sense of Russian messianism, and one feels a clear dissatisfaction with the representatives of extreme national pride. The story ends on a loud Westernizer note, with the suggestion that it is probably Russia that should be historically rejuvenated and not Europe.

Crises: Romantic Pain

Leontiev was to undergo two crises, one at the beginning of the 1860s which changed him from a liberal to a conservative, the second in 1871 which brought him to a new sense of Orthodoxy and, finally, to monastic vows. The years in between the two crises, roughly extending over the decade of the 1860s, were the most productive for his fiction and the time when he began to formulate key principles of his mature sociopolitical views. The turn to conservatism went hand in hand with a revitalized sense of aesthetics inspiring his major novels, while religious involvements during this middle period acted as an internal creative stimulant invigorating literary form rather than as the dominant force leading away from fiction to the Optina cloister in the last years of life.

There were several key reasons for the initial shift in political and literary viewpoint. Like Tolstoy, Leontiev experienced the Crimean War at first hand, and being a doctor he met death at a much closer distance which made optimistic appraisals of social direction and human perfectibility hard to maintain. The operating and dissecting rooms, moreover, provided him with a distrust for abstract political programs that was similar to the disquiet felt by Chekhov. Leontiev himself explained that the great change in his thinking occurred during a conversation with a young representative of the radical camp. Prior to this moment, he writes, he was not really worried about radical views expressed in The Contemporary, the journal of the left. As late as 1857, in fact, he still considered himself to be a liberal of "uncertain direction."[11] But while walking with Piotrovsky, a contributor to The Contemporary, Leontiev stopped before the intricately constructed mansion of Prince Beloselsky-Belozersky. Looking at the building he asked his young companion if he really desired that neat, comfortable homes and barracks built on exactly the same pattern would replace the beautiful rococo complexity of the aristocrat's domicile. Piotrovsky's answer, in the best socialist traditions of the day, was "what could be better?" And from that moment on, Leontiev concludes, "I was not [their] man."[12]

This rejection of what Leontiev imagined to be simplifications and vulgarizations in the left's ideology was impelled by a reworking into romantic perspectives of aesthetic and transcendent realities already glimpsed during childhood in the church.[13] The literary influences were clear enough and included Goethe, Byron, Béranger, Pushkin, Batyushkov, and Lermontov. "[They] corrupted me in this direction in the highest degree," Leontiev remarks late in life forgetting to note the equally important debt he owed to Appolon Grigoriev's kindred reformulation of Orthodoxy.[14] As a result of combining such cultural models with a religious maximalization of values and ideas, Leontiev begins to follow the Russian romantic tradition, even in the strongly antiromantic atmosphere of the 1860s, while carrying aesthetic sensibility to an extreme rarely seen in traditional lives. A basic impulse manifested itself in the typical romantic intransigence which refuses to accept the unseemly and imperfect things of our world; in everyday practice such aesthetic dissatisfaction meant an ever-present feeling of revulsion for soiled and rumpled sheets, shoddy furniture, and unshaven waiters. We can find him describing with obvious sincerity the nausea that he feels in a particularly unpalatable hotel room. Conversely, he shows himself to be at peace with clean and perfumed linen, the air of flowers, and the melody, discovered anew, of the Orthodox service.[15] In defining the cultural situation in which Leontiev was located, it is useful to link these feelings to two particular impulses of the romantic tradition: the rejection of the real world of ugly and banal reality, commonly expressed through ridicule, irony, or withdrawal, and a yearning for another more perfect sphere of existence in which religious principles, particularly those of Byzantine Orthodoxy, suggest the possibilities of beauty and eternity.

Despite intellectual and emotional affinities, however, as a writer of the second half of the nineteenth century Leontiev could not permit himself to be fully content either with religious beliefs or with the romantic tradition. The earlier forms of romantic disillusionment in Western literatures, the sensibilities of *Weltschmerz* or *mal du siècle* for example, were now inadequate, because a more direct approach was necessary in a period of growing skepticism, science, and materialism. After Feuerbach's *The Essence of Christianity,* Darwin's *Origin of Species,* and the Crimean War, a writer who chose a romantic viewpoint could no longer withdraw into the pessimism of a Lermontov, the fantasy of an Odoevskii, or the mystery and terror of Zhukovsky, nor could he intelligently argue for the eternal verities of God and church without considering modern secular thought. It was clear that more direct modes of attack on the imperfections of reality were necessary if the new reading public were to be drawn at all to a fiction expressing dissatisfaction with the temporal and secular concerns of life.

Leontiev echoed a number of these new modes of attack—ridicule of the bourgeoisie, of rationalism, and of modern-day banality— which men like Nietzsche later used in a manner only hinted at earlier in the century. More important, however, he also suffered from the pivotal problem of romanticism in modern culture, of finding a goal or purpose for intransigence and the critical spirit. Unlike Schelling, Coleridge, or Wordsworth, the modern romantic could no longer depend on idealism to provide an alternative reality or a metaphysical hope. Leontiev showed himself to be thoroughly modern in this sense, for he steadfastly refused to view existence as a reflection of some hidden life process. Indeed, the major tensions of his fictional writings as we see them in the 1860s had their source in an inner romantic paradox. Without ever being able to completely stifle the underlying impulses of Orthodoxy and idealism, he turned the critical imperative of his aesthetic vision against, rather than toward, the companion yearning for transcendent absolutes, for the future development of reason and abstract realms of the beautiful.[16]

Podlipki

This intellectual bias—a variant of what M. H. Abrams defines as "displacement from a supernatural to a natural frame of reference"— affected the change of direction which Leontiev introduced into the predominant romantic view of history in his writings on Russian society and politics. Bolstered by the pessimism of Herzen and Danilevsky, he moved away from the German idea of a vast, organic force of nature progressing to ultimate perfection and arrived at a historical interpretation based on biological principles of inevitable decay. But the same romantic skepticism and dissatisfaction deprived of an outlet to the Absolute also provides the ideological key to most of the familiar features of his fiction, including his so-called aesthetic immoralism, his concern for the immediate sensual image, and his ridicule of liberal plans for future political utopias. *Podlipki*, his first novel published in the *Annals of the Fatherland* toward the end of 1861, already reflects the essence of this fictional response. The romantic influence is not hard to single out. In *Podlipki* Leontiev rejects the ugliness and banality of reality—and the literary technique of naturalistic realism most often used to depict it in Russian fiction—by creating another world and an opposite narrative mode to approach it.

In contrast to the sometimes gross detail and extensive description of Russian realistic works—a constant concern of Leontiev's literary criticism—*Podlipki* unfolds through the chance, unstable memory of a young protagonist, Volodia Ladnev. The first person prism of Ladnev is effectively used to convey an impressionistic, many-colored sense of experience; we catch brief glimpses and bright moments of life rather than the squalor, poverty, and madness that the Russian reader could expect in fiction devoted to clerks and merchants. The technique is not unlike that developed later in *La porte étroite* and *Speak, Memory*, with much of the narrative constructed out of snatches of memory floating in evasive images from the hazy past: "Or I remember myself as though in a deep mist . . . I do not see the house or the trees in front of me, but only the railing of a balcony and on the balcony, three girls. I—still very small it must be—come out . . . and blow bubbles out of my mouth. I do not remember the faces of the girls at this moment, but the bright printed calico of one seems familiar; it is brightly colored in red designs."[17] The bubbles are just the right touch here, providing both humor and the appropriate image to catch the evasiveness of Ladnev's memory.

Anticipating Nabokov's faded photographs, Leontiev uses pictures to create an aesthetic world colored by memories and chance details. The recollection of his uncle, a soldier, does not introduce an actual description, but makes Ladnev think of the uncle's gift to Ladnev's aunt, a small box with a colorful battle between Turks and Cossacks drawn on the lid. The young boy, we are told, spent countless hours daydreaming over the exotic picture (a comparison with Nabokov's box of Turkish delights inevitably comes to mind). Or Ladnev's older friend, Sergei, draws pictures for him which he remembers better than the actual events of his past: "A ship is sailing, on the ocean my aunt and I look out over the railing . . . and coming towards us from Podlipki is a rowboat, and inside the rowboat are Ol'enka, Verochka, and Klashenka, and the watchman Egor Ivanovich is rowing . . ." (pp. 24–25).

The indirect, impressionistic style of narrative construction was to be used by Leontiev throughout his life and to attain its strongest expression much later in such works as *The Egyptian Dove*. Understandably, therefore, in the few instances when Leontiev's fiction has been studied, critics have tended to emphasize this aesthetic strategy.[18] The main literary enterprise of *Podlipki*, however, does not end with the static production of hazy, beautiful images, but involves the growth of Ladnev *out of* the haze of romantic imagery and fancy into the actual world. Although we can appreciate the sensuous detail and wonderful impressionism of the novel, Leontiev's text requires a more complex aesthetic perspective than the point of view that his own protagonist transcends.

Podlipki, the estate where Ladnev spends his childhood, is a magical fairyland where the snow is perfectly white, the air is crystal clear, and cleanness and light prevail. The queen of the kingdom is Ladnev's kindly, portly aunt. Her estate is the setting for Ladnev's first feelings of beauty, friendship, and love. As the novel takes shape, however, we become increasingly aware that recollections of this magic edifice are constantly being set off against Ladnev's awareness of the cracks in the structure. There is the beautiful melody, the mystery of the Orthodox religious service which forms one of his fondest memories, and next to it the image of the priest's wife, a pretentious, horrible woman who unmercifully hounds her husband. There is the kindly aunt who keeps a "harem" of serf girls, household servants subject to the gentry's whims and caprice. Ladnev particularly dwells upon one youngster who was beaten, shorn, and tied to a tree for a theft she did not commit, and he notes with wry amusement his inability to understand then why the child wanted to run away. There is Ladnev's brother, a handsomely sculptured youth and a typical romantic hero in the Pechorin mode, who does not hesitate to send his huge borzois after a peasant's small mongrel and to laugh with stupid glee at the brutal attack. There is, finally, Ladnev's uncle, a nobleman of the old school who instructs peasants with his fist and whose wife is mad. When Ladnev reaches eleven he is sent to his uncle's city mansion and there, he tells us, he learns conclusively to "reconcile fancy with reality."

From this point on, Ladnev's disillusionment and the growing up process become decidedly more painful. Particularly effective are his recollections of his cousin Modest, the victim of a grave injustice perpetrated by Ladnev's family, and a wonderful tool to deflate the romantic-sentimental expectation that his plight arouses. Ladnev expects to meet "a poor youth who is aristocratically attractive, [who is] graceful even within poverty," and encounters instead "a tall, thin, freckled, curly-haired and fat-lipped young man, who is not very careful about his appearance."[19] Modest seduces the serf girl whom Ladnev loves, and turns out to be a cynical groveler without pride or honor. The young narrator discovers that the injustice suffered does not make Modest noble or tragic, but simply vulgar.

The unfrocking of Ladnev's youthful ideals is made effective by the free structure of the novel. Leontiev does not hesitate in breaking time sequence to juxtapose the romantic pictures of Ladnev's childhood with the actual reality he is eventually forced to face. A case in point is the same Sergei who drew pictures for him as a young man. Sergei and his wife, a former ward of Ladnev's aunt, are held up as paragons of virtue and religious feeling by the old woman. Ladnev remembers the wonderful moment when, thanks to her help, the two young people finally got married, and he imagines the scene when the newlyweds left Podlipki, full of life, happiness, and what he assumes to be boundless gratitude. At this point, the narrative abruptly takes a huge skip in time to the description of a visit that Ladnev later made to the couple, when they had already settled down to their new life. They receive him in a cluttered hotel room with "bad tea but a warm welcome." Almost from the first words they utter, they begin to criticize Ladnev's aunt, accusing her of being a miser of the worst sort and bitterly complaining of the hardship she caused them. In place of his imagined idyll of protector and grateful wards, Ladnev is forced to confront the true nature of a relationship conditioned by ingratitude on one side and petty miserliness on the other.

Ladnev finally returns to Podlipki, hoping to rediscover his youthful world. He finds, instead, a young peasant girl who is no hazy faerie, but a snub-nosed, sexually enticing young woman. Ladnev is at the point of seducing her but stops at the last moment under the dual influence of a vision of Christ and nostalgia for the old Podlipki. In spite of his sexual impulses he does not want to "dirty the pure vision" of childhood religious beliefs and his dilemma clearly reflects Leontiev's own troubled merger of religious and romantic values. Christ's hazy spiritual image provides an aesthetic-moral reminder and measure of the inadequacies of reality but it is clear that the ideal is only appropriate for nostalgia rather than for a direct interpretation of what real life involves.

In One's Land

In One's Land (1864), Leontiev's next major literary text, is constructed on a design similar to the earlier novel's: a young man comes into maturity and learns to face up to an existence that is not simple, moral, or beautiful in the traditional sense. In comparison with the first work, however, the thematic structure is noticeably different for Lontiev puts greater emphasis on the philosophical odyssey of the hero and throws a wider net over the intellectual environment. The protagonist, Rudnev, is neither a naive boy exposed to the gradual erosion of a romanticized childish world, nor is he quite the disillusioned romantic that Ladnev came to be. Leontiev draws him as a determined, introspective, somewhat straitlaced young man who sets out to find his role in life by clear thought and deliberate choice.

The alternatives open to Rudnev are varied and far from clear-cut. Leontiev consciously makes the reader's task difficult by refusing to delineate black and white guidelines or to set up a ready-made goal toward which his protagonist can strive. A not particularly successful literary effect of this ambiguity is an extremely loose plot structure full of sudden sharp corners and dead ends. In respect to Rudnev himself, however, Leontiev achieves a fascinating counterpoint to the simplistically easy moral solutions depicted in Chernyshevsky's just published What Is to Be Done? The thematic impetus is similar to Dostoevsky's antiradical fiction but is played out in a different key.

Rudnev's first intellectual conflict, not unlike Leontiev's own, is brought about when he begins the study of medicine. He is haunted by the images of dissected corpses. Under the pressure of science, and with the biological certainty of death grating on his earlier religious training and faith, Rudnev decides to withdraw to the small country estate of his uncle where he intends to put his intellectual house in order by extensive reading in Rousseau and other philosophers. His ideal is uninvolved contemplation of the outside world, and the kind of withdrawal he imagines for himself unmistakably reflects the romantic cult of isolation from civilization's woes. As in the case of Ladnev, however, Leontiev does not permit this initial romantic situation to remain intact, but draws Rudnev out of his self-imposed exile into the life around him. There he is made to face a wide spectrum of the ideological realities of Russia and a world far more complex than he originally imagined.

He meets, on the one hand, the seminarist Bogoiavlensky (or "God-manifestensky"), an obvious caricature of the Feuerbach-inspired radicals on the Russian left. Bogoiavlensky constantly uses the terminology of progressive German thought, but his openly admitted purpose in life is the simplest of materialist doctrines: he wants to get his share no matter what the moral cost. In this pursuit he does not hesitate to spread malicious gossip about the people who house and feed him or, in spite of his socialist convictions, to assure himself of a warm bed and full board by marrying a rich member of the merchant class. Although mildly attracted by the impulse to get down to brass tacks, Rudnev is far from satisfied with this type of crude materialism or with Bogoiavlensky's theory of self-interest.

Another mode of life is represented by Sardanapal, a member of the landed gentry and, of course, a complete debaucher. Although he spends most of his days in a thoroughly inebriated condition, Sardanapal is not unaware of current economic theory, which he puts into effect in his harem of serf girls. The maidens are organized on the strict principle of division of labor, with Khavronia, a fat girl, taking the major role in winter, and Fevronia, a thinner favorite, coming to the fore during the summer. There is a hint of social criticism here, but more obviously, Leontiev wants to caricature an unpromising way of life open to the young Russian nobleman in order to contrast it to the deeper intellectual search of his hero.

By far the strongest ideology which Rudnev comes up against is that of Mil'keev, a young teacher living on a neighboring estate. Mil'keev is a proponent of unbridled beauty; aesthetics is the only "sure measure" of all things for him and this doctrine has usually been taken to represent Leontiev's own views.[20] In reality, Mil'keev represents only one of the alternatives open to Rudnev—the most important, it is true—and while he helps to shape the protagonist's thought, his own aesthetic principles are firmly rejected in the course of the novel.

In contrast to Rudnev who is withdrawn and pessimistic, Mil'keev is exuberant and optimistic almost to the point of caricature. He loves the fervor and play of life and wants to gambol through it in great skips and jumps of Dionysian enjoyment. This intense feeling for pleasure and beauty helps Mil'keev to draw Rudnev out into the world, but is quickly exposed to be unrealistic and inadequate in the face of life's crueler elements. Mil'keev is unable to break through the psychological defenses of the woman he loves; he almost kills a man in a foolish duel; he leaves to join the armies of Garibaldi but can only manage to get arrested in Petersburg, and so on. Mil'keev wants revolution for the paradoxical reason that revolution will arouse reaction, and in this, as in other issues, he reflects some of Leontiev's own views. But the point is that Leontiev does not let political convictions interfere with the greater inner struggle of his protagonist.

Rudnev gradually learns to compromise between his earlier rejection of the world and Mil'keev's exuberant acceptance. Although recognizing the limitations of science which he calls an "illuminated corner in the drunkenness of eternity," Rudnev marries and opens a hospital, resolving to do his own small part as a doctor. He is grateful to Mil'keev for showing him "an aristocracy of mind," the many faces of beauty, but he moderates this concern with the down to earth medical care of peasants and a recognition that all visions of beauty must be adjusted to the actual world. Thus, at the conclusion of the novel, when a friend is impressed by the carefree happiness of Mil'keev's former wards, Rudnev objects to this overly optimistic appraisal. He points out that individual flaws in each child, ill health, pride, and stubbornness, are the kernels of future sorrow and tension in their lives. Addressing himself directly to Mil'keev's legacy, he concludes that the children's happiness lies not in "eternal gaiety" but in "something else." We have the right to suspect that this "something else" is represented by his own growth into a complex life of struggle and difficulty transcending his initial romantic impulses.

A Husband's Confession

In *A Husband's Confession*, a novella written three years later in 1867, Leontiev has his protagonist directly confront the key tenets of romanticism. The first person narrator is another recluse who, like Rudnev, takes to pondering over philosophical questions at a crucial moment of his life. At one point in his random thoughts he decides to examine the colors of nature, but, not being content with simple admiration for the surface of things, he plunges into a fundamental problem of perception: what makes us think we see what really is, what gives us the right to assume that "trees are green, dawn red, and cliffs black?" The question is used to approach reality in a manner not unlike that of the famous Schellingian, Pavlov: "An ethereal substance is active in infinity, its ... waves strike the nerve of the eye ... But what is a nerve? The conductor of electricity to the cell? But what is electricity? What is a cell? And who will swear that ... a bottomless abyss of life does not seethe in its depths?"[21] With the metaphysical uncertainty of this "bottomless abyss" inspiring his speculations, the narrator goes on to question rationalism and the modern ways of morality as a "madness of steadfastness, common sense, and utility." Bolstered by his recognition of the beauty and power in nature's irrational movement, he can accept an unconventional moral situation and permit his wife, who is much younger than he, to take a lover closer to her own age. He cannot, however, force himself to separate emotionally either from her or from her lover, for whom he also feels deep affection, and indeed he does not want to. When they drown in a storm, he commits suicide.

The important romantic elements we have already encountered are crystallized in this short piece. Accepting the traditional romantic images of abyss and storm as metaphysical principles, Leontiev deprives them of purpose and hope while indicating that conventional morality can hardly exist in such a state of the world. The protagonist experiences his best moments as a result of a type of aesthetic immorality, that is, when he is both enjoying the full power and beauty of the cruel world and when he is free of conventional prejudices about marriage and love. But he is also a victim of this process, for the metaphysical and ethical situation which we see has no hidden design or extraterrestrial dimension. The predominant point of view in the story suggests the rejection of bourgeois morality and banal reality, but instead of another sphere of existence, indicates tragedy and death as a resolution of romantic despair.

Conclusion: Religious Return and Later Work

Leontiev left for consular service in the Balkans four years before *A Husband's Confession* was published. Most of his later work shows the influence of the southern countries, particularly in ethnographic descriptions of native dress, customs, and mores. While this exotic environment provided a rich store of images and sensations, its surface literary reflections should no more be taken to sustain the dynamic of Leontiev's fiction than the imagery of *Podlipki* and *In One's Land*. It is true that Leontiev himself thought that he had reached a new stage of his creative life by moving in the direction of a less skeptical view of the world. His rejection of "Gogolishness," of narrative modes that emphasize the abhorrent or vulgar aspects of reality, attained a kind of apotheosis in the south. He felt that in such stories as "Hrizo," "Polikar-Kostaki," and "Hamid and Manoli," he had finally found a way of writing truly beautiful, nonprosaic literature which did not lower life with excessively vulgar detail and naturalistic emphasis.[22] The fictional perspective is obviously dependent on the transcedental yearning of his religious-romantic self. In the south, Leontiev was still searching for the unflawed and perfect essence of reality untainted by the commonplace and temporal of this world. The Balkans, in the Byronic tradition to which he refers in one of his stories, would seem the ideal place to find beauty and spiritual purity. Yet in the southern tales and novels, as in his earlier work, Leontiev is completely unable to get away from "ugliness," constantly turning to his ideological pursuit of it for catalysis. His major target, as for Herzen and Nietzsche, is again the bourgeoisie and the "European Man." In almost every piece of the southern fiction, Leontiev either explicitly or implicitly contrasts the Balkan natives to the European middle class, the epitome of *poshlost'*, narrrowmindedness, and petty calculation, whose dress, habits, and convictions serve to stimulate his critical sensibility.

The full implications for Leontiev's fiction will have to be worked out in a more exhaustive study, but clearly he retained the spark of intransigence in his literary texts and, as previously, the sense of rejection—intensified by what he imagined to be a Byzantine

Orthodox legacy of disparagement of everything earthly—led to despair and painful impulses of pessimism and tragedy. The religious crisis which began the last twenty years of his life was in itself made up of profound suffering, cholera, and acute fear of dying. Against the measure of inevitable death the socialists no less than the "average man" could only be considered to be shortsighted "spiritual bourgeoisie." "Only one thing is certain—one thing and only one thing," he writes in a characteristic outburst directed at the left, "that is that everything here must perish. And why, therefore, all this feverish concern for the earthly well-being of future generations? What is the purpose of these childish, sickly dreams and raptures?"[23] In broad outline this ideological course, evident both in fiction and sociopolitical essays, was one of doctrinal religious return accompanied by a romantic revival; the more Leontiev attempted to deal with the life beyond in his historical and theological writings, the more he was drawn to a romantic life-vision made up of exotic images from the Balkans. Yet the lure of transcendental verities constantly gave way to disillusionment for its own sake. The cruel beauty and "flowering complexity" of life was transitory and subject to inevitable decay, but try as he could Leontiev never managed to give up the pain of this experiental vision even for spiritual rest and eternal salvation.

Indeed, throughout his later work intransigence became a kind of intellectual method. Leontiev's most characteristic way of forming ideas was to take up the weapons of opposing philosophical camps to criticize, more than to create, turning his training in biology and the empirical method into ridicule of the offshoots of the Hegelian vision and the Absolute Idea's evolution, while professing the traditional romantic distrust of empiricism and logic and rejecting rational procedures:

> . . . "progress" implies the manifestation of some terrible pathological process which gradually reduces a complete organism to the secondary simplification of a corpse, a skeleton, and a heap of ashes.[24]

> If I humbled myself it was not because I came to have less faith in my own reason, but in human reason in general.[25]

Such fundamental skepticism, leading at times to contradictory premises, inspired Leontiev to produce most of his better known turns of thought. When he criticized Dostoevsky and Tolstoy in

1882 for their "rose-water Christianity," he was accusing the writers of participation in humanity, of uncalled-for optimism resulting in what he felt to be a failure of tragic vision and a crucial weakness in ontological sense. The "New Christians," he thought, were simply too involved in the world; they had lost the hard texture of Byzantine Christian objectivity substituting in its stead a murky hope of earthly paradise. His own thought permitted no such hopeful *engagement*, and we can see him turning again to his biological self to question all attempts to create earthly well-being: "It is stupid and shameful for people who have some respect for realism to believe in such an unreal thing as man's happiness, even his approximate happiness. ... It is ridiculous to uphold such an ideal which is neither compatible with historical experience, nor with the laws and examples of natural history."[26] It is not hard to see how the doctrine of "transcendental egoism," Leontiev's formula for salvation, was formed out of a similar cruel and biological sense of life. His core theological argument was for a "personal Christianity" motivated by "animal fear" of death and by the egotistic impulse to save oneself.[27] And while the forthright selfishness of such principles has provoked a strong debate between Russian theologians over the propriety of Leontiev's religious speculations, such an understanding of Orthodoxy was ultimately fully in keeping with the visions of individual salvation that figured so strongly in Russian culture after Nil Sorsky.[28]

The same painful egocentricity, expressing a modern revision of an older cultural value, was the ideological component which can be seen to shape much of the self-involvement of Leontiev's later fiction. As George Ivask has aptly noted, the elegant romantic images of his texts are a reflection of Leontiev's self, an expression of a pervasive narcissism. And yet it should not be forgotten that this was an uncommon and unsettled Narcissus who felt anguish in the very beauty of his own vision. The southern tales and novels are bright, well-polished gems reflecting conflict, cruel passion, banality, and disorder that stand in strange and painful opposition to other images of harmony, grace, and love. Ladnev, the hero of *The Egyptian Dove*, refers to another flower peculiar to Leontiev's sense of metaphor that goes straight to this aesthetic involvement in the pressure of being. It could serve very well as an epigraph to the fiction discussed above: "I knew how to admire roses without forgetting for an instant the pain which I felt from even the smallest of its thorns."[29]

CHAPTER 6

Tolstoy's Ideological Order:
Herzen and *War and Peace*

UNCERTAINTY about the aesthetic function of Tolstoy's ideology is one of the more familiar critical responses to his work. The uncertainty is most frequently evident in studies dealing with his fiction after *Anna Karenina* and his religious crisis, but it has touched the earlier stories and novels as well. *War and Peace* has particularly suffered in this regard, for it is easy to sense a gnawing and persistent suspicion that Tolstoy's core values and intellectual speculations as he expressed them in his philosophy of history can be separated from the intrinsic movement of the novel without causing excessive damage to its artistic merit. The most extreme and obvious manifestation of such criticism can be found in the popular abridged paperback, which in the case of *War and Peace* has usually been carefully pruned of the epilogue and all other overly forceful and direct attempts by the author to express his thought. Editions of this sort have been justified by critics on the grounds that Tolstoy's philosophy is of dubious literary merit and that the writer has failed to weave the crude threads of his ideas into the otherwise fascinating tapestry of the novel.[1]

Such a perspective is not original but has an imposing history behind it, including most notably the works of Henry James and Percy Lubbock.[2] James was the first to suggest to a Western audience that Tolstoy's "loose and baggy monsters" had no design or guiding intellect supporting them; Lubbock, in *The Craft of Fiction* (1921), offered a solution to this supposed chaos by showing how Tolstoy's fiction should be reconstructed to erase the flaws in his aesthetic standards. In both instances there was no attempt to find structure

and order in Tolstoy's text by working from his own ideas as distinct
from the ideas of the critic, and in this sense there was undoubtedly a
kind of spiritual abridgement of War and Peace long before editors
actually brought out their scissors. This is not to say that there is not
an equally distinguished critical tradition behind the notion that
Tolstoy's fiction should be examined and valued for its own intellectual imperatives. The studies of Dmitry Merezhkovsky, Boris Eikhenbaum, and Isaiah Berlin have, in fact, shown us too much of
Tolstoy's mind for us to doubt its importance in his art.[3]

But more work needs to be done, for even in the most interesting
modern exegeses of Tolstoy's texts—John Bayley's Tolstoy and the
Novel (1966) or George Steiner's Tolstoy or Dostoevsky (1959), for
example—the insights of the critic have frequently lacked the hard
realities of ideological context to prove the validity of interpretation.
It is, in fact, a neglect of context which most directly undercuts the
proper use of James's critical legacy—the concern for point of view
and the controlling intelligence of a piece of fiction—even if James
sometimes preferred his own idea of what a viewpoint should be to
the one actually held by another writer. A serious discussion of the
presence or absence of what James called the "center of interest" in
War and Peace surely requires some consideration of the cultural
elements which helped Tolstoy shape his own ideological interests
and point of view.

In this instance, as in the others we have noted, effects of native
Orthodox culture appear in ideological formation at crucial points in
childhood development, in mature reformulation of early values into
secular concerns, in spiritual crisis, and in new gradations of religious
understanding reached at later stages of life. Biographical evidence
for such religious contacts is well documented in critical and biographical literature and includes the devout female guardians who
took young Tolstoy to church and who stimulated his moral sensibilities even in the course of providing him with a largely secular education, the pious peasants and "holy fool" types found in the Tolstoy
household, the funeral services and rituals of confession the young
man participated in and incorporated into early fiction like Childhood, Boyhood, Youth, the intense study of the Bible and church
fathers in the course of formulating key principles, and the later
religious involvements copiously charted by contemporaries, disci-
ples, and Tolstoy himself.[4] Tolstoy's ideology, as clearly as any
Russian writer's, demonstrates the effects of a native religious tradi-

tion, but it also shows the secularization of such cultural material and its transformation into a personal literary vision far removed from accepted Orthodox dogmas. As one scholar who has worked extensively with Russian fiction points out, "Tolstoy was essentially a man who tried to live a religious life [but] ... without links with an established church or religious organization."[5]

It is an understandable temptation to attempt to find constants in this ideological course. Tolstoy was always moved by a strong sense of the moral measure of himself against the principles, originally demonstrated to him by his pious female relatives, of ascetic self-control, kenotic humility, and love. He reworked such fundamental values into the ethical postulate of passive nonresistance, and he never stopped yearning for a free, natural, and commonsensical life in which moral beliefs could be expressed consistently and at maximum force without the hindrance of social artifice, hypocrisy, or temptation. But, as has been amply described in scholarly literature, he received values and ideas through numerous cultural prisms, of which Enlightenment thought and literary sentimentalism were only two of prime importance.[6] Moreover, he reacted differently to ideological stimulants at different stages of his life, and in each instance he changed the meanings of his fiction. Tolstoy's biography reminds us once again that the definition of ideology as it appears in some one text must originate in the local and specific work of a writer as much as in larger cultural patterns. Indeed, in the key case of *War and Peace* the critical task is made considerably easier not only by an awareness of religious origins, but by the basic reexamination of immediate, secular sources. For a major influence on Tolstoy has remained untapped, an influence which can give us a sense of the cultural ambiance necessary both to understand the novel on the author's own terms and to explore the secular transformations and literary uses of at least two long-standing religious concerns—for the self and moral freedom—in one of his important works.

Predispositions: Ideological Stimulants

On 29 January 1857, approximately six years before *War and Peace* was printed, Tolstoy left Russia for the first of two trips to Europe. Paris offered obvious distractions for a young man, and Turgenev, who was said to know France better than his own estate, provided an introduction to Parisian night life the day of the writer's arrival. Turgenev, however, also took the time to arrange a more serious matter, a meeting with Herzen, who by then was living in London. Altough the tête-à-tête came about only during Tolstoy's second voyage, Herzen assured Turgenev by post: "I will be very happy to meet Tolsoy. Tell him from me that I am a true admirer of his talent." The compliment was sincere. Herzen had praised Tolstoy's "Detstvo" ("Childhood") in the second number of his journal *Poliarnaia zvezda* ("The Polar Star") and had written to an acquaintance, M.K. Reichel, that he considered the young author to be "very talented" and his short sketch "Metel'" ("The Snowstorm") a "miracle." Turgenev answered Herzen on 5 March: "I gave your regards to Tolstoy; he was very happy to receive them and asked me to tell you that he has wanted to make your acquaintance for a long time and already likes you as he likes your literary work."[7]

Turgenev's letter is among the first indications of Tolstoy's interest in Herzen's ideas. In the majority of Western studies which have dealt with the two men, this correspondence and various other biographical materials have been treated as the chance data of an interesting but irrelevant acquaintanceship which left no lasting mark on either man.[8] There are two major reasons why critics have dismissed the material in question. First, it is only recently that Western scholarship has begun to place proper emphasis on the unparalleled importance of Herzen's work in Russian culture; second, Tolstoy's response to Herzen was ambiguous and can only be fully understood through the clarification of what Herzen meant to the Russian intelligentsia of the nineteenth century.

A significant point is that Herzen was undersood to wear two hats: the hat of political activist and the hat of a writer and thinker who rejected politics at crucial and creative periods of his life. The first Herzen was the man who left Russia to live in Europe and publish *Poliarnaia zvezda* and *Kolokol* ("The Bell"), forbidden journals read by everyone, and who was accepted both by Western and Russian men of letters alike as one of the progenitors of Russian socialism. The other Herzen was the man who wrote what was one of the nineteenth century's most biting critiques of the revolutionary mentality, *S togo berega* ("From the Other Shore"), who profoundly influenced conservatives like Dostoevsky and Constantine Leontiev, and whose style, grace, and wit in his fiction and his monumental autobiography, *Byloe i dumy* ("My Past and Thoughts"), had little to do with the crude literary manners often found on the Russian political left.

We know how Tolstoy would respond to that Herzen whose *Kolokol* was the symbol and the inspiration of Russian radicalism because we know of Tolstoy's disapproval of Nicholas Cherny-shevsky and his colleagues.[9] It should not be surprising that the writer would speak unfavorably of Herzen in the context of political discussion and polemic, for Herzen inspired journalists and writers whose views were diametrically opposite to his. Such differences, however, do not mean that Herzen's work was entirely lost to Tolstoy for, as we have seen, it often rose above the issues of everyday politics to focus on more basic and subtle questions of existence. Indeed, Tolstoy read the part of Herzen's *oeuvre*, written after he left Russia, that revealed a bitter disappointment with political activity. And it was the philosophical concern evident in this disappointment which held his attention after he had spoken to the émigré.

Tolstoy finally visited Herzen during his second trip abroad in 1860–61. In the two weeks that he spent in London, the two writers met often and discussed various topics at some length; Tolstoy's own comments, made at a much later date, indicate that he saw Herzen "almost everyday."[10] The memoirs of N. A. Tuchkova-Ogareva, G. Rusanov, and Herzen's daughter Natalie, provide additional evidence, but the most interesting material is found in P. A. Sergeenko's interview with Tolstoy given during January 1908. The writer is quoted as saying: "Lively, responsive, interesting, Herzen immediately fascinated me by his personality.... Since then I have never found such a rare combination of depth and brilliance of mind.... He is incomparably above all political men of that time and of this time."[11] Sergeenko's notes are invaluable if we consider the date when they were taken down and Tolstoy's later criticism of many of his early ideological infatuations. Herzen, in short, was one of the few thinkers whose effect withstood the exposure to new ideological influences and Tolstoy's inner battles.

One explanation for this lifelong interest in Herzen's work is that Tolstoy's journey to London occurred during one of the pivotal moments of his life. His diary and letters at the end of the 1850s and during the early years of the next decade reveal an acute if not unusual crisis brought about by the conflicting demands of literature and interests such as agriculture and education. In this period Tolstoy was dissatisfied with the kind of fiction that he had written; it seemed irrelevant to him, and he was constantly troubled by the suspicion that there was more serious work to occupy one's life. On 9 October 1859, approximately half a year before his journey, he wrote to the author and literary critic Alexander Druzhinin renouncing "novels that are charming and entertaining" while wishing that "there was some subject that was really prodding me on to be bold, proud, and strong."[12]

The most obvious result of this dissatisfaction is a radical change in Tolstoy's fiction. We can sense it without difficulty because the style of *War and Peace* and *Dekabristy* ("The Decembrists") is quite obviously not the style of *Detstvo, Otrochestvo, Iunost'* ("Childhood, Boyhood, Youth"), or *Kazaki* ("The Cossacks"). Tolstoy is inspired by a new skepticism; he is less prone to sentimental or romantic colors and more critical than before of all that comes into his field of vision. The first step to understanding *War and Peace* lies within the genesis of this new sensibility, and although its vital ideological dynamic had not yet been given full expression in 1861, the problems which would shape it and Tolstoy's novel had already appeared in hints and glimmers.

Major Issues: Self and History

The primary problem Tostoy confronted was that of structuring his own life, the direction and the form, the moral program of living to follow. The role of planning in personal and social life in relation to destiny, "fatum" or the "natural course of events," can be clearly discerned in the *Sevastopol'skie rasskazy* ("Sebastopol Tales") and the war sketches of the Caucasus, and the concern is obvious as well in Tolstoy's diary and the daily schedules that he made for himself. Is one free to control one's life, to chart a personal map to the moral life? But there was also his concern for events in Russia, the new Russia after the disaster of the Crimean War, which called for a more sweeping view of things and for a philosophy of history in which one's own role in the vast movements and conflicts of nations could be examined. Tolstoy met Herzen during this first mature confrontation between his personal imperatives and the larger designs of Russian society. It was a time when his mind was hungry for work and his fiction ripe for the impetus of intellect. Indeed, the startling intellectual impression produced by Herzen, a brilliant conversationalist, was so strong that Tolstoy immediately took up Herzen's journal *Poliarnaia zvezda* and, in his own words, read it "properly" after leaving London. Here in the article "Robert Ouen" ("Robert Owen"), he again encountered the full force of Herzen's thought, and in a letter he subsequently wrote to his new acquaintance he came to grips with the central issues of Herzen's works:

> I was just preparing to write to you, dear Alexander Ivanovich, when I received your letter. I was preparing to write about the *Poliarnaia zvezda*, which I just now read properly, in its entirety. The journal is wonderful. This is not only my opinion but the opinion of all whom I have seen. . . . Your article about Owen, alas, is too, too close to my own heart. In truth, it could only be possible in our time for an inhabitant of Saturn, come to earth, or a Russian. There are Russians who from fear will not believe your idea (and in parentheses let it be said that it is very easy for them to do so, thanks to the too light tone of your article). It seems that you only address yourself to wise and brave people. The people who aren't wise and brave will say that it is better to keep quiet when one has come to such results, where this result shows that the path was wrong. And to a certain extent you give them the right to say this, in that in place of broken idols you place real life, free will, the design of life, as you say. In the place of huge hopes of eternity, eternal perfection, historical laws, and so forth, this concept is nothing—a button in the place of a colossus. It would be better not to give them this right. Nothing in its place. Nothing with the exception or that force which has toppled the colossus. . . .[13]

Important to note in the letter is Tolstoy's remark that his heart is "too, too close" to Herzen's essay on Owen. From other biographical sources we know that he was equally fond of *S togo berega*, which he read a number of times.[14] His interest is not difficult to understand, for both of these works deal with the problems then foremost in his own mind: what is the course of the world—or more directly the course of European history—and how am I, the individual, to react to it? In "Robert Owen" Herzen approached the first of these issues by defining life as a free, dynamic process where "an abyss of possibilities, episodes, discoveries slumber in [history] and in nature at every step."[15] The world is in a state resembling chaos, but it is a chaos where free will is possible and where the individual has a place. Contact with native religious ideas, German idealism—particularly Schelling's philosophy of nature—and Left Hegelianism inspired both the metaphysical and personal components of this intellectual syndrome. By the time Tolstoy met him, however, Herzen's disappointment with the events of 1848 and the failures of liberal political predictions led him to an even greater emphasis on individualism and his religious legacy of free will. By looking to himself rather than placing his hopes on the Absolute Spirit or future utopian societies, he decided, the individual can find a sphere of existence that makes sense even in the midst of vast and apparently uncontrollable historical events.[16] In attempting to delineate this personal realm, man has to approach the conditions of his being as an open-ended process, for "only in depriving history of any predetermined path do man and history become something serious and real. . . ."[17]

Tolstoy was obviously aware of these issues: "free will" and "huge hopes of eternity, eternal perfection, historical laws," he writes. After coyly remarking that Herzen's concept of free will and "real life" is only for "wise and brave people," he quite forcefully comes out in favor of "that force which has toppled the colossus." The "force" is in part the ironic style with which Herzen ridicules notions of a predetermined future for mankind; but Tolstoy must also have had in mind the pragmatic defintion of the individual's self-interested existence which provides Herzen with much of the inspiration for his attacks. In "Robert Owen" the message of Herzen's irony is particularly clear: "People will not, after all, stop eating and drinking, loving and propagating children, wondering over music and a woman's beauty when they find out that they eat and listen, love and have pleasure for themselves and not for the fulfillment of a higher predetermination and the *quicker* attainment of the *eternal* development of the whole."[18] In *S togo berega* this same response to 1848 and all the other instances of dashed liberal hopes then troubling the European intelligentsia could not be more direct: "My advice is not to quarrel with the world, but to begin an independent, self-reliant life, which would find salvation within itself were the whole world around us to perish."[19] Herzen's point then, Tolstoy must have noted, is that the world is in a state of chaos where human hopes and expectations are often unfulfilled, but that man has a personal sphere of existence in which he *can* operate with relative freedom and moral control.

One the one hand, Tolstoy's response to such a formulation of things should not be oversimplified; it is clear, for instance, that he approached free will with some reservations, both in his letter and later in *War and Peace*. On the other hand, it is even more inadequate to follow the example of a number of important Western studies that emphasize these reservations—with the enthusiastic support of most Soviet scholars—at the expense of the *positive* things that the writer also saw in free will. *War and Peace*, on the whole, has been taken to show both a complete denial of free will and Tolstoy's supposedly categorical acceptance of determinism, the inverse of Herzen's position and a radical break with the native religious emphasis on moral freedom of choice.[20] It is this critical approach, unenlightened by the writer's own interpretation of determinism, which has most contributed to the confusion surrounding Tolstoy's point of view.

Free Will—Historical Skepticism

The "message" of *War and Peace* is that events control men, not men events, for there is some kind of a "dependence" (*zavisimost'*) to which everything is subject. Tolstoy does not involve the protagonists of his novel in a dependence on easily demonstrable causes such as those we find in *An American Tragedy* or a Zola novel, however, but shapes their story out of a vast number of apparently disconnected moments occurring during one of the most confused periods he could find in modern Russian history. The problem is that *War and Peace* brings together something akin to Blok's galloping polka of history, Henry James's refined drawing room waltz, and a multitude of other motifs and melodies, while the usual interpretation of Tolstoy's ideas calls for the steady march of inevitability. The lack of unity between idea and form in this view has never been satisfactorily explained; instead, by some strange critical metamorphosis it has been suggested that there is no unity in *War and Peace* at all.

The cultural issues that troubled Herzen suggest a different perspective and provide the necessary context to an interpretation within which *War and Peace* is not a "loose and baggy monster" dancing to the tune of some mystical artistic cacophony or loosely exuberant appreciation of life. The apparent disorder of the novel is both a definition of things and the controlling technique of the text; it is Tolstoy's way of saying that not only historians or emperors but *writers* as well can never know the absolute nature of the world because the world consists of an infinite number of elements that are beyond human awareness. The vital point missed by such critics as James and Lubbock is that Tolstoy's method of composition has a higher, unifying purpose—the grasp of events which is strikingly reminiscent of Herzen's reaction to the chaos of the world.

Both men discover innumerable, transcendent forces at work in the universe (their movement is precisely the historical process intuitively grasped and accepted by Platon Karataev and General Kutuzov) and both go on to form an epistemology out of the impossibility of fully understanding these basic world forces. When Tolstoy breaks the link of cause and effect—"an event happened only because it had to happen"—he has such a view of existence and the frailty of human cognition in mind. When he writes about the "spontaneous" movement of entire nations, which has nothing to do with the attempts of leaders to guide them, he, like Herzen and the Slavophiles, is thinking of the uncontrollable forces at play in the world and along with them is rejecting important tenets of the Enlightenment.

The puzzling aspects of Tolstoy's definition of freedom and necessity are explainable when set against this intellectual background. At a crucial moment in the epilogue of *War and Peace* we arrive at the conclusion that free will is the "content" of life, necessity is the "form," and "only by their synthesis is a clear conception of the life of man attained."[21] Thus, while Tolstoy is apparently advocating *both* determinism and freedom, his argument is not as paradoxical as it may seem. By necessity as form, Tolstoy means that human beings can ascribe fixed and determinate patterns to similar phenomena and recurring movements of history but that such patterns are only the superficial outlines attainable through human knowledge. The true metaphysics of life is an infinite chaos of elements which is beyond man's finite capabilities. It is indicative that Tolstoy should write about war, one of the clearest symbols of his thought, in these terms: "An innumerable collection of freely acting forces (and nowhere is a man freer than the field of battle, where it is a question of life and death) influence the direction taken by a battle, and that direction can never be known beforehand" (p. 930). In a similar vein, Tolstoy goes to great lengths to distinguish between causes and man-made "laws" of nature. For while true causes are unknowable, the possibility may still exist, in a limited framework and with the recognition of the frailty of man and artist, "to seek the laws common to all the equal and inseparable, interconnected, infinitesimal elements of free will" (p. 1134).

The determinism that Tolstoy and Herzen accept, then, derives from their belief in mankind's depedence on nature's unknowable causes, causes so dark in substance, vast in number, and unpredictable in movement that the vision of universal irrationality and freedom is allowed to prevail in both men's work. And while the objective conclusion of Tolstoy's doctrine, unlike Herzen's, is that God and these elemental forces guide the universe toward some unknown, predetermined end, the emphasis in his ideas lies on the play of life rather than its end, exactly in the spirit of Herzen's disillusionment with the future.

Such a metaphysical tradition, it is true, was not uniquely Herzen's, for writers such as Turgenev and Tiutchev were in its mainstream. But the particular ramifications of Herzen's ideas can serve to illuminate many of the important details of War and Peace as well. Tolstoy, hostile as he was to the Russian left wing in the person of Chernyshevsky, could not have failed to derive strong satisfaction from Herzen's various sieges on all the liberal abstractions which simplified the real, diverse nature of life. Previous to his ecounter with Herzen's work, Tolstoy's fondness for the past and dislike of the "new man" were expressed in such fiction as "Dva gusara" ("Two Hussars") where father and son represent, respectively, the grace and bon ton of the older generation and the crudeness and vulgarity of the new. Tolstoy's early antagonism toward the younger generation, however, was more a reflexive feeling of contempt for social manners outside his own circle than a fully thought-out response, while War and Peace deals with a specific ideological reaction to the ideas of the raznochinets, the "new man" of the Russian intelligentsia, which strikes out much further.

The first indication of this side of War and Peace can be found in the unfinished first draft that Tolstoy mentioned in his correspondence with Herzen. According to Eikhenbaum, the returning exile Labazov of Dekabristy was conceived by Tolstoy as a contrast "to the 'new people' who know no other religion but the religion of progress and no other laws but the laws of history."[22] If Eikhenbaum's hypothesis is correct, Tolstoy's ideological intention had noticeably progressed from the period of "Dva gusara," where the conflict of generations was played out in a charmingly harmless anecdote about the success of the father and the failure of the son in matters of seduction. Tolstoy's more sophisticated ideological foils in *Dekabristy* are the men who, in Herzen's words, spun the "fairy tale of a Golden Age behind us and of eternal progress ahead of us."[23] Apart from the epilogue, where Tolstoy chides the younger generation for using zoological principles to prove that there is no soul and no freedom, there are, of course, no "new men" in *War and Peace*. But, as we will see below, Tolstoy deals with the Napoleons and Speranskys of his novel in the same cruel manner with which he criticized the secular builders of progress living in the 1850s and 1860s.

There is no better introduction to Tolstoy's growing interest in contemporary ideological issues than the opening paragraph of *Dekabristy*, which is very similar to Herzen's work. In this first draft of his novel Tolstoy, like Herzen, directs a caustic, ironic attack on "civilization, progress, questions, the resurrection of Russia" and does so in the same journalistic style which Herzen made famous. *War and Peace* follows the spirit of this nihilistic rhetoric from Tolstoy's opening tongue-in-cheek description of Anna Pavlovna's salon to the sweeping virulence that he develops in a broad historical context. Such passages of the novel as the parody of scholarly historical accounts could easily be interpolated into *From the Other Shore* or "Robert Owen" without doing any noticeable damage to Herzen's style or intentions. Again, I do not want to overstate the case. Indications of Tolstoy's cruel tongue were already present in the second and last sketch of *The Sebastopol Tales*, but in them we find only a glimmer of the sharply polished barbs and wit which run throughout the whole of *War and Peace* as an integral element of style. Obviously Tolstoy had sharpened his literary weapons somewhere, and the ideological shop of "The Russian Voltaire," as Herzen was known, gives us a glimpse of some of the best apparatus then available.

Interestingly enough, one of Herzen's cherished targets was Napoleon; he was, in fact, among the first writers to attack a virtual Napoleonic cult in early nineteenth-century Russian literature (Lermontov's poetry provides an obvious example).[24] The Soviet critic A.A. Saburov has pointed out the striking kinship of specific passages in *Byloe i dumy* with Tolstoy's methods of description.[25] The assault on this "colossus," if we use the terminology of Tolstoy's letter, can also be found in "Robert Owen." In both instances,

Herzen's cutting description of the emperor complements his criticism of the men who profess to determine history. And Tolstoy, as can be expected, follows Herzen's lead in using the same subject to attack notions of predeterminism.[26]

The Salvation of Ego

Tolstoy's critical sensibility is not an end in itself, however, but has a larger purpose within the total design of the novel. The main effect of his ironic attacks on the abstract visions of a predetermined historical movement or the human involvements in war is to make "peace"—the sections of his novel devoted to family life and, in particular, the life of the Rostovs and Pierre and Natasha—an alternative, "real" sphere of existence. This side of War and Peace has been delineated with some clarity by John Bayley. War and Peace, he points out, excludes all "tormenting problems which might be solved by actions other than those of growing up, growing old, marrying, and dying."[27] The intellectual point of this exclusion, however, is best understood in the light of Tolstoy's reading of Herzen. For Herzen, as we have seen, tempered his skeptical view of progress and determinism by indicating that the withdrawal of the individual into his own immediate realm of life offered a free and relatively controllable existence in the midst of uncontrollable historical processes. The recognition of the immediate, pragmatic terms of one's destiny, in part seen as the gratification of self-interest, was the "force" that could provide man with a concrete alternative to the abstract, personless search for a "fulfillment of a higher predetermination."

It would be difficult to find a closer juxtaposition of personal life and the uncertain movement of vast historical events than is made in War and Peace. War, for Tolstoy, represents the same impersonal, chaotic progress of history which Herzen saw in 1848, and if we take peace to mean the individual's existence defined by Herzen from native religious tradition, German idealism, and Left Hegelianism, then the withdrawal of Pierre to his estate and his family becomes understandable as a response to Herzen's advice to "begin an independent, self-reliant life, which would find salvation within itself were the whole world around us to perish." In his own explanation of War and Peace, Tolstoy defined freedom precisely in these terms. "It is very hard to establish the boundary of freedom and necessity," he writes in "Neskol'ko slov po povodu knigi *Voina i mir*" ("A Few Words on the Book *War and Peace*"). "But, in observing the conditions under which our greatest freedom and our greatest dependence appear, it is impossible not to see that the more alienated and therefore the less involved is our activity with the activity of other people, the freer it is, and conversely, the more our activity is involved with other people, the more it is unfree."[28]

The limits of freedom that Tolstoy arrived at, then, were strikingly similar to the peculiar, alienated vision Herzen formulated out of Orthodox ideas of free will and Left Hegelian individualism. Moreover, there is a strong indication that Herzen's detailed views of personality also left their mark on *War and Peace*. In a central passage of the novel Tolstoy follows Herzen's example by contrasting the concreteness of egoism to the abstractions of terms like "patriotism." His answer to the patriot's view of the war is that the majority of people who were involved in and who managed to live through Napoleon's invasion were rightly concerned only with their own personal interest. In fact, those people "who were striving to grasp the general course of events, and trying by self-sacrifice and heroism to take a hand in it, were the most useless members of society." The soldiers who did the actual fighting were not thinking of saving Mother Russia or of a patriot's revenge but were concerned by the quite selfish and immediate detail of the "next quarter's pay, of the next halting place, of Matryoshka the canteen-woman."[29] Herzen's use of egoism as a touchstone of reality in a world permeated with generalizations and abstractions, provides us with an important clue to Tolstoy's perspective on human nature in *War and Peace*.

Conclusion

There is, of course, much more to the novel than issues of freedom and the self but in such a frame of reference the relationship of "war" and "peace" is intelligible, and the conficting and chaotic elements of Tolstoy's text can be seen as an explicit literary response to persistent ideological accents of his culture. Herzen's philosophy of history permits us to go beyond the vague notion of fatalism which is usually imposed on *War and Peace* and to grasp the true intellectual-emotional dynamic of Tolstoy's point of view and his arrangement of fictional material. It is reasonable to suggest, in fact, that Herzen's complex reworking of long-standing values and ideas should be placed next to the purely literary examples of Sterne and Stendhal when we evaluate the sources that helped shape this novel. For the relationship of these two men is a strong argument against the incongruity of form and idea which is commonly attributed to *War and Peace*. It is a disservice to the unity and meaning of Tolstoy's fiction, in short, not to be aware of its ideological affinities with Herzen's search for real freedom of choice in life, his skepticism before secular historical idols, and his emphasis on the central importance of individual existence.

PART III

CHAPTER 7

Ideology as Control:
Tolstoy and Fadeyev

AN APPROPRIATE measure of the value judgements proposed in the preceding chapters would be a literary situation in which the neglect of the self and moral-spiritual issues produces some essential weakness in Russian fiction. If the creative responses to ideology, on the suggested terms of individuality and identity, are indeed integral components of the Russian writer's vitality and insight, then a condition of ideological deprivation, it would have to follow, would critically injure the important textual attributes. The tragic misfortune of Russian culture, of course, is that such a measure is provided in the twentieth century through the evolution of ideas and letters in the Soviet Union.

There has been much of lasting value produced in the Soviet period, it is true, and a number of writers have continued the proud traditions of Russian literature after 1917. Bulgakov, Pasternak, Zamyatin, Sholokhov, and Solzhenitsyn, or even the less-talented Fedin, Leonov, Katayev, Kaverin, and Gorky offer ample evidence of both literary vitality and insight. The truly Soviet literature, however— in a sense impossible for the nineteenth century when there was no "Russian" literature attached to a homogeneous sociopolitical program—is quite a different order of art. This body of fiction is represented by Alexander Fadeyev, Dmitry Furmanov, Fedor Gladkov, Semen Babayevsky, Boris Polevoi (Kampov), and other writers, whose texts are marked by sterility and banality and who provide the key examples of socialist realism, the officially sanctioned aesthetic program of the USSR throughout much of its history.

One typical explanation of the inadequacy of socialist realism—

that it is *too* ideological, too committed to society, politics, and moral rhetoric—fails to take into account the actual internal relationship of the Soviet writer with his culture. Differences of achievement between past and present Russian texts only become more puzzling in this view, for contact with moral and sociopolitical issues enhanced rather than detracted from the typical Russian vitality. Indeed, the telling weakness of Soviet fiction lies not in its social or moral commitments but in the prohibitions which make a true self-involvement in ideology impossible. Soviet literature is not unlike the Soviet constitution in this regard in that its principal failure is the spirit rather than the letter of the law. For in spite of a very sound system of legal codes, everyone in the Soviet judiciary recognizes his impotence before orders issued from someone higher in the bureaucracy, just as every Soviet writer knows that the values he expresses in his fiction are ultimately determined not by his own moral interests and beliefs but by the current program of the party. Deming Brown's thorough and penetrating study of literature after Stalin reaches a similar judgement in suggesting that the avoidance of "serious ideological confrontations" and the absence of "questions of ideological belief" are indications of what has gone wrong.[1] It would be more appropriate, in this regard, to speak of the ideological hypocrisy, rather than the ideological enthusiasm, of Soviet fiction. The distinction is important to make because it helps us not only to justify our value judgements about the soundness of Russian literature and the relative weakness of orthodox Soviet texts, but also suggests a definition of the internal mechanisms and core formulations of a unique and cautionary literary process in the twentieth century.

A clear view of socialist realism from within is provided by the evolution of basic Russian values during its tenure. The native responses to love, brotherhood, sacrifice, and humility are no longer present as a spiritual moral reference brought into fiction by writers, but are evoked, frequently by order of committee, for purposes of propaganda and social control. Most typically, brotherhood, courage, and humility are used by protagonists who argue for some form of sacrifice by citizens and consumers to the larger needs of the state and the future, while inclinations to protest are channeled into the uncomfortable fictional positions of villainous selfishness and egoism which the reader is warned in various ways to avoid. The moral platitudes and external features of Soviet positive heroes are thus related, as in the instance of older Russian positive types, to the perennial kenotic standards, except that they are cynically used in literature, as in various social mechanisms, for political domination rather than for moral catalysis and self-confrontation.[2]

Such ideological hypocrisy is most clearly evident in Soviet responses to the individual. While the rights of the self and personality are strongly defended in media and literature, it is ultimately understood by all except the most naive that the individual is not an independent value standing outside historical and economic forces, but is the tool of government policy. A pioneering student of Soviet literature, Ernest J. Simmons, has described the effect on fictional processes as follows: "Perhaps for the first time in the history of literature art has utterly repudiated the subjective ... and the artist has been forced to kill within himself the desire to convey a personal vision of humanity in his work. The primary purpose of literature in the Soviet Union is to instruct, and the obligation of the writer is to employ his medium to instruct in conformity with the spirit and letter of the latest ideological position of the Communist party."[3] This is not to say that there are no Soviet writers who believe in Marxism-Leninism and who make it their own ideology (although, in fact, very few of the minimally talented ones ever did), but that a true creative commitment even to orthodox doctrine is impossible because the government does not allow any ideology except its own. Vladimir Mayakovsky, one writer who believed in communism and attempted to make it an active part of his poetry, ultimately committed suicide—in large part, we can assume, because of government prohibitions which prevented him from true ideological expression. Such political impositions from the outside had strong technical implications for literary procedure. For the writer's inability to involve his own self in ideology created difficulties of aesthetic discovery and inspiration which lead directly to the sterility of style and form in socialist realist texts.

The acute problem for those Soviet authors who wanted to continue writing after the relatively free environment of the twenties gradually passed into history must have been how to create metaphors, characters, and plots without the active and honest involvement of their own thought and emotional commitments. The practical solution that was agreed upon, I would like to suggest, can be understood in the socialist realist response to Russian literary tradition. Just as the use of older, native values for purposes of social and political control, the development of the formal properties of Soviet literature—as, for that matter, all other aesthetic technique whether it be in the ballet, architecture, painting, or music—ultimately came to depend on a gross imitation of methods and style created in the past. In his "On Socialist Realism," Andrei Sinyavsky, writing under the pseudonym of Abram Tertz, defined the result as a "loathsome literary salad [in which] characters torment themselves though not quite as Dostoevsky's do, are mournful but not quite as Chekhov's, create happy families which are not quite like Tolstoy's, and, suddenly becoming aware of the time they are living in, scream at the reader the copybook slogans which they read in Soviet newspapers, like 'Long live world peace!' or 'Down with the warmongers!' "[4] It can be postulated that by disrupting the normal interaction of a writer and his culture through the interjection of politics into the creative process, socialist realism prevented the kind of intense personal commitment to art which inspires experiment and new literary forms, and forced instead a dulled imitation of already available plots, characters, metaphors, and stylistic devices. The two major characteristics of socialist realism, in fact, can be seen to be the repetition of whatever government policy is current—to the extent, as Sholokhov, Fadeyev, and a number of other writers knew, of rewriting already published novels to adjust for changes in the political situation—and the imitation of past stylistic and thematic conventions to decorate an impersonal ideology.

The suggested literary procedures can be found in most Soviet fiction, but a particularly useful example is provided by the process through which Alexander Fadeyev created *Razgrom* ("The Rout"). Written in 1926-27, the novel portrays the adventures of a Bolshevik troop of soldiers in the period of communist consolidation after the revolution. The principal characters are all stock figures: Levinson, a commissar and positive hero; Morozka and Metelitsa, courageous Soviet guerrillas; Metchik, a representative of the intelligentsia and a foil for Fadeyev's polemic with it; Goncharenko, a factory worker; and Varya, a peasant girl who provides love interest. The troop fails, as can be expected from the title, but their defeat is not consequential and is only meant to illustrate the trials and hardships that communists must go through before the inevitable socialist victory. The importance of this novel should not be gauged only by this dubious thematic structure, for Fadeyev's key role in the politics which impregnated Soviet culture, as well as his methods of using literature, had larger repercussions in the course of socialist realism.[5] Indeed, *The Rout's* essential contribution was to demonstrate a practical way of imitating one particular writer taken from the Russian fictional heritage. The writer was Leo Tolstoy, and it was his stylistic examples and literary devices which allowed Fadeyev to provide an important model for those who remained within the ideological pale created by the government. Such a response to Tolstoy helped produce key components of socialist realism by demonstrating a two-step process of following an older writer's fictional technique while criticizing his ideology and interjecting in its place some of the major tenets of Lenin's party.

Although the published references which Fadeyev made to Tolstoy before and during the period when *The Rout* was being written are very sparse, they demonstrate a thorough knowledge of his work. Among these is a citation taken from Tolstoy's texts which appeared in Fadeyev's notebooks for 1927 (March 3) and, in April of the same year, a note on literary method in "Hadji Murat."[6] In 1928, when *The Rout* was already finished, Fadeyev mentioned Tolstoy in "Against Superficiality," an article aimed at M. Semenov's critical analysis. It "should and could" be shown, he writes, "what is the nature of Tolstoy's world view . . . , how Tolstoy was limited by his class."[7] Much later in 1944 and then in 1955, Fadeyev revealed his intimate knowledge of Tolstoy's diaries, although it would be difficult to establish when he read them. In 1955–56, Fadeyev also examined Tolstoy's use of a number of themes to illuminate one central idea and concluded that such stylistic procedure should be "a canon of artistic work."[8]

However, it was in 1932, approximately six years after finishing *The Rout* and in a time of decisive importance for Soviet literature, that Fadeyev gave the clearest signs of his particular preoccupation with Tolstoy. In the article "About Socialist Realism" he writes: "The contradiction is well known between the idealistic philosophic views of L. Tolstoy and the basic realistic tendency of his work; it is this [contradiction] that has enabled us to call his work 'a step forward in the creative maturity of humanity.' "[9] Two aspects of the statement should be stressed. First, the citation is from Lenin and it shows that Fadeyev knew he could use Tolstoy for his own purposes supported by the most important political authority. Second, in this passage Fadeyev takes his first firm step in separating form and idology, a separation that was an integral part of his reaction to the past. That same year, in the article "My Literary Experience—To the Beginning Author," he went on to give the best exposition of such a process:

> I wrote this novel [*The Rout*] in two years. What basic principles did I use for the work? First of all, in contrast to the pretentious language of my first piece (*The Overflow*), I attempted to write much more simply, to express my thoughts clearly. I subjected the entire work to this task: write it so that it would more clearly, persuasively, exactly, show all of what I see, what I conceive. . . .

> As you know, critics have noted that *The Rout* was influenced by a great Russian writer, Leo Tolstoy. This is partially true, partially not. It is not true in the respect that there is not a trace of Tolstoy's world view in this work. But Tolstoy always captivated me by the life and validity of his artistic images. . . . While working on *The Rout*, I involuntarily assumed certain characteristic elements of Tolstoy's language, of the rhythm of a phrase. This circumstance doesn't worry me particularly: any artist who is beginning to work depends on the experience of the past. . . . If an artist succeeds in revealing new elements of reality, in developing new ideas, then the influence which the more experienced master has exerted on him in the process of study, does not affect his independence, and it becomes more and more solid during the artist's growth. Undoubtedly, for each of us who learns his trade from a classic writer, it is necessary to study critically both the ideological content of [that writer's] legacy and [his] formal method of artistic expression.[10]

A discrepancy here should be singled out. Fadeyev was not beginning his literary career and his own remarks about an abrupt change in style from his early work to *The Rout* point to this earlier fiction. But *The Rout* was, in a certain sense, a new departure for him, for the political conditions which helped create this novel did not strongly affect his earlier texts, nor did they affect the ornamentally rich fiction of Boris Pilnyak, Artyom Vesyoly (Kochkurov), Babel, and Vsevolod Ivanov. The reason for the error is understandable because Fadeyev is speaking of a literature in which he is beginning to work and which differs markedly from the daring and highly individualistic literary responses to the communism of the twenties. Furthermore, perhaps as a result of the creative vacuum fostered by the change in political conditions, he goes on to offer a practical method of promulgating the new type of fiction. And as can be seen from the second part of the citation, this method hinged on utilizing the past in terms of the dichotomy discussed earlier.

The reaction of one writer, no matter how important his position in literary circles or in the circles that exercise literary control, does not, of course, entirely explain the drastic change in the mode of Soviet fiction in the 1930s; the demand for simplicity and unsophisticated prose undoubtedly reflected five-year-plan sensibilities which needed propaganda and feared the nonutilitarian. But the fact that an ornamental style had not been noticeably present in Russian culture since the period of the baroque, with the possible exception of Gogol, and was consequently a step toward creative independence from the established tradition of the past century, could not fail to influence the Soviet writer in his search for a workable solution to totalitarianism. It can be ventured that while the spirit of innovation and experiment in twentieth-century ornamentalism demanded a commitment to art which was rapidly becoming impossible, the past century offered a familiar and rich store of literary formalities which could easily, with a minimum of intellectual labor, be called upon. Indeed, as Fadeyev hastens to point out, the only problem was maintaining the separation of ideological content and formal method as a precaution against any alien intellectual moments in the work of the classics. Thus, we can expect *The Rout* to mimic Tolstoy's literary devices and to interject current sociopolitical doctrine where Tolstoy would depend on his powers of speculation.

Perhaps the most obvious use of Tolstoy's work can be seen in the syntactical structure adopted in *The Rout*. Typical of *War and Peace*, *Anna Karenina*, and most of Tolstoy's fiction are phrases, sentences, or even paragraphs which convey the sense that "a given situation happened not because ... but because." Syntax, in this instance clearly reflects attempts to discard the false core of things and to get at the real principles of life. The beginning of the short story "After the Ball," for one example, shows a character at the height of such a process: "You say that man can not understand by himself what is good, or what is bad, that everything depends on the event.... I will tell you of myself.... My whole life has been formulated, one way or another, not by the environment but from something completely different." Obviously, Fadeyev could not accept the idea of this

particular paragraph: to say that man is not created by his environment would be too contrary to the spirit of Marxism-Leninism. But
Fadeyev does accept the bare form, and we can trace numerous
instances in *The Rout:*

> He went on even more carefully and warily, not because he wanted to
> remain unobserved, but so that he might not frighten the smile off the
> guard's face.[11]

> When he recognized Levinson, Metchik was embarrassed, not so
> much because his rifle was out of order, but because he had been taken
> unawares with such thoughts [p. 142].

> Stashinsky could see that he praised Levinson not only because Levin-
> son was clever, but because it pleased the man to ascribe to somebody
> qualities he himself did not possess [p. 82].

> It seemed to her that he alone, so good-looking, so modest and tender,
> could satisfy her yearning for motherhood, and that she had fallen in
> love with him for no other reason. (In reality this feeling had arisen in
> her only after she had fallen in love with Metchik, while her infertility
> had physical reasons behind it which did not depend on personal
> desires.)[12]

Another link between Fadeyev's and Tolstoy's literary devices can
be seen in the psychological approach to characterization used by
both men. Particularly relevant are the frequent internal monologues
that are often found in *The Rout*. Metchik, Morozka, Levinson, and
other protagonists all carry on unmistakably Tolstoyan conversa-
tions with themselves.[13] Not only are they depicted through a
method of characterization typical of Tolstoy's texts, but their very
thoughts carry the unmistakable tone of Tolstoy's characters. The
"smoke of gunpowder and heroic deeds" of Metchik's dreams and
their contrast to the brutal reality of war bear an obvious resemblance to young Petya Rostov's flights of imagination. The Soviet
warrior's reaction to the first horse given to him ("What am I—a
little boy?") is colored by the same childish desire to be accepted as a
grown man which worries Petya and the protagonist of *Childhood,
Boyhood, Youth*. Metelitsa, once he realizes that death is imminent,
accepts his fate in a manner virtually identical to Prince Andrey's:
"However, he groped on and on until he eventually realized with
final, desperate certitude that this time there was no chance of escape.
And once he was convinced of this, the question of his own life and
death ceased to interest him" (p. 165).

But there is a further parallel which can be drawn between Metelitsa's death and Tolstoy's work. The particular chapter in which
Metelitsa is shot is entitled "Three Deaths," the title which Tolstoy
gave to one of his stories. Tolstoy was largely concerned with showing the differences between the deaths of a noblewoman and a
peasant. The peasant accepts his fate and faces death calmly and
without futile struggle, to the point of giving away his boots on the
condition that the recipient erect a tombstone over his grave. The
noblewoman does not accept her fate, cannot face the thought of her
death, and dies foolishly, striving to the end to find a miraculous cure
which will save her life. In the process she betrays her human dignity
and makes life miserable for all around her. Metelitsa, like the
peasant and unlike the noblewoman, dies a brave death. In contrast, a
man shot in reprisal by Levinson's partisans dies ingloriously, plead-
ing for his life. Thus, in all probability, the idea of presenting a
positive virtue through the "proper" sacrificial death of a partisan
came out of Tolstoy's story, although the exploration of ultimate
experiential issues was replaced by Fadeyev with the current political
demand for sacrifice and defense of the party.

Another law of psychological dynamics which we can observe in
Tolstoy's characters is the sudden, abrupt nature of changes in their
feelings. It is typical for Tolstoy's heroes to be suddenly struck by
something, to sharply change their intentions under the jolting
awareness of some essential truth. Pierre's reawakening to his love of
Natasha is of this nature. Pierre has no thoughts about his feelings till
he meets Natasha at Princess Marya's residence: "But at that moment
Princess Marya said, 'Natasha!' And the face with the intent eyes—
painfully, with effort, like a rusty door opening—smiled, and
through that opened door, there floated to Pierre a sudden, overwhelming rush of long-forgotten bliss, of which, especially now, he
had no thought. It breathed upon him, overwhelmed him and swal-
lowed him up entirely. When she smiled, there could be no doubt. It
was Natasha, and he loved her" (p. 1038).

This abrupt awareness of a profound thought, of real feeling, is
also typical of Fadeyev's characters. For one example, Varya's
thoughts about Metchik go through this process: "And suddenly she
felt that she did not at all want to harbor resentment and evil notions
directed against him, or to suffer from them herself when everybody
around was so contented and nobody worried their heads about

anything, and when she too might be thoughtlessly happy. There and then she made up her mind to cast all other things from her head and to go to Metchik; now she no longer saw anything humiliating about such a step" (pp. 131–32). Metchik himself undergoes a sudden emotional reaction which smacks of Tolstoy's method of characterization: "Metchik's chance remark had evidently awakened a host of unwanted memories in Baklanov. With sudden passion, Metchik began to argue that it was not in the least a bad thing, but quite good, that Baklanov had not been in high school" (p. 99). The difference between the two sets of responses is that in Tolstoy's texts the character's sudden realization led to basic truths and complex issues of experience the writer wants to confront; in Fadeyev's work the shock of awareness introduces banal notions of feminine sexuality and social class. Both Varya's and Metchik's platitudes are derived from Marxist-Leninist doctrine; Varya is stimulated by a sexual drive based on the most vulgar of materialistic views of personality, and Metchik defends, with a gross Marxian sentimentalism, the rights of the lowly and uneducated.

In striking out for the new ways of literature, Fadeyev argued against the persistent lyrical descriptions of nature which created much of the beauty of early Soviet prose. The Soviet critic Bushmin was entirely right when he wrote that "the author of The Rout followed the traditions of the old masters of realism in his methods of description."[14] Fadeyev's nature, in the main, is simple and uncolored by extreme flourishes in language. Bushmin describes this particular aspect in detail and there is no need for extensive analysis. But Bushmin does not clarify a major characteristic of Fadeyev's style and its origins in Tolstoy. Strikingly enough, Fadeyev himself pointed out where he was remiss to Bushmin after reading his critical essay. In a letter of 11 October 1948, Fadeyev writes: "The landscape often serves [Tolstoy] the function of expressing a deep thought (remember Prince Andrey and the old oak, and later this same oak, covered with green) and—even more than with Turgenev—serves to express feelings which give emotional color to the condition of characters."[15]

Fadeyev was focusing on a literary technique that he had already incorporated into his own text using Tolstoy's method of introducing environment and setting to develop characterization. The following example from *The Rout* is typical: "Every morning when they were carried out of the stuffy barrack hut, the quiet fair-bearded old man Pika came up to Metchik. He made Metchik see an old forgotten picture: in tranquil stillness, near an ancient, moss-grown hermitage, a quiet and clear-browed old man wearing a calotte sits fishing on the emerald-green bank of a lake. A peaceful sky above the old man's head; fir trees, peaceful and languorous, all around; the peaceful lake overgrown with rushes. Peace, dreams, silence ..." (p.20). Bushmin cites this passage in his article but does not explain that the rustic scene is clearly supposed to reflect Fadeyev's criticism of Metchik's impractical, idealistic character, as does this following excerpt: "His thought carried him far away—into the radiant days of the future; they were light and airy and melted imperceptibly like the gentle, rosy clouds over the glades of the taiga. He pictured himself returning together with Varya to the town in a jolting train with open windows, beyond which clouds as gentle and rosy as these would sail above the distant, hazy mountain ranges. The two of them would sit at the window, side by side, very close to each other, Varya murmuring soft words to him, he stroking her head and her plaits, as golden as burning daylight ..." (pp. 62–63). After Morozka realizes that Varya loves Metchik, we read: "He felt forsaken and lonely. It seemed to him that he was sailing over a huge, deserted field and its terrifying emptiness only accentuated his loneliness" (p. 71).

Tolstoy's work further served Fadeyev in constructing a new type of protagonist—the political commissar or party representative—who would be used throughout socialist realist fiction to argue for immediate government goals. Earlier, writers such as Vsevolod Ivanov and Dmitry Furmanov had created amazing Bolshevik heroes—Nikita Vershinin, Chapayev, Serafimovich's "Iron-Jaw" Kozhukh—who were hardly credible but strikingly forceful giants fighting for the glorious future. Such fictional types were all too representative of poetic fancy and unbridled literary imagination to be the reliable spokesmen of government needs. Some one stock protagonist was needed for this function and Fadeyev provided a solution by using Tolstoy's fiction to invent Levinson, a much more ordinary, "realistic" protagonist who directly interjects party ideas into the text. Below, I will examine Levinson as a particularly representative model of technical imitation and ideological sterility but first I would like to show some of the typical modes of description taken from Tolstoy which are shared by almost *all* of Fadeyev's protagonists.

In 1935, Fadeyev made the following notation after reading Stanislavsky's My *Life in Art:* "An example of the approach from the external to the internal: one half of the mustache pasted higher than the other helped to reveal a character. (L. Tolsoy—the role of a stearine spot in one of the works of the artist Mikhailov in *Anna Karenina)."*[16] In other words, our writer's notebooks show that he related the use of a particular detail in characterization—a stearine spot, a mustache—to the work of Tolstoy. Indeed, one of Tolstoy's favorite devices was to force the impression of one particular element of a character's physique on the reader's awareness. We remember Elena most vividly for her "white shoulders," her brother for his harelip and idiotic speech, Pierre for his huge clumsy figure, Kutuzov for his tired old face. Tolstoy selects one or two physical details and by constantly repeating them in the activity of his characters, creates a central leitmotif of description from which the reader can generalize to the entire nature of a personality. As Fadeyev points out, each of these external details carries with it a higher, "internal" meaning. Elena's white shoulders symbolize her depravity and sexuality; her brother's grotesque lip, the nature of court figures whom Tolstoy thoroughly satirizes; Pierre's bearlike clumsiness, his groping and awkward search for the meaning of life; Kutuzov's tired face, the acceptance of fate and the understanding that men do not determine the course of events. Fadeyev carries this technique into his own work.

A typical physical detail which is used extensively throughout *The Rout* involves the eyes of the characters. We read of Levinson's "foreign, big eyes," Morozka's "green-hazel" and Varya's "smoky" ones, and of Metchik's "poor, lost look." Varya's and Morozka's eyes are also used to convey the feeling of a particular moment. After one of their excursions into the forest, the two return "hiding their eyes from each other, tired and languid." These "tired and languid" eyes are indications, we can assume, not only of the essence of their sexual experience but also of the nature of their entire relationship and Varya's escape from it in Metchik's arms.

There are numerous other details which serve the same function of characterization. Interesting in *The Rout* are Goncharenko's "large, knotty hands." While Varya's large hands, like her large bosom, should convey her primitive, peasant nature, Goncharenko's hands help to establish his love for work and proletarian determination. Morozka's disobedient locks of hair crudely prepare us for his thievery and reckless spirit. Metelitsa's "sharp nostrils" characterize his keen mind and lithe body. Doctor Stashinsky's unbending figure and rigidly tough spine form the physical detail which is best supposed to predispose the reader to understand the doctor's unwavering act of mercy killing. Finally, Levinson's small body is an important part of Fadeyev's differences with the conventions of early Soviet literature. For in this period, it is not the "iron jaw" of Kozhukh or Chapayev's legendary figure which would lead the party to victory but the ideas of Marxism-Leninism which govern Levinson's puny physique. Thus, we are brought to the question of Fadeyev's response to Tolstoy's ideological heritage; as we have seen, the formal side of Tolstoy's fiction was imitated directly and without embarrassment.

During his career as a cultural bureaucrat Fadeyev was chairman of a committee which was preparing Tolstoy's work for publication. In March of 1949, he wrote out a list of suggestions to its members. One suggestion was:

> It is doubtful that one can put out the texts of even Tolstoy's fictional work without a short introduction which will help the reader to understand and judge properly Tolstoy's ideological-artistic development. . . . It is impossible, for instance, not to comment on the challenging, 'aristocratic,' remarks of Tolstoy. . . . It is no less important to contrast the first variations of Kutuzov's and Bagration's images with the final embodiment of their images in the novel. Such differences present a particularly good opportunity to place Tolstoy's views on the historic role of these generals under criticism. . . .[17]

In 1950, Fadeyev repeated the same demand after V.F. Lebedev naively submitted his memoirs of Tolstoy for comment. Fadeyev returned the manuscript with this criticism: "Insofar as your meeting with Tolstoy was connected with his religious search, one just cannot write that the reason for the meeting was Tolstoy's book *God's Kingdom is within You*; one must dwell longer on Tolstoy's religious views, they must be explained and they must be criticized."[18] As we will see, Fadeyev had much earlier attempted his own criticism in the figure of Levinson.

The one particular motif of Tolstoy's thought which Fadeyev, as a good party member with a firm knowledge of Lenin, could not possibly admit, was the wavering and seemingly inconclusive historical determinism of *War and Peace*. For Tolstoy, as we have seen, many causes, many elements, went into shaping the course of things. The major ideological argument of *War and Peace* was directed at the historians, writers, and politicians who saw history not in the many unexplainable causes which really determine events but through the simplified view of a predetermined future. Tolstoy's devastating portrayal of Napoleon and of the generals on both sides who thought they controlled the flow of battle was created with such a polemic in mind. Obviously, given Lenin's history-creating vanguard, with its finger supposedly placed firmly on the pulse of the world, Fadeyev could either pretend not to notice this aspect of Tolstoy's work or directly pick up the gauntlet. In the figure of Levinson, we see that he chose the latter path.

Levinson stands opposite to the hero of *War and Peace* in one vital respect: General Kutuzov feels he does not control events; Levinson knows he does. Because Fadeyev maintains his formal debt to Tolstoy in creating Levinson no less than in the depiction of the other protagonists we noted, his character structure is one of the most obvious examples of the separation between literary convention and ideology which took place in the creative process that brought forward *The Rout*. For instance, Levinson has Kutuzov's "rare patience and doggedness," the same ability to communicate with soldiers and peasants, the same sly approach to his subordinates. In order to inspire confidence in his men, he, like Kutuzov, pretends to have a sure draft to the fate of his soldiers. Both, in reality, have none. As we will see, later Fadeyev does give Levinson the power to understand and control events; here, however, Levinson is identical to the Russian general in his ability to put up a good bluff. Another technique meant to build morale in Levinson's soldiers is taken straight out of *War and Peace*. After Borodino, Kutuzov's famous response was "The battle is won," although nothing of the sort had happened. Levinson gives commands with the same assurance and the same neglect of cold facts. Last of all, in a scene strikingly reminiscent of the legendary Council of Tilsit, Levinson, like Kutuzov, listens calmly to the various arguments of his lieutenants and, when all are finished, gives his unequivocal decision to retreat. The formal similarities that exist between the two leaders are obvious, and it is not too extreme to say that one appears to be the caricature of the other.

On the other hand, Kutuzov's success in *War and Peace* was due entirely to the fact that he did not attempt to understand or control the stream of events. Fadeyev provides the opposite argument for Levinson: "Not that he believed, either then or now, that an individual was incapable of influencing events in which masses of men were involved—no, this view seemed to him the worst sort of human hypocrisy, a camouflage for the weakness of those who had recourse to it, for their lack of the will to action. . . . In this second period he acquired the power to direct events; the more clearly and accurately he divined their genuine course and the mutual relation of forces and of the men involved—the more complete and more successful was this power of his" (p. 173). The passage is all dead weight in the ideological sense; it is an insertion into the text, without any intellectual work on the part of the author, of Lenin's theory of the conscious vanguard. Levinson's power and will to action are ultimately hypocritical, in the sense of ideological hypocrisy noted previously, for they are not independent, self-explored values but are shown to be valid only in expressing the victory of the party and the inevitable triumph of Marxism-Leninism. The character's spiritually emasculated political meaning is a far cry, of course, from the personally felt, ideological exploration of the individual and historical context that Tolstoy undertook in protagonists like Pierre Bezukhov.

Most of such examples serve to illustrate a crucial pattern of Soviet aesthetic reaction to an environment which prohibited the natural relationship of ideology and literary form. It is true that the correlation between the death of creative formal experiments and literary technique and the imposed end of ideology is not necessarily direct, and the purpose of this essay was not to establish irrevocable proof of a direct relationship. Moreover, no attempt to demonstrate a unique influence on Fadeyev's work was intended since other writers could have been used to provide similar material for imitation. But I would like to suggest that the outlined reaction to the past is, at the very least, an indication of an abnormal development of literature—of an environment which spoiled the intellectual reservoirs of its writers, forced a rabid dependence on the purely mechanical elements of its legacy, and prohibited the normal reformulation and growth of its complete heritage. By speaking of this total heritage, I do not mean to say that Fadeyev should have mimicked or even concerned himself with Tolstoy's philosophy but that the results of his labor would have surely been more valuable to the existence of literature as a living, ever-changing force if he, like Tolstoy, had been allowed to extend his own mind and vision beyond the boundaries established by the state. The telling examples of a literature in which ideology is deprived of the writer's identity can only remind us again of the decisive role played by values of the self in past literary achievements.

CHAPTER 8

The Hopes of Ideology:
Conclusion

IT WOULD NOT do justice either to the historical strength of Russian culture or to the state of letters in the USSR at the time this book is being written to end on the disheartening ideological note of socialist realism. There was, it is true, ample ground for pessimism after the period of political thaw in the 1950s and 1960s failed to produce substantial changes in Soviet society or in the prevalent mediocrity of its fiction. Giving proper credit to the creative forces of the Russian literary tradition, on the other hand, suggests that some hope for future literary growth is a reasonable critical expectation as long as the vital, internal values which sustained writers in their past achievements remain active.

Such a hopeful appraisal requires a strict discrimination between the organic health of Russian literature and its nineteenth- and twentieth-century derangements. In particular, sociopolitical history should not be confused with literary tradition which has always, even at the worst of moments, found writers to maintain its independence. There is, it is true, a strong sociopolitical line within the culture leading from members of the radical intelligentsia such as Belinsky and Chernyshevsky to the policies of Fadeyev and Zhdanov. The victory in socialist realism of their argument for a literature geared to immediate social problems, however, was hardly the representative course of Russian fiction in past or present. Belinsky and Chernyshevsky no more represented the texts of Dostoevsky and Tolstoy than Zhdanov can be said to have represented Russian literature in arguing that Soviet writers use nineteenth-century realism to create propaganda.[1] In such instances, of course, it is more appropriate to speak of *misrepresentation* created with the purpose of integrating literary texts into the designs of political activists.

In making such discriminations I am not arguing against the premise, stated earlier in this study, that the vitality of Russian fiction in part derived from writers grappling with the immediate and pressing problems of their society. Indeed, because the issue of sociopolitical involvements cannot be limited to the radical intelligentsia but goes straight to the heart of the ideological intensity we have noted in all the Russian writers, it is important to distinguish between two different types of social response. There were, after all, both those men of letters such as Chernyshevsky for whom society and politics were ultimate concerns, and those for whom the literary exploration of social issues was the occasion for an involvement in larger, basic problems of human experience. My major premises have been that key values of the native religious heritage stimulated the second, most important literary sensibility—although Chernyshevsky and the radical intelligentsia can also be seen to have been influenced by other, equally persistent religious forces—and that it was in this realm of ideology that the insight and vitality we value in Russian texts arose.

Insufficient differentiation between politics and literature, Chernyshevsky and Dostoevsky, nineteenth-century fiction and socialist realism, suggests a partial explanation for a long-standing paradox in value judgements about Russian culture. The genius of Herzen, Tolstoy, Dostoevsky and other writers is universally recognized and yet there is a fundamental belief accompanying the recognition of literary merit of some essential backwardness in the Russian milieu, of a "silence" in its intellectual-aesthetic tradition, or a lack of originality and a dependence on the West in its creative vigor. Clearly such negative judgements are most valid in the important sectors of the socially committed literature noted above, and are much harder to defend in the instance of a Tolstoy or Dostoevsky. Aside from a blurring of distinctions, however, the evaluative paradox also stems from the important internal dilemmas of Western culture and, in particular, the ambivalent attitude of twentieth-century intellectuals toward their own religious heritage. In its deep attachment to native religious roots Russian literature acts as a constant reminder of values and beliefs that have been eroded or completely lost in the West as well as in the Soviet Union; and it is not surprising, therefore, that our painful modern transitions to analytical sensibilities and scientific technology inspire both criticism of such past cultural commitments as well as a sense of loss and appreciation. Tolstoy, Dostoevsky, and Solzhenitsyn are often judged to be reactionary but also elicit our praise for the exploration of spiritual and humanistic problems that touch some older, cherished sense of values.

Much of what has been said in the preceding pages suggests that the crippling defeat in Russian literature during the Soviet period was not in Western sensibilities, as has been postulated by some literary scholars, but in this same native religious-moral tradition which invigorated earlier literary appraisals of society and politics with the larger, eternal questions of man's self and existence on earth. If we place the proper emphasis on internal sources of the Russian creative endeavor, moreover, then the twentieth-century defeats are less likely to be taken to be a permanent condition, and hope of a cultural rebirth is suggested by the very persistence of Orthodox and kenotic values even in their perverted uses. An optimistic appraisal of Soviet literature suggests that the values themselves of individuality and dignity, of spiritual pride, free will, love, brotherhood, and humility continue to be strong among the Russians, and that it only requires recognition of their perversion in Soviet history for a fundamental shift to occur. Indeed, the predominance of ideological commitment— of ideas and values received in their ultimate meanings— over other historical and social forces points to a literary future opposite from the one imagined by party theoreticians. If Soviet communism demonstrates anything it is that ideologies or perversions of ideologies determine economic and social forms rather than the other way around. It is not difficult to imagine, then, that even a slight shift to a healthier and more honest sense of values than now prevails in the USSR will bring down propaganda superstructures, topple literary mausoleums, and allow an unobstructed involvement of Russian writers with their true cultural selves.

Some literary texts, along with theatre and painting, have already provided such culture shock by asserting, once again, the traditional ideological function of confronting society with spiritual visions of the self. The period of the thaw was marked by Vladimir Dudintsev's *Ne khlebom edinym* ("Not by Bread Alone," 1956), a work that clearly looked back to older, spiritual traditions.[2] In retrospect Edward J. Brown seems right in judging the novel to be unsuccessful.[3]

The central situation of a brave scientist fighting for new ideas against the establishment is grossly derivative and sentimental, the characters are wooden, and the language is uninspired. And yet Dudintsev's work was immediately taken to be a sign of hope, both in the East and the West. The reason for the enthusiastic response, I suspect, was a recognition by readers that the novel had brought back literary exploration of morals in the classic Russian form of the individual's sacrificial struggle in the name of verities higher than those of society and politics. There seemed then to be a strong possibility that Russian fiction would once more respond to the author's sense of values rather than to the legislated morality of socialist realism; Dudintsev's achievement was to provide a strong reminder of this native source of strength, if not to attain a high degree of craftsmanship.

The expectations generated by *Not by Bread Alone* were soon justified by the Italian publication of *Doctor Zhivago* (1957). Out of a complex and multidimensional use of religious, philosophic, and historical motifs, Pasternak focused on one key situation, the conflict between Marxism-Leninism's triumphant ideologial course and the native concern for identity represented by Zhivago. Identity was defined through three major themes in the novel: the exploration, reminiscent of Tolstoy and Herzen, of the individual's stand against historical intrusion; the opposition of personal moral freedom to moral doctrine imposed by external forces; and the anguished appraisal of the writer's aesthetic task in the midst of political terror. The dominant issues were formulated throughout the novel and crystallized in Zhivago's poems by the skillful use of traditional Christian symbols and ideas. Of particular importance was the religious sense of communion with a transcendent order of things; it created the principal hope for each variety of identity, and inspired Zhivago's primary role of organic participation in the cosmic order, his derivation of moral and aesthetic strength from it, and his personal and literary expression of a spiritual human destiny greater than materially limited or socially determined meanings. The wholeness of life that Zhivago experiences, as Rufus Mathewson noted, was ultimately a product of the Russian writer showing once again how individuals "know communion—akin to Walt Whitman's 'knit of identity'—with time and immanent being."[4]

Nothing more clearly pointed to the hidden strength of the native literary tradition, however, than the publication in 1966–67 of Mik-

hail Bulgakov's *The Master and Margarita*. Written at the height of
Stalinism, the novel demonstrated the supreme independence of
literature in sociopolitical history while sabotaging society and politics through the exploration of ultimate issues and the creation of a
magnificent religious vision. Bulgakov's fiction was anticipated most
directly by Gogol, both in the depiction of moral grotesqueness and
vulgarity and in the use of humor and the supernatural to make
readers aware of essential deficiencies in the fiber of the profane. The
use of the Christ story in juxtaposition with Soviet urban life offered
an inspired continuation of deep-seated religious concerns, but it
also incorporated a highly original sense of narrative, myth, philosophy, and comedy. Fully in keeping with the best of his literary
heritage, Bulgakov skillfully linked his talent with basic literary-
religious values to undermine a superficial sociopolitical reality and
confront essential questions of morality and being.[5]

Approximately six years after the publication of *The Master and
Margarita*, Alexander Solzhenitsyn wrote in his monumental *Gulag
Archipelago*: "Thanks to *ideology* the twentieth century was fated to
experience evildoing on a scale calculated in the millions."[6] In both
his fiction and polemical texts it was evident that Solzhenitsyn was
most concerned with those ideological systems in which a spiritual
human identity is rejected or neglected. *One Day in the Life of Ivan
Denisovich* (1962) introduced this literary perspective by combining
Shukhov's triumph over political impositions with the routine exercise of his human capacities. In his banality Ivan Denisovich expressed the victory of the human mean over history and social arrangement. Nerzhin pointed to the same concern for identity in *The
First Circle* (English edition 1968). Whatever the sociopolitical situation, Solzhenitsyn wrote, the first human task is "to be oneself"; the
basic values of the Russian people, his protagonist learns, do not
depend on class origin, work, or education but are formed by an
assertion of one's soul.[7] The same vision of individual moral responsibility arising out of transcendent qualities is glimpsed by Kosto-
glotov in his struggle with repressive social forms, cancer, and the
inevitability of death. Olda in *August, 1914* (1971) defends the
"spiritual life of the individual" against the notion that life is totally
dependent on material conditions. "Each individual," she decides,
"has . . . in spite of his environment, a personal responsibility," and
this principle was clearly at the center of the large historical pano-

rama Solzhenitsyn imagined.[8] Finally, the 1978 commencement address, "A World Split Apart," reminded a Harvard audience of "the moral heritage of Christian centuries with their great reserves of mercy and sacrifice" and argued against the secular debasements incipient in technology and modern life.[9]

Solzhenitsyn was joined by a host of other writers motivated by similar impulses to reach out to their literary heritage not only for the methodological procedures of their craft but for an appraisal of ideologies and a revitalization of basic values. The response to the native tradition may proceed in a number of ways; it may include the discovery of the religious revival before the revolution which went into the essays of *Vekhi* and which later inspired the contributors of *Iz-pod glyb*. It may take the form of the village subjects and deep-seated values which writers such as Vasily Shukshin use as a counterpoint to modern Soviet beliefs and urban life, or the form of Andrei Voznesensky's poetry with its exploration of twentieth-century antihumanism. It may incorporate folk psychology and emotional nuance such as that analyzed by Valentin Rasputin, or it may encourage, as in the case of the Taganka Theatre's Yuri Liubimov, interpretations of Gogol and Dostoevsky reminiscent of Dmitry Merezhkovsky's nightmares of twentieth-century materialism. Whatever the cultural forms they produce, however, we can surely expect the persistence of the perennial Russian standards and the intensity of commitment to them to eventually bring about organic and self-motivated change. The literary hints that are available suggest that such a change, if it does occur, will bring a new intensity and insight to the particular Russian explorations of ideology, and to the problems of totalitarianism, technology, and dehumanization which trouble the twentieth century.

Notes

CHAPTER 1

1. See A. Naess, *Historia del Termino Ideologia desde Destutt hasta Marx* (Buenos Aires, 1964). See also Clifford Geertz, "Ideology as a Cultural System" in *Ideology and Discontent*, ed. David E. Apter (New York, 1964), pp. 47–52; Daniel Bell, "Ideology and Soviet Politics," *Slavic Review*, 24, 4 (Dec., 1965): 591–603, and *The End of Ideology*, rev. ed. (New York, 1965); Henry D. Aiken, "Philosophy and Ideology in the Nineteenth Century," in *The Age of Ideology, the Nineteenth Century Philosophers*, ed. Henry D. Aiken (New York, 1956), pp. 13–26. For a typical use of ideology in American literary criticism to designate the habit or the ritual of showing respect for certain formulas, see Lionel Trilling, "The Meaning of a Literary Idea," in *The Liberal Imagination* (Garden City, N.Y., 1953), p. 277. The more neutral sense of "a body of ideas" still tends to be associated with pejorative nuances as in René Wellek and Austin Warren's chapter on "Literature and Ideas," in *Theory of Literature* (New York, 1942), pp. 110–24, and in studies of literatures and cultures as throughout Dmitry Chizhevsky, *Russische Geistesgeschichte II, Russland zwischen Ost und West* (Hamburg, 1959–61). On the other hand as early as the 1930s Roman Jakobson referred to ideology in a constructive, formal analysis of Czechoslovakian literature. See "K casovym otkazam nauky o ceskem versi," *Slovo a slovesnost*, 1 (Prague, 1935): 46. An even earlier use is M. M. Bakhtin's, in *Problemy tvorchestva Dostoevskogo* (Leningrad, 1929).

2. Frederic R. Jameson, "Ideology and Symbolic Action," *Critical Inquiry*, 5, no. 2 (Winter, 1978): 417.

3. David Apter, for instance, sees ideology as a "link between action and fundamental belief" which "helps to make more explicit the moral basis of action." *Ideology and Discontent*, p. 17.

4. A particular debt should be acknowledged at the outset to E. D. Hirsch, Jr., *Validity in Interpretation* (New Haven, Conn., 1967); "Objective Interpretation," *PMLA*, 75 (Sept., 1960): 413–79; "Three Dimensions of Hermeneutics," *New Literary History*, 3, no. 2 (Winter, 1972): 245–61; and *The Aims of Interpretation* (Chicago, 1976). The concern for authorial identity is

also inspired—although in much lesser part and without any consistent attempt to use the personality models in question—by psychoanalytic theory, in particular the work of Rollo May, *Man's Search for Himself* (New York, 1953) and *Love and Will* (New York, 1969), and Erik Erikson, *Childhood and Society* (New York, 1950), *Young Man Luther* (New York, 1958), and "Identity, Psychosocial," in *International Encyclopedia of the Social Sciences*, 1965. See also Daniel Yankelovich and William Barrett, *Ego and Instinct*, (New York, 1970).

5. Representative studies from different disciplines which include bibliographical notations pertinent to this sense of ideology are: for psychology L. B. Brown, *Ideology* (London, 1973); for psychiatry Thomas Szasz, *Ideology and Insanity* (Garden City, N.Y., 1970); for philosophy Aiken, *Age of Ideology*, pp. 13–26, Eugenio Trias, *Teoria de las Ideologias* (Barcelona, 1975), and Richard T. De George, *Patterns of Soviet Thought* (Ann Arbor, Mich., 1966), pp. 226–33 (a comparison of Soviet "ideology" with Western "philosophy"); for history Louis Althusser, *Pour Marx* (Paris, 1965) and *Lénine et la philosophie* (Paris, 1969), Hayden White, "Interpretation in History," *NLH*, 4, no. 2 (Winter, 1973): 281–314, and Gordon Leff, *History and Social Theory* (Garden City, N.Y., 1971), especially pp. 141–217; for sociology Apter, *Ideology and Discontent*, Karl Mannheim, *Ideology and Utopia* (London, 1966), and Raymond Aron, *German Sociology* (New York, 1964); for cultural anthropology, Geertz in Apter, *Ideology and Discontent*; for literature the volume entitled "Ideology and Literature" of *NLH*, 4, no. 3 (Spring, 1973), Terry Eagleton, *Criticism and Ideology* (London, 1978), Jameson, "Ideology and Symbolic Action," pp. 417–22, *Marxism and Form* (Princeton, N.J., 1971), pp. 375–90. "The Ideology of the Text," *Salmagundi*, no. 31–32 (Fall, 1975/Winter 1976), 204–46, and *The Political Unconscious* (Ithaca, N.Y., 1981), the latter two authors for intelligent Marxist perspectives.

6. See René Wellek's remarks in *Concepts of Criticism* (New Haven, Conn., 1963), p. 13.

7. See Jonathan Culler, "Structure of Ideology and Ideology of Structure," *NLH*, 4, no. 3 (Spring, 1973): 471–82.

8. Roland Barthes, *S/Z* (Paris, 1970).

9. "Research in semiotics remains an investigation which discovers nothing at the end of its quest but its own ideological moves, so as to take cognizance of them, to deny them, and to start in anew." Translated by Culler, p. 472, from *Semiotike: Recherches pour une semanalyse* (Paris, 1969), pp. 30–31.

10. See William Youngren, "What is Literary Theory?" a review of *In Search of Literary Theory*, ed. Morton W. Bloomfield, in *Hudson Review*, 26, no. 3 (1973): 562–71. See also Frederic Jameson, "Metacommentary," *PMLA*, 86, no. 1 (Jan., 1971): 9–18, and *The Prison House of Language* (Princeton, N.J., 1972).

11. Helen Muchnic, *An Introduction to Russian Literature* (New York, 1964), p. 80.

12. Northrop Frye, *Anatomy of Criticism* (Princeton, N.J., 1971) and

"New Directions from Old," in *Fables of Identity* (New York, 1963). On inductive reasoning and literary interpretation see Maria J. Valdes, "Toward a Structure of Criticism," *NLH*, 3, no. 2 (Winter, 1972): 263–78, Thomas Munro, "Scientific Method in Aesthetics" in *Towards Science in Aesthetics* (New York, 1956), pp. 1–84.

13. Carl H. Hempel, *Philosophy of Natural Science* (Englewood Cliffs, N.J., 1966), especially pp. 11–18.

14. Ludwig Wittgenstein, *Philosophical Investigations* (Oxford, 1953); *Tractatus Ligico-Philosophicus* (London, 1953); *The Blue and Brown Books* (New York, 1965); and Thomas S. Kuhn, *The Structure of Scientific Revolutions*, 2nd ed. (Chicago, 1970).

15. Ernest Gellner, *Words and Things; A Critical Account of Linguistic Philosophy and a Study in Ideology*, intro. Bertrand Russell (Boston, 1960), p. 37.

16. Mr. Kuhn's relativism raises the same problems as the structuralist analysis noted earlier. See Karl Popper's remarks in "Normal Science and Its Dangers," in *Criticism and the Growth of Knowledge*, ed. Imre Lakatos and Alan Musgrave (Cambridge, 1970), pp. 51–58. A discontented and intelligent appraisal of modern linguistic philosophy and Wittgenstein is offered in Erich Kahler, *Out of the Labyrinth* (New York, 1967), pp. 184–87. For an enthusiastic integration of Mr. Kuhn's insights into literary theory see Martin Steinmann, Jr., "Cumulation, Revolution, and Progress," *NLH*, 5, no. 3 (Spring, 1974): 477–90.

17. Wellek, *Concepts of Criticism*, p. 14.

18. See Edward Wasiolek, "Wanted: A New Contextualism," *Critical Inquiry*, 1, no. 3 (Mar., 1975); Albert William Levi, "D Interpretatione: Cognition and Context in the History of Ideas," *CI*, 3, no. 1 (Autumn, 1976): 153–78; Hayden White, "The Problem of Change in Literary History," *NLH*, 5, no. 1 (Autumn, 1975): 97–111; and in the same issue Quentin Skinner, "Hermeneutics and the Role of History," pp. 209–32, including an extensive bibliography on the topic.

19. On the Hegelian roots of aesthetic anti-individualism see Richard Kuhns, *Structures of Experience* (New York, 1970), p. 84, and Arnold Hauser, "The Philosophical Implications of Art History: 'Art Theory Without Names,'" in *The Philosophy of Art History* (New York, 1959), pp. 117–276.

20. In *Literature as System* (Princeton, N.J. 1971), pp. 443–44, Claudio Guillén shows Georg Lukács slipping into such a stance by neglecting the writer's (Schiller's in this instance) personal insight.

21. Wilhelm Dilthey himself, of course, rather than neglecting the individual aesthetic process attempted both to define it in the fullest sense and to provide a detailed exploration of the subject-object problems raised here. See H. Stuart Hughes, *Consciousness and Society*, (New York, 1958), and William Dilthey, "The Rise of Hermeneutics," *NLH*, 3, no. 2 (Winter, 1972): 229–44, with an introduction by Frederic Jameson.

22. Hirsch, *Validity in Interpretation*, p. 469.

CHAPTER 2

1. Erich Auerbach, *Mimesis. The Representation of Reality in Western Literature*, trans. Willard Trask (Garden City, N.Y., 1957), pp. 459–60.

2. Irving Howe, "Dostoevsky: The Politics of Salvation," in *Dostoevsky*, ed. René Wellek (Englewood Cliffs, N.J., 1962), p. 53; Hugh McLean, "The Development of Modern Russian Literature," in *The Development of the USSR*, ed. Donald W. Treadgold (Seattle, 1964), pp. 87–98. For the Russian sublimation of politics into literature see Martin E. Malia, "Adulthood Refracted: Russia and Leo Tolstoi," *Daedalus*, 105, no. 2 (Spring, 1976): 169–83. An extreme variant of the hypothesis that literature is dependent on political repression is offered by Herbert Marcuse, who argues that the development of *any* culture without social constraints would result in the total demise of art. See *Eros and Civilization* (Boston, 1955).

3. Alexander Solzhenitsyn's *The Gulag Archipelago* (New York, 1973,) provides a reminder of the differences between Soviet and Russian political repression. For Russian censorship see Sidney Monas, *The Third Section. Police and Society in Russia under Nicholas I* (Cambridge, Mass., 1961); N. Drizen, *Dramaticheskaia tsenzura dvukh epokh* (St. Petersburg, 1917); A. M. Skabichevskii, *Ocherki po istorii russkoi tsenzury (1700–1863)* (St. Petersburg, 1892); N. A. Engel'gardt, *Ockerk istorii russkoi tsenzury v sviaszi s razvitiem pechati (1703–1903)* (St. Petersburg, 1904); and M. K. Lemke's frequently cited *Nikolaevskie zhandarmy i literatura 1826–1855 gg.* (St. Petersburg, 1908), as well as *Ocherki po istorii russkoi tsenzury i zhurnalistiki XIX stoletiia* (St. Petersburg, 1904). A view from the inside is provided by the civilized Aleksander Nikitenko (1804–77) whose diary is now available in an abridged English version as *The Diary of a Russian Censor*, ed. and trans. Helen Satz Jacobson (Amherst, 1975).

4. Monas, *Third Section*, pp. 194, 136.

5. The prevalent and imprecise view of Russian political repression in the nineteenth century has been shown to be invalid in many specific instances by Frederick S. Starr, *Decentralization and Self-Government in Russia, 1820–70* (Princeton, N.J., 1972).

6. The hypothesis of a Russian cultural underdevelopment that merges with an "attitude of total commitment" was considerably stimulated by Sir Isaiah Berlin's influential essay originally entitled "The Silence of Russian Culture," *Foreign Affairs*, 36 (1957): 1–24, reprinted under "Social Change and Cultural Stagnation" in *Soviet Society, A Book of Readings*, ed. Alex Inkeles and Kent Geiger (Boston, 1961), pp. 76–89. An extreme statement of Russian retardation, bordering on the outrageous, is Werner Keller, *East Minus West = Zero* (New York, 1962). James Billington in *The Icon and the Axe* (New York, 1966) argues that the Russians "repeatedly ... sought to acquire the end products of other civilizations without the intervening process of slow growth and inner understanding" (p. 595). An occasional awkward judgement, such as the reference to the "crude mentality of the average Russian" (p. 539), does injustice to one of the important Western cultural histories of Russia.

Such critical attitudes extend as far back as the nineteenth-century work by Germain de Laguy entitled bluntly *The Knout and the Russians* (New York, 1854). Tomas Masaryk's not unsympathetic remark in his influential *Russland und Europa. Studien über die geistigen Strömungen in Russland* (Jena, 1913), translated and reprinted as *The Spirit of Russia*, 2 vols., rev. ed. (New York, 1955), that "Russia preserved Europe's childhood" can lead to a similar underestimation of both the complexities of the native religious-philosophical tradition and the responses to it by Russians like Dostoevsky and Tolstoy. See also Rufus W. Mathewson, Jr., "Russian Literature and the West," in Treadgold, *The Development of the USSR*, pp. 101–7. For an extensive bibliography of Western attitudes with polemical commentary from a Soviet perspective see A. L. Grigoriev, *Russkaia literatura v zarubezh-nom literaturovedenii* (Leningrad, 1977).

7. Mathewson, "Russian Literature," p. 103.

8. The preparatory theoretical work and historical research is offered in Dmitry Likhachev, *Chelovek v literature drevnei Rusi* (Moscow-Leningrad, 1958), and *Razvitie russkoi literatury X–XVII vekov* (Leningrad, 1973). See also V. E. Vetlovskaia, *Poetika romana "Brat'ia Karamazovy"* (Leningrad 1977). Auerbach succinctly analyzed the religious nature of Russian fiction in *Mimesis*, pp. 459–63. I am indebted to Victor Terras for his reminder that Apollon Grigoriev had also emphasized the organic link between pre-Petrine and modern Russian literature.

9. E.g., Isaiah Berlin's statement that "The Russian priesthood [lacked] conspicuously ... the intellectual resources and tradition of the Western churches" in "Social Change and Cultural Stagnation," p. 77. Richard Pipes offers a similar generalization ("The Russian clergy was unbelievably ignorant") partially based, as the scholar himself admits, on Soviet sources published by the Union of Militant Atheists, in *Russia under the Old Regime* (New York, 1974), p. 227. The counter-argument deriving from an intimate knowledge of both the Western and Orthodox religious traditions is most tellingly provided in Georges Florovsky, *Puti russkago bogosloviia* ["The Ways of Russian Theology"] (Paris, 1937). See also Wladimir Weidle, *Russia: Absent and Present* (New York, 1961) and Marc Raeff, *Imperial Russia* (New York, 1971) for the positive influence of the clergy on higher education and the arts. The review essay of Richard Pope, "But the Literature Does Not Fit the Theory: A Critique of the Teleological Approach to Literature," *Slavic Review* (Dec., 1977), pp. 667–75, points out the detrimental effects on criticism of Western and Russian anti-religious bias. The inadequacy of Western historical research in Russian Orthodoxy is noted by Hugh Seton-Watson in "Russia and Modernization," in Treadgold, *Development of the USSR*, p. 192, in Cyril Black's reply, p. 203, and in the essay by Robert L. Nichols, "Orthodoxy and Russia's Enlightenment, 1762-1825," in *Russian Orthodoxy under the Old Regime*, ed. Robert L. Nichols and Theofanis George Stavrou, (Minneapolis, Minn., 1978), pp. 65–89.

10. On the traditional opposition of the nineteenth-century Russian

intelligentsia to religion see Nicholas Berdiaev, "Filosofskaia istina i intelligentskaia pravda," in Vekhi ["Landmarks"] (Moscow, 1909; reprint ed., Frankfurt, 1967), pp. 1–22; see also the essays by S. N. Bulgakov and P. Struve in the same work. For the development of Western attitudes see Owen Chadwick, The Secularization of the European Mind in the Nineteenth Century (Cambridge 1975).

11. See Herbert E. Bowman's remarks on the dangers and attractions of Russian engagement with literature in "Literary and Historical Scholarship," Transformation of Russian Society, ed. Cyril E. Black (Cambridge, Mass., 1960), especially p. 373; Nicolas Zernov The Russian Religious Renaissance of the Twentieth Century (New York, 1963), pp. 3–34; V. V. Zenkovsky, A History of Russian Philosophy, trans. George L. Kline (New York, 1953), 754–920.

12. For the following discussion see P. Znamensky, Dukhovnye shkoly v Rossii do reformy 1808 g. (Kazan', 1881); M. L. Demkov, Istoriia russkoi pedagogiki, 3 vols. (St. Petersburg, 1897); N. Konstantinov and V. Struminskii, Ocherki po istorii nachal'nogo obrazovaniia v Rossii (Moscow, 1953).

13. Znamensky, Dukhovnye, p. 43.

14. Konstantinov and Struminskii, Ocherki, pp. 42–99, 169. For an analysis of "the overwhelming presence of religious books . . . well into the twentieth century in Russia," see Jeffrey Brooks, "Readers and Reading at the End of the Tsarist Era" in Literature and Society. 1800–1914, ed. William Mills Todd III (Stanford, 1978), pp. 132–35.

15. Billington, The Icon and the Axe, p. 290. See also Demkov, Istoriia, pt. 2, p. 395, and Gregory Freeze, The Russian Levites, (Cambridge, Mass., 1977).

16. Florovsky, Puti, p. 231.

17. Ibid., p. 242.

18. See Aleksandr Nikolaevich Pypin, Religioznyia dvizheniia pri Aleksandrie I (Petrograd, 1916); Billington, The Icon and the Axe, pp. 269–306; Florovsky, Puti, pp. 128–331.

19. Berdiaev, in this as in other matters, has had a strong effect on Western scholars. See his The Meaning of History, trans. George Reavey (Cleveland, 1962), and The Russian Idea, trans. R. M. French (Boston, 1962); see also the foreword by Serge A. Zenkovsky to Dmitry Chizhevsky, History of Nineteenth-Century Russian Literature, trans. Richard Porter, 2 vols. (Nashville, 1974), 1: viii.

20. See the two works of Likhachev metioned in n.8 and Dmitry Chizhevsky's History of Russian Literature from the Eleventh Century to the End of the Baroque (The Hague, 1960).

21. Florovsky, Puti, pp. 30–128; Billington, The Icon and the Axe, pp. 102–306 and bibliography, p. 609.

22. Marc Raeff in his important study Origins of the Russian Intelligentsia (New York, 1966) stumbles a bit on the issue of individualism as a Russian value by arguing that the individual personality was unimportant in Moscow (p. 146) while recognizing, in seeming contradiction, the native at-

tachment to Christianity on an"individual basis only" (p. 162).

23. See George P. Fedotov, *The Russian Religious Mind* (Cambridge, Mass., 1946); and Nadejda Gorodetzky's *The Humiliated Christ in Modern Russian Thought* (New York, 1938). The latter work often depends on Florovsky.

24. Joseph Frank, *Dostoevsky. The Seeds of Revolt, 1821–1849* (Princeton, 1976), pp. 42–53. The religious family background of leading radical critics like Chernyshevsky and Dobroliubov is also to the point. "While rejecting all the traditional ideas of their homes," writes D. S. Mirsky, "they retained much of the moral atmosphere they had been brought up in: they were puritans—almost ascetics—and fanatics" (*A History of Russian Literature* [New York, 1960], p. 214).

25. Ernst Benz, *The Eastern Orthodox Church. Its Thought and Life*, trans. Richard and Clara Winston (Garden City, N.Y., 1963).

26. Timothy Ware, *The Orthodox Church* (Baltimore, 1963), pp. 269–314.

27. Fedotov, *The Russian Religious Mind*, p. 196.

28. James Joyce, *A Portrait of the Artist as a Young Man* (New York, 1964), pp. 145–46.

29. Marcel Bataillon, *Le roman picaresque* (Paris, 1931).

30. Donald Fanger, *Dostoevsky and Romantic Realism* (Chicago, 1965). See also the remarks which continue to influence Soviet literary scholarship in Maxim Gorky, *Sobranie sochinenii*, 24 (Moscow, 1953): 471.

31. M. H. Abrams, *Natural Supernaturalism* (New York, 1971), pp. 65–66. See also N. A. Guliaev, "Sotsial'no-esteticheskaia i gnoseologicheskaia sushchnost' romantizma," in *Russkii romantizm* (Moscow, 1974).

32. E.g., Alain Besançon, *Les Origines intellectuelles du léninisme*, ed. Calmann-Levy (Paris, 1978).

CHAPTER 3

1. W. K. Wimsatt's essay, "The Affective Fallacy," in *The Verbal Icon* (New York, 1965), pp. 20–39, has been followed by more optimistic appraisals of the part readers take in creating texts. For the theoretical background to my conclusions see Roman Ingarden, *Das literarische Kunstwerk* (Tübingen, 1960), and *Vom Erkennen des literarischen Kunstwerks* (Tübingen, 1968); Wolfgang Iser, *The Implied Reader* (Baltimore, 1974), and "The Reading Process: A Phenomenological Approach," *New Literary History*, 3, no. 2 (Winter, 1972): 279–99; Stanley Fish, "Literature in the Reader: Affective Stylistics," *New Literary History*, 2, no. 1 (Autumn, 1970): 123–62.

2. Quentin Skinner, "Hermeneutics and the Role of History," *New Literary History*, 7, no. 1 (Autumn, 1975): 212; J. L. Austin, *How to Do Things with Words* (Oxford, 1962).

3. Vissarion Belinsky was the first important reader in this regard. See Victor Terras, *Belinskij and Russian Literary Criticism* (Madison, Wis., 1974) and Herbert E. Bowman, *Vissarion Belinski* (Cambridge, Mass., 1954). The sociophilanthropic view of 1830s–40s fiction is most often expressed in

studies of the natural school. Fundamental works on the subject are V. V. Vinogradov, *Evoliutsia russkogo naturalizma* (Leningrad, 1929), and *Gogol' i natural'naia shkola* (Leningrad, 1925). See also Ernest J. Simmons, *Introduction to Russian Realism* (Bloomington, Ind., 1965); V. I. Kuleshov, *Natural'-naia shkola v russkoi literature XIX veka* (Moscow, 1965); and the essays of Yurii Mann, "Filosofiia i poetika natural'noi shkoly," in *Problemy tipologii russkogo realizma* (Moscow, 1969), "Utverzhdenie kriticheskogo realizma. Natural'naia shkola" and "Formirovanie teorii realizma v Rossii v pervoi polovine XIX v.," in *Razvitie realizma v russkoi literature* (Moscow, 1972). All of the critics mentioned maintain the sociophilanthropic interpretation, although Vinogradov and Mann are too aware of the complex issues involved to maintain it rigidly. The more common Soviet treatment of natural school writers is well expressed in the unsigned article on Dostoevsky published in the *Large Soviet Encyclopedia*, 2nd ed. (Moscow, 1952). He is described as "truthfully portraying the sufferings of ... people, revealing their human dignity, spiritual purity and nobility ... and [evoking] profound sympathy for them on the part of the reader" (XV, p. 148). D. S. Mirsky offers an essentially similar view in *A History of Russian Literature* (New York, 1960), especially p. 170. For a typical Soviet analysis of Herzen see A. A. Krundyshev, *Gertsen. Biografiia pisatelia* (Moscow-Leningrad, 1967), especially pp. 48–50.

4. Martin Malia, *Alexander Herzen and the Birth of Russian Socialism* (New York, 1965), p. 42, 43.

5. Leonid Piper illustrates the problem of Soviet scholars who, because of an antireligious bias, can only afford to see discontinuity between Herzen's early religious attachments and his later work. The perspective makes impossible exploration of an organic ideological development involving core values and ideas. See *Mirovozrenie Gertsena* (Moscow-Leningrad, 1935). Raoul Labry goes against all existing evidence in stating "La religion n'a touche ni (Herzen's) imagination ni son coeur," *Alexandre Ivanovič Herzen. 1812–1870* (Paris, 1920), p. 27. Malia argues that Herzen's education was "essentially secular in content if not entirely in form" (*Alexander Herzen*, p. 27), and Mirsky makes a similar observation that "though the content of his ideas was materialistic and scientific, their tone and flavor always remained romantic" (*A History of Russian Literature*, p. 210). The following interpretation is based on the reverse hypothesis: that Herzen's ideas took secular form but originated in religious principles and moral codes. A comprehensive bibliography of works on Herzen is available by combining three sources: Malia, *Alexander Herzen*, pp. 427–28; A. I. Gertsen. *Seminarii*, ed. M. I. Gillel'son, E. N. Dryzhakova, M. K. Perkal' (Moscow-Leningrad, 1965); and *Letopis' zhizni i tvorchestva A. I. Gertsena*, 2 vols. (Moscow, 1976). Of particular interest are Lidia Ginzburg, *"Byloe i dumy" Gertsena* (Leningrad, 1957), and A. G. Rozin, *Gertsen i russkaia literatura 30–40kh godov XIX veka* (Krasnodar, 1976). *A. I. Gertsen khudozhnik i publitsist*, ed. L. I. Matiushenko (Moscow, 1977) and V. A. Putintsev, *Gertsen-pisatel'* (Moscow, 1963) are uneven in quality and display stereo-

types of Soviet literary scholarship. Western essays are Sir Isaiah Berlin, "Introduction," in *From the Other Shore* (Cleveland, 1956), pp. vii–viii, and "Herzen the Great," in *The New York Review of Books*, 10, no. 5 (Mar. 14, 1968); and, for an introduction only, George Steiner, "Displaced Person," in *The New Yorker* (Feb. 8, 1968).

6. The basic studies of Herzen's religious inspirations, although without the literary implications I draw, are S. N. Bulgakov, *Dushevnaia drama Gertsena* (Kiev, 1905); V. V. Zenkovsky, *History of Russian Philosophy*, 2 vols., trans. George L. Klein (New York, 1953), especially 1: 276; Georges Florovsky, *Puti russkago bogosloviia* (Paris, 1937), "Iskaniia molodogo Gertsena," *Sovremennye zapiski*, 39: 274–305, 40: 335–67 (1929), and "Die Sackgassen der Romantik," *Orient und Occident. Blätter für Theologie und Soziologie*, 4 (1930): 14–27. See also W. Piroschkow, *Alexander Herzen. Der Zusammenbruch einer utopie* (Munich, 1961), and Gustave Shpet, *Filosofskoe mirovozrenie Gertsena* (Petrograd, 1921).

7. Alexander Herzen, *Sobranie sochinenii v tridtsati tomakh* (Moscow, 1954–65), 1:267 (hereafter cited as *Sochineniia*). All translations are my own. Although I do not use it for purposes of citation, the older edition of collected works compiled by M. K. Lemke, *Polnoe sobranie sochinenii i pisem*, 22 vols. (Petrograd, 1915–25) is valuable for its commentary.

8. *Sochineniia*, 8:148.

9. Ibid., pp. 181–82.

10. Ibid., 2:361.

11. Dates in parentheses given after titles refer to the first edition or, if the work in question was not published, the year when it was completed.

12. "O meste cheloveka v prirode," *Sochineniia*, 1:13–25.

13. Ibid., pp. 81–84.

14. For biographical detail see P.V. Ivanov-Razumnik, *A.I. Gertsen: 1870–1920* (Petrograd, 1920), pp. 10–45, and Malia, *Alexander Herzen*, pp. 155–62.

15. *Sochineniia*, 1:139.

16. No satisfactory explanation has ben offered why Herzen refers to a different ending—in which the Prince recovers—in *My Past and Thoughts*. The editors of the Academy edition suspect that the reference is to another, lost version. Another possibility is that Herzen intentionally, or forgetfully, drew up a weaker ending in his memoirs as part of his later ironic depiction of the story's religious–supernatural content.

17. Elena's innocence is also questionable since she earlier offers to live with the Prince as his mistress. Moreover her sickness is described in too light a tone for a true sentimental tragedy. On the other hand, she does turn down the Prince's offer of money in a manner closer to a Pamela or a Liza.

18. "Gofman," *Sochineniia*, 1:62–80.

19. Ibid., p. 186.

20. In the lost version, Apostle Paul brings Licinius back from death. *Sochineniia*, 1:339.

21. Ibid., p. 507. The Academy edition editors argue for this interpreta-

tion without adequately considering Herzen's Orthodox involvements. See Nadejda Gorodetszky, *The Humiliated Christ in Modern Russian Thought* (New York, 1938), p. 19, for the kenotic themes of the work.

22. *Sochineniia*, 1:258.

23. Dmitry Chizhevsky, "About Gogol's 'Overcoat,'" in *Gogol from the Twentieth Century*, ed. Robert A. Maguire (Princeton, 1974), especially pp. 311–13; "Neizvestnyi Gogol," *Novy zhurnal*, no. 27 (1951), pp. 126–58. See also Fanger, "Gogol and His Readers," in *Literature and Society. 1800–1914*, pp. 61–95.

24. Ia. El'sberg, *Gertsen* (Moscow, 1951), p. 92.

25. *Sochineniia*, 2:199–413.

26. Ibid., p. 238.

27. Ibid., p. 231.

28. Alexander Herzen, *Selected Philosophical Works* (Moscow, 1956), p. 79.

29. *Sochineniia*, 2:365.

30. Malia argues that for Herzen "all ideas, including religion, were simply emanations of man's nervous system" (*Alexander Herzen*, p. 328.) He mentions two of Herzen's letters and two entries in the diary as evidence. A review of this material, however, does not substantiate the statement.

31. See vol. 3 of *Sochineniia* and *Selected Philosophical Works*, pp. 126, 138.

32. *Sochineniia*, 2:92.

33. Ibid., p. 93, ff. for passages cited below.

34. Ibid., p. 220.

35. Ibid., p. 49.

36. Ibid., p. 228.

37. Compare the choice of pronouns in Chernyshevsky's *What Is to Be Done?* (1863) with its hint of impersonal process.

38. For Herzen's reading of George Sand see Malia, *Alexander Herzen*, pp. 265–74. The accompanying interpretation of *Who Is to Blame?* should be consulted with care, however, for it includes an incorrect paraphrase of the plot (p. 271).

39. Letter of 31 Dec. 31 1834, *Sochineniia*, 2:29.

40. See Gogol's uses of the King of Spain or the reading matter Dostoevsky provides Devushkin in *Poor Folk*.

41. Georg Lukács, *Studies in European Realism* (New York, 1964), p. 112.

42. Ibid., p. 11.

43. See Yurii Mann's remakrs in *Poetika russkago romantizma* (Moscow, 1976).

44. Lidia Ginzburg, *O psihologicheskoi proze* (Leningrad, 1971), p. 431.

45. *Sochineniia*, 4:120.

46. *Sochineniia*, 6: 481.

CHAPTER 4

1. Such, certainly, is the importance of Joseph Frank's literary biography, *Dostoevsky. The Seeds of Revolt. 1821–1849* (Princeton, 1976). Geoffrey C. Kabat's interesting *Ideology and Imagination. The Image of Society in Dostoevsky* (New York, 1978) is inspired by similar considerations but lacks analysis of Dostoevsky's early ideological formation on which to build a reading of his mature works.

2. The literature on Dostoevsky is too vast to attempt a full bibliography. Vladimir Seduro lists basic sources in his *Dostoyevski in Russian Literary Criticism, 1846–1956* (New York, 1957), and *Dostoevski's Image in Russia Today* (Belmont, Mass., 1975). See also *F. M. Dostoevskii. Bibliografiia proizvedenii F. M. Dostoevskogo i literatury o nem. 1917–1965*, ed. A. A. Belkin, A. S. Dolinin, V. V. Kozhinov (Moscow, 1968); for Western bibliographical sources see *Dostoevsky. A Collection of Critical Essays*, ed. René Wellek (Englewood Cliffs, N.J., 1962), the special number of *Modern Fiction Studies*, 4, no. 3 (Autumn, 1958), and the yearly bibliographies published in the *International Dostoevsky Society Bulletin*. For a Russian view of Dostoevsky's influence on Western writers see *Dostoevskii v zarubezhnykh literaturakh* (Leningrad, 1978).

3. See Frank, *Dostoevsky*, pp. 25–28, 379–91.

4. In the 1960s and 1970s a number of Western critics published such religio-philosophical studies. See, for instance, A. Boyce Gibson, *The Religion of Dostoevsky* (Philadelphia, 1974); George Panichas, *The Burden of Vision: Dostoevsky's Spiritual Art* (Grand Rapids, Mich., 1977); Konrad Onasch, *Dostojewski als Verführer* (Zurich, 1961), and *Der verschuregene Christus: Versuch uber die Poetisienung des Christentum in der Dichtung F. M. Dostoewsky* (Berlin, 1976); Roger L. Cox, *Between Heaven and Earth: Shakespeare, Dostoevsky, and the Meaning of Christian Tragedy* (New York, 1969); and Ellis Sandoz, *Political Apocalypse. A Study of Dostoevsky's Grand Inquisitor* (Baton Rouge, 1971).

5. For example, see the basic works of V.S. Nechaeva, *V sem'e i usad'be Dostoevskikh* (Moscow, 1939) and *Rannii Dostoevskii, 1821–1849*, (Moscow, 1979); the biographical material available in *F. M. Dostoevskii v vospominaniakh sovremennikov*, ed. A.S. Dolinin, 2 vols. (Moscow, 1964); and Dostoyevsky's letters in *Pis'ma*, ed. A.S. Dolinin, 4 vols. (Moscow, 1928–59) (hereafter cited respectively as Nechaeva, for the first of her studies, *Vospominaniia*, and *Pis'ma*).

6. See Jean Piaget's remarks on parental influence in the evolution of a child's moral feelings, "The Mental Development of the Child," *Six Psychological Studies* (New York, 1968), expecially pp. 33–38. In his memoirs Andrei Dostoevsky notes that both parents were "very religious" but "especially mother," *Vospominaniia*, 1:61. In the same collection Andrei and others attest to Marya Dostoyevsky's frequent acts of charity, the help she gave to destitute peasants, and the love and respect she seemed to inspire among most of her acquaintances.

7. S. D. Yanovsky, "Vospominaniia o Dostoevskom", *Russkii Vestnik* (Apr., 1885), p. 813. Unfortunately the edited version of Yanovsky's memoirs in *Vospominaniia* cannot be trusted in this instance The abridgements made by Soviet editors include important passages on Dostoevsky's religious beliefs in which Yanovsky characterizes him as a "believer" and in which this remark occurs.

8. Nicholas Lossky, *Dostoevskii i ego khristianskoe miroponimanie* (New York, 1953), pp. 52–53.

9. Apparently Dostoevsky suffered a loss of voice and other psychosomatic symptoms. See Andrei Dostoevsky's remarks in *Vospominaniia*, 1:83–86. Konstantin Mochulsky is a bit insensitive on this point in suggesting that Pushkin's death left a greater impression on Dostoevsky than that of his mother. *Dostoevskii. Zhizn' i tvorchestvo* (Paris, 1947), p. 14. Professor Frank is much more to the point. (*Dostoevsky*, p. 37).

10. *Vospominaniia*, 1:86.

11. Frank, *Dostoevsky*, p. 43.

12. Piaget, "Mental Development," pp. 61–64.

13. *Khristianskoe chtenie*, vols. 11–12 (1881): 763–64. On Filaret, see Robert Louis Nichols, "Metropolitan Filaret of Moscow and the Awakening of Orthodoxy," (Ph.D. diss., University of Washington, 1972); Nadejda Gorodetsky, *The Humiliated Christ in Modern Russian Thought*, pp. 108–14; Georges Florovsky, *Puti russkago bogosloviia* (Paris, 1937), pp. 166–84, and the extensive bibliography on pp. 542–43.

14. From "The Apocalypse of Our Times," in *Four Faces of Rozanov*, trans. and intro. Spencer E. Roberts (New York, 1978), p. 199. Filaret was no Thomas Aquinas but Gibson is clearly wrong in suggesting that "Dostoevsky's religious education did not supply him with the means to meet an intellectual challenge" (*The Religion of Dostoevsky*, p. 9).

15. Gorodetzky, *The Humiliated Christ*, pp. 113–14.

16. Cited by R. Pletnev in "Serdtsem mudrye," *O Dostoevskom*, ed. A. L. Bem (Prague, 1929), p. 77. The following hypothesis of Dostoevsky's concern for self–affirmation and identity is my own but a number of critics have provided approaches to the same issue. Mikhail Bakhtin's *Problemy poetiki Dostoevskogo* (Moscow, 1963) offers a still-stimulating appraisal of Dostoevsky's ideology and identity in a sense of these terms that is close to mine, although I am in basic disagreement with his conclusions about the multiplicity and relativism of Dostoevsky's "voices." Victor Terras, *The Young Dostoevsky (1846–1849)* (The Hague, 1969), did much to shift critical emphasis from the social humanitarian view of the writer; Rudolf Neuhaüser, "Re–reading *Poor Folk* and *The Double*," in *Bulletin of the International Dostoevsky Society*, no. 6 (Nov. 1976), pp. 29–32, provides a suggestive although undeveloped argument. Dragutin Prohaska, *Fedor Mikhailovich Dostoevskii* (Zagreb, 1921); S. Askol'dov, "Religioznoe–eticheskoe znachenie Dostoevskogo," in *Dostoevskii. Stat'i i materialy*, ed. A. S. Dolinin, 1 (Petersburg, 1922); B. M. Engel'gardt, "Ideologicheskii roman Dostoevskogo," in *F. M. Dostoevskii. Stat'i i materialy*, ed. A.S. Dolinin (Lenin-

grad- Moscow, 1924); Viacheslav Ivanov's study "Dostoevskii i roman-tragedia," in *Borozdy i mezhi* (Moscow, 1916); D. Chizhevsky's numerous essays; and Leo Shestov, "Dostoevsky and Nietzsche. The Philosophy of Tragedy," in *Essays in Russian literature; the Conservative View: Leontiev, Rozanov, Shestov,* ed. and trans. Spencer E. Roberts (Athens, Ohio, 1968), pp. 3–183—all offer insights into Dostoyevsky's ideas about personality and the self that make up the theoretical foundation of modern Dostoevsky scholarship.

17. Mary-Barbara Zeldin, "Chaadayev as Russia's First Philosopher," *Slavic Review*, 37, no. 3 (Sept., 1978), p. 479.

18. F.M. Dostoevsky, *Polnoe sobranie khudozhestvennikh proizvedenii,* ed. B. Tomashevsky (Leningrad, 1926–30), 13:157, cited hereafter as *Polnoe sobranie.* I use Frank's translation of this passage; see p. 133 of his study. Although pertinent critical and biographical material from the Russian edition of Dostoevsky's works begun in 1972 is incorporated into my discussion, I rely on Tomashevsky's edition because it includes material not yet published in the newer *Polnoe sobranie sochinenii* (Leningrad, 1972–).

19. See Erikson's hypothesis of adolescent imitation in *Childhood and Society* (New York, 1950), and *Young Man Luther* (New York, 1958).

20. *Pis'ma,* 1:56.

21. Ibid., p. 46.

22. Ibid., p. 47.

23. Ibid., pp. 58–59.

24. See Weidle, *Russia,* pp. 161–68.

25. Richard Pipes, "Solzhenitsyn and the Russian Intellectual Tradition," *Encounter*, 52, no. 6 (June, 1979):53.

26. *Pis'ma* 1:46, 61.

27. Ibid., p. 51.

28. Ibid., pp. 54–55.

29. Mochulsky, p. 31.

30. V. L. Komarovich, "Iunost' Dostoevskogo," in *O Dostoevskom,* intro. Donald Fanger (Providence, R.I., 1966), p. 77.

31. Leonid Grossman mentions one of the few times that the young Dostoevsky did write about the benefits of communal living in *Dostoevskii* (Moscow, 1962), p. 88. The joking tone of the letter in question, however, hardly suggests a serious commitment to Utopian Socialist theories. Rudolf Neuhaüser argues for a Utopian Socialist influence on Dostoevsky's psychological views in "Social Reality and the Hero in Dostoevskij's Early Works: Dostoevskij and Fourier's Psychological System," *Russian Literature*, 4 (1973): 18–56.

32. Viktor Vinogradov, *Evoliutsiia russkogo naturalizma* (Moscow-Leningrad, 1929).

33. Ibid., p. 385.

34. Edward Wasiolek, *Dostoevsky, the Major Fiction* (Cambridge, Mass., 1964), p. 7.

35. See *Pis'ma,* 1:86.

36. Ibid., pp. 66–67.

37. Ibid., p. 82.

38. Ibid., p. 140.

39. N. N. Stakhov proposed this interpretation in *Biografiia, pis'ma i zametki iz zapisnoi knizhki F. M. Dostoevskogo* (St. Petersburg, 1883). Mochulsky strongly influenced Western critics through a similar reading: "Dostoevsky having mastered the technique of the Gogolian school of literature," he writes, "tears it apart from the inside. He makes the funny protagonist human" (*Dostoevskii*, p. 29 ff.). Victor Terras offers a much more complex and nuanced interpretation, as does Frank.

40. Dmitry Chizhevsky, "Neizvestnyi Gogol,'" *Novyi Zhurnal*, 22 (1951): 154–55. See also Georges Florovsky, "Three Masters," in *Comparative Literature Studies*, 2, no. 2 (1966): 122–28. On Dostoevsky's use of Devushkin to criticize sentimental fiction see Neuhaüser, "Re–reading *Poor Folk*," pp. 29–32.

41. F.M. Dostoevsky, *Sobranie sochinenii* (Moscow, 1956), 1:187, 196.

42. Ibid., p. 172.

43. For a more detailed analysis of Herzen's influence on Dostoevsky see my dissertation, "Herzen in Russia" (Princeton, 1972). Professor Frank sees a similar ideological congruence between the two men (*Dostoevsky*, p. 233).

44. Wasiolek, *Dostoevsky*, p. 10. See also Prohaska, *Dostoevskii*, and Terras, *The Young Dostoevsky*, p. 63.

45. Vissarion G. Belinsky, *Selected Philosophical Works* (Moscow, 1948), p. 385.

46. See Maximilien Rubel, *Karl Marx, essai de biographie intellectuelle* (Paris, 1957).

47. Pavel V. Annenkov, "Zamechatel'noe desiatiletie," *Literaturnye vospominaniia* (Moscow, 1960), pp. 343–51.

48. *Polnoe sobranie*, 11:6–11. Dostoevsky's subsequent remarks on Belinsky are taken from this edition.

49. N. F. Bel'chikov, *Dostoevskii v protsesse Petrashevtsev* (Moscow-Leningrad, 1936), p. 85.

50. See T.D. Usakina, "Belinskii i literaturno-teoreticheskie printsipy Petrashevtsev," in *Belinskii i sovremennost'* (Moscow, 1964), pp. 172–96.

51. Ibid., p. 173.

52. Annenkov, "Zamechatel'noe," p. 349

53. Belinsky, *Selected Philosophical Works*, p. 375.

54. Ibid., pp. 368-69.

55. Ibid., p. 420.

56. *Polnoe sobranie*, 11:9.

57. V. N. Maikov, *Sochineniia* (Kiev, 1901), 1:58.

58. *Pis'ma*, 1:106.

59. Grossman, *Dostoevskii*, p. 115.

60. F. M. Dostoevsky, *Fel'etony sorokovykh godov*, ed. Iu. G. Oksman (Moscow-Leningrad, 1930). The commentary by V. Nechaeva in *F. M.*

Dostoevskii, Peterburgskaia letopis' (Petersburg-Berlin, 1922) is also useful.

61. Dostoevskii, *Fel'etony*, p. 129.

62. Ibid., pp. 176–77.

63. Bel'chikov, *Dostoevskii*, p. 107.

64. *Fel'etony*, pp. 176–77, ff; also F. M. Dostoevsky, *Occasional Writings*, sel., trans., and intro. by David Magarshack (London, 1964).

CHAPTER 5

1. See Constantine Leontiev, *Moia literaturnaia sud'ba* (New York, 1965), p. 96; I.S. Turgenev, *Sobranie sochinenii v dvenadtsati tomakh*, 12 (Moscow, 1958): 136; for Strakhov's remarks to Rozanov, see *Literaturnye izgnanniki* (St. Petersburg, 1913); for Rozanov's own views, "Neuznannyi fenomen," in *Pamiati K.N. Leont'eva* (St. Petersburg, 1911); also T. Masaryk, *The Spirit of Russia*, 2 (London, 1919): 207–20; S. Bulgakov, *Tikhie dumy* (Moscow, 1918), p. 119.

2. George Ivask has done much in the way of translation to introduce Leontiev's fiction to a wider audience; see *The Egyptian Dove* (New York, 1969) and *Against the Current: Selections from the Novels, Essays, Notes, and Letters* (New York, 1969). His own essays in *Vozrozhdenie*, beginning with no. 118 of Oct., 1961, and continuing to no. 138, and the more recent *Konstantin Leont'ev: Zhizn' i tvorchestvo* (Bern, 1974), offer somewhat diffuse biographical data and one of the few attempts in Western scholarship to discuss Leontiev as a writer. Soviet sources have only recently begun to show promise with P. Gaidenko, "Naperekor istoricheskomu protsessu," *Voprosy literatury*, no. 5 (1974), pp. 159–205. The material is scarce in other instances. In "Konstantin Leontiev's Fiction," *American Slavic and East European Review*, 20, no. 4 (Dec., 1961):622–29, Professor Ivask interprets Leontiev in the framework of the Narcissus myth. In a review of the translations, Clarence F. Brown recognizes Leontiev's fictional craftsmanship but pessimistically separates it from his ideas in "Slightly to the Right of the Czar," *New Republic* (Apr. 19, 1969), pp. 25–27. Eduard Swoboda in *Wiener slavistisches Jahrbuch*, 13 (1966):83–89, examines biographical background and analyzes stylistic devices used in *The Egyptian Dove*. Critical studies which place greater exphasis on Leontiev's intellectual history are: N. Berdiaev, *Leontiev* (London, 1940); V.V. Zenkovsky, *A History of Russian Philosophy*, 2 vols., trans. George L. Klein (New York, 1953), vol. 1, chap. 15; and Georges Florovsky, *Puti russkago bogosloviia* (Paris, 1937), p. 305, and "Die Sackgassen der Romantik," *Orient und Occident*, 4 (1930):14–27. Berdiaev follows Rozanov in comparing Leontiev to Nietzsche but is scarcely interested in literary issues which arise out of the comparison. Zenkovsky's chapter on Leontiev is one of the better general introductions available; my own essay often follows Florovsky's interpretation of the romantic "blind alley." See also my dissertation "Herzen in Russian Literature," for a more detailed exploration of Leontiev's ideological background. I agree with Robert E. MacMaster (*Slavic Review*, 28,

no. 1 [Mar., 1969]: 134–35) that "a fuller, analytic consideration of . . .
cultural, social, and situational matters" would have greatly improved
Stephen Lukashevich's study Konstantin Leontiev (1831–1891): A Study in
Russian "Heroic Vitalism" (New York, 1967). In this instance, unfortunately, Erikson and the psychoanalytic approach have contributed much to
Leontiev's bizarre image in scholarship, and little to an understanding of his
fiction or its intellectual and literary context.

3. See Leontiev's reminiscences. Constantine Leontiev, "Moe obra-
schenie i zhizn na sv. afonskoi gore," Sobranie sochinenii, 9 (Moscow,
1912–14): 21–34.

4. Ibid.

5. Ibid., especially p. 25.

6. Ibid.

7. Ibid., p. 23. "In his childhood Leontiev assimilated his mother's moral
Christianity and, simultaneously, was inspired by a 'poetic' Christianity."
Ivask, Leont'ev, p. 34 (my translation).

8. Otechestvennye zapiski, no. 5 (1855), pp. 3–70 (hereafter cited as O.z.).

9. O.z., no. 9 (1858), pp. 105–58.

10. O.z., no. 119 (1958), p. 221–52.

11. Ivask, Leont'ev, p. 74.

12. Ibid., pp. 86–89.

13. Controversy over the use of the term "romanticism" is summarized in
René Wellek's essays "The Concept of Romanticism in Literary History,"
Comparative Literature, 1 (1949):1–23, and 2 (1949):147–72; and "Roman-
ticism Re-examined," in Northrop Frye, ed., Romanticism Reconsidered
(New York, 1963), pp. 107–33 (first printed in Concepts of Criticism [New
Haven, 1963]). As will become obvious further on, I do not share Arthur
Lovejoy's view that romanticism is a vague or impractical concept; nor do I
agree with Northrop Frye's suggestion that a "conceptual approach" to
romanticism is unwise. In the last instance, our differences seem to arise
from a question of genre. Professor Frye shows a marked predilection for
poetry, while I prefer to emphasize prose writers such as Leontiev, Stendhal,
and Dostoevsky, whose often romantic images are best understood with a
conceptual critical sensibility. I do, however, accept the critical principle
adhered to by Mr. Frye and René Wellek that the real meaning of romanticism should not be formulated outside of the concrete textual situation of
some one writer's or poet's work. Much of the following discussion is
indebted to two other studies which still retain their vigor in our time:
Oskar Walzel, German Romanticism (New York, 1966), and Irving Babbitt,
Rousseau and Romanticism (Cleveland, 1955). In both works, the chapters
dealing with romantic irony and Schlegel are particularly relevant to my
discussion of idealism and the notion of a romantic crisis in modern
conditions. Morse Peckham, in "Toward a Theory of Romanticism,"
PMLA, 61 (1951):5–23, suggests the view of romantic nihilism that I share
but comes to different conclusions than those proposed in this essay.
Florovsky, "Die Sackgassen der Romantik"; I. Zamotin, Romantizm dvadtsa-

tykh godov XIX stoletiia v russkoi literature, 2 vols. (St. Petersburg, 1911); and Dmitry Chizhevsky, *History of Nineteenth-Century Russian Literature*, 1 (Nashville, 1974) and *Outline of Comparative Slavic Literatures* (Boston, 1952), pp. 85–103, provide pertinent material dealing with the Russian tradition.

14. Cited by Zenkovsky, *History of Russian Philosophy*, 1:440. On Grigoriev's romantic transformations of Orthodoxy and influence on Leontiev see Ivask, *Leont'ev*, pp. 82–86, and Florovsky, *Puti*, pp. 305–8.

15. For the biographical details used here see Leontiev's memoirs *Moia literaturnaia sud'ba* (also published in N. Mescheriakova, ed., *Literaturnoe nasledstvo [Moscow, 1935]*), and the material Ivask has accumulated in *Vozrozhdenie*.

16. See Zenkovsky, *History of Russian Philosophy*, 1:439–42, 445–47, for an extensive discussion of Leontiev's aesthetics and ethics from a religious perspective. Leontiev's paradoxical religious views often reflect the tensions of his romanticism; his reading of Herzen on Mt. Athos, and his refusal, even as a monk on his deathbed, to speak of an afterlife, would seem to be indications of the same rejection of idealism within the romantic tradition. See also A. Konopliantsev, "Zhizn' K. N. Leont'eva i sviazi s razvitiem ego mirosozertsaniia," in *Pamiati K. N. Leont'eva*.

17. Leontiev, *Sobranie sochinenii*, 1:24–25.

18. Ivask, *Leont'ev*; Brown, "Slightly to the Right of the Czar"; Swoboda, in *Weiner Slavistisches*.

19. Leontiev, *Sobranie sochinenii*, 1:133.

20. For example, by Lukashevich, *Konstantin Leontiev*, p. 47.

21. Pavlov left a clear imprint on Russian intellectual history. See Zenkovsky, *History of Russian Philosophy*, 1:274, and James H. Billington, *The Icon and the Axe* (New York, 1966), p. 312.

22. Leontiev, *Moia Literaturnaia sud'ba*, *Literaturnoe nasledstvo*, p. 461.

23. Cited by P.F. Preobrazhensky, in "Aleksandr Gertsen i Konstantin Leont'ev," *Pechat i revoliutsiia*, 2 (1922): 84.

24. Cited by Berdiaev, *Leontiev*, p. 84.

25. *Moia litereturnaia sud'ba*, p. 467.

26. Berdiaev, *Leontiev*, p. 76.

27. See Leontiev's letter of Aug. 14, 1891, published by Rozanov in *Russkii vestnik*, 6 (1903); 420–23.

28. See Florovsky, *Puti*, p. 304, and Zenkovsky's defense of Leontiev in his *History of Russian Philosophy*, pp. 444–47.

29. Konstantin Leontiev, *Egipetskii golub; Rasskaz russkogo* (New York, 1954), p. 148.

CHAPTER 6

1. See Leon Tolstoy, *War and Peace*, ed. E. J. Simmons, trans. A. and L. Maude (New York, 1970); L. Tolstoy, *War and Peace*, ed. M. Komroff (New York, 1956). In the introduction to the latter, Clifton Fadiman writes:

"All of this [Tolstoy's thought] is interesting but not at all essential to the enjoyment of his novel" (p. xii).

2. Henry James. *The Tragic Muse* (New York, 1908), p. x; Percy Lubbock, *The Craft of Fiction* (New York, 1921). It is probably indicative of how closely he read the novel that James referred to Tolstoy's work as *Peace and War*. R. P. Blackmur was one of the first to note James's "rudderless attention" in "The Loose and Baggy Monsters of Henry James," *The Lion and the Honeycomb* (New York, 1955), p. 272.

3. See especially Isaiah Berlin, *The Hedgehog and the Fox* (New York, 1957), and "Tolstoy and Enlightenment," in *Tolstoy*, ed. R. E. Matlaw (Englewood Cliffs, N.J., 1967); B. M. Eikhenbaum, *Lev Tolstoi*, 2 vols. (Leningrad–Moscow, 1931); D. S. Merezhkovsky, *Tolstoy as Man and Artist, with an Essay on Dostoevski* (New York, 1902).

4. Out of a vast body of critical literature Tolstoy's own notations and reminiscences still provide the most effective evidence of his childhood ideological development. See "Vospominaniia," in Leo Tolstoi, *Polnoe sobranie sochinenii*, ed. V. G. Chertkov *et al.*, 90 vols: (Moscow, 1925–58), 34:345–93. On Tolstoy's pious guardians, see pp. 263–64, 369. On the kenotic mentality of the peasants and the holy fools in the Tolstoy household, in the same volume, see "Vstavki i zamechaniia k rukopisi 'Biografii L. N. Tolstogo,' sostavlennoi P. I. Biriukovym," p. 395. "There were many different *iurodivye* (holy fools) in our home," Tolstoy writes, "and I—for which I am deeply grateful to my guardians—became accustomed to regard them with the utmost respect ... I am glad that from childhood, I subconsciously learned to understand the grandeur of their heroic deed." Also on the peasants, M. N. Gusev, *Lev Nikolaevich Tolstoi, Materialy k biografii s 1828 po 1855 god*, (Moscow, 1954), pp. 72–73; for religious effects on Tolstoy of the death of his father and grandmother "Prilozhenie," see p. 402. Nicolas Weisbein, *L'Evolution religieuse de Tolstoi* (Paris, 1960) offers a recent, detailed map of Tolstoy's later religious involvements.

5. R. F. Christian, Introduction, *New Essays on Tolstoy*, ed. Malcolm Jones (Cambridge, 1978), p. 10.

6. Tolstoy's reformulation of underlying religious views with the aid of eighteenth–century thinkers like Rousseau is analyzed in E. B. Greenwood, "Tolstoy and Religion," *New Essays on Tolstoy*, pp. 149–71.

7. For most of the biographical data used here, see M.N. Gusev, "Gertsen i Tolstoi," *Literaturnoe nasledstvo*, nos. 41–42 (1941), pp. 490–525.

8. Berlin, "Tolstoy and Enlightenment," p. 44, typifies this critical view when he states that Tolstoy's attitude toward Herzen was "at all times ambivalent." R. F. Christian in *Tolstoy's War and Peace* (Oxford, 1962) mentions the strong evidence that indicates Herzen's influence on Tolstoy, then goes on to speak of the "more direct influence [of] Hegel" (pp. 92–93). Tolstoy, of course, never met Hegel in person. On the other hand, Soviet criticism in particular the first-rate article by Gusev, has performed an invaluable service in bringing to light basic information. Recent studies that touch upon the Herzen-Tolstoy relationship are S. Bychkov, *Lev Tolstoy*

(Moscow, 1954); A. A. Saburov, *Voina i Mir L. N. Tolstogo* (Moscow, 1959); V. Shklovsky, *Lev Tolstoy* (Moscow, 1963); and S. Rozanova, *Tolstoi i Gertsen* (Moscow, 1972).

9. See Gusev, "Gertsen i Tolstoy," p. 491, for a typical incident in which Tolstoy attacked Herzen's views in the course of what appears to be largely a political discussion.

10. Ibid.

11. To prevent a misunderstanding it should be pointed out that Berlin does not properly translate this excerpt in "Herzen the Great," *New York Review of Books*, 10, no. 5 (Mar. 14, 1969): 9, for he omits without an ellipsis the very sentence that most clearly connects Tolstoy's views with Herzen's. For the correct text, see *L. N. Tolstoy v vospominaniiakh sovremennikov*, 2 vols. (Moscow, 1960), 2:352.

12. Leo Tolstoy, *Sobranie sochinenii v dvadtsati tomakh*, 20 vols. (Moscow, 1960–65), 17: 205.

13. The letters Tolstoy wrote were in Prague when Eikhenbaum was working on his study. They were donated to the USSR at a later date. Gusev's study and A. Izioumov, "Leon Tolstoi et A. I. Herzen," *International Review for Social History*, 1 (1936):17–272, provide the full text.

14. Gusev, "Gertsen i Tolstoy," p. 514. Shklovsky, *Lev Tolstoy*, p. 295, points out that Herzen's essay "Voina i mir" was also available to Tolstoy.

15. Alexander Herzen, *Byloe i dumy*, 2 vols. (Minsk, 1957), 2:397.

16. See Malia, *Alexander Herzen and the Birth of Russian Socialism* (New York, 1965), especially chaps. 5 and 10.

17. Herzen, *Byloe i dumy*, 2:393.

18. Ibid., p. 400.

19. Alexander Herzen, *From the Other Shore, and the Russian People and Socialism: An Open Letter to Jules Michelet* (Cleveland, 1963), p. 141.

20 See Berlin, "The Hedgehog and the Fox," p. 44 ff.: and E. J. Simmons, *Leo Tolstoy*, 2 vols. (New York, 1960), 1:313. A. A. Saburov's monograph and Ia. El'sberg, "Ideinaia bor'ba vokrug naslediia Gertsena," in *Problemy izucheniia Gertsena* (Moscow, 1963), pp. 432–50, provide pertinent examples of Soviet interest in determinism and unhappiness over questions of free will.

21. Leo Tolstoy, *War and Peace*, trans. C. Garnett (New York: Random House, n.d.), p. 1132 and preceding. Further references to *War and Peace* are taken from this text unless otherwise noted.

22. Eikhenbaum, *Lev Tolstoy*, 2:199.

23. Herzen, *Byloe i dumy*, 2:397.

24. In *War and Peace*, Tolstoy describes the meeting between Herzen's father, Captain Iakovlev, and Napoleon. It is doubtful that he could have found the exact detail he uses in any other source outside Herzen's memoirs. See Tolstoy, *War and Peace* (trans. Garnett), p. 933, and Herzen, *Byloe i dumy*, 1: 8–12.

25. In particular see Herzen, *Byloe i dumy*, 1:10–11.

26. In "The Hedgehog and the Fox," Berlin makes a well-known case for

the influence of another famous expatriate, Joseph de Maistre, on many of these same aspects of Tolstoy's thought. Sir Isaiah has permitted a notable flaw in his argument, however, by failing to explain why Tolstoy's characterization of de Maistre's fictional counterpart in *War and Peace*, the vicomte of Anna Scherer's soirée, is sarcastically drawn and why this characterization shows so little of the respect one would expect to be shown an admired thinker.

27. J. Bayley, *Tolstoy and the Novel* (New York, 1967), p. 119.

28. Leo Tolstoy, "Neskol'ko slov po povodu knigi *Voina i mir*," *Polnoe sobranie sochinenii*, 16:16.

29. Tolstoy, *War and Peace* (trans. Garnett), p. 876.

CHAPTER 7

1. Deming Brown, *Soviet Russian Literature since Stalin* (New York, N.Y. 1978), pp. 377–78.

2. For the cultural background and literary typologies I mention see Gleb Struve, *Soviet Russian Literature, 1917–1950* (Norman, Okla., 1951); E. J. Brown, *Russian Literature since the Revolution* (New York, 1963); Rufus Mathewson, *The Positive Hero in Russian Literature* (Stanford, 1975); and Vera Dunham, *In Stalin's Time: Middleclass Values in Soviet Fiction* (New York, 1976). Herman Ermolaev, *Soviet Literary Theories. 1917–1934. The Genesis of Socialist Realism* (Berkeley, 1963), offers an invaluable investigation of the men and ideas that made up socalist realism, including Fadeyev's key contributions.

3. Ernest J. Simmons, *Russian Fiction and Soviet Ideology* (New York, 1958), p. 1.

4. Abram Tertz, "On Socialist Realism," *"The Trial Begins" and "On Socialist Realism"* (New York, 1965), p. 213.

5. See Ermolaev, *Soviet Literary Theories*, especially pp. 5, 62–72, 82, 147, 150, 156.

6. Alexander Fadeyev, *Sobranie sochinenii*, 5 (Moscow, 1961):103, 119 (hereafter cited as *Sobranie*). All translations are my own.

7. *Sobranie*, 4:46.

8. Ibid., pp. 20, 233.

9. Ibid., p. 88.

10. Ibid., pp. 98–111.

11. Alexander Fadeyev, *The Rout*, trans. O. Gorchakov (Moscow, 1957?). All further references, except where noted, are to this text.

12. This citation is taken from an early article on Fadeyev by M. El'sberg, entitled (in translation) *"The Rout* by A. Fadeyev and L. N. Tolstoy's Influence," *Oktiabr*, no. 8 (1927), pp. 156–78. In later editions, and in the English translation I use, this excerpt has been omitted.

13. Apparently the first use of the term "interior monologue" took place in Chernyshevsky's article "L. N. Tolstoy's *Childhood and Boyhood*, and Military Tales," which Fadeyev was likely to know. See *Belinsky, Cherny-*

shevsky, and Dobrolyubov: Selected Criticism, ed. Ralph E. Matlaw (New York, 1962), p. 99.

14. *Voprosy sovetskoi literatury*, 2 (1958): 131–79.

15. *Sobranie*, 5:365.

16. Ibid., p. 272.

17. Ibid., 373–74.

18. Ibid., p. 425.

CHAPTER 8

1. See the suggestive essay of Gleb Struve, "Soviet Literature in Perspective," in *Soviet Literature in the Sixties*, ed. Max Hayward and Edward L. Crowley (New York, 1964), pp. 130–49.

2. Vladimir Dudintsev, *Not by Bread Alone*, English ed. (New York, 1957).

3. Edward J. Brown, *Russian Literature since the Revolution* (New York, 1963), pp. 260–63.

4. Rufus Mathewson, *The Positive Hero in Russian Literature* (Stanford, 1975), p. 262.

5. For a fuller discussion of some of the issues I raise see Ellendea Proffer's "*The Master and Margarita*," in *Major Soviet Writers*, ed. Edward J. Brown (New York, 1973), pp. 388–411.

6. Alexander Solzhenitsyn, *The Gulag Archipelago, 1918–1956*, 1–2, trans. Thomas P. Whitney (New York, 1973), p. 174.

7. Alexander I. Solzhenitsyn, *V kruge pervom* (New York, 1969), p. 62–63.

8. Alexander Solzhenitsyn, *August, 1914* (New York, 1972), p. 548.

9. Alexander Solzhenitsyn, *A World Split Apart, Commencement Address Delivered at Harvard University June 8, 1978* (New York, 1978), p. 51.

Index

Note on the Author

Nicholas Rzhevsky was born in Linz, Austria. He received his B.A. (1964) from Rutgers University, and his M.A. (1968) and Ph.D. (1972) from Princeton University. He has taught at Oberlin College, Livingston College of Rutgers University, and the University of Illinois. His previous publications include journal articles in *Encounter*, *Slavic Review*, *Russian Review*, *Slavic and East European Journal*, and *Comparative Literary Studies*.